T0371759

The Economic
Viability of
Micropolitan America

PUBLIC ADMINISTRATION AND PUBLIC POLICY
A Comprehensive Publication Program

EDITOR-IN-CHIEF

DAVID H. ROSENBLOOM

Distinguished Professor of Public Administration
American University, Washington, DC

Founding Editor

JACK RABIN

RECENTLY PUBLISHED BOOKS

The Economic Viability of Micropolitan America, Gerald L. Gordon

Democracy and Public Administration in Pakistan, Amna Imam and Eazaz A. Dar

Personnel Management in Government: Politics and Process, Seventh Edition, Katherine C. Naff, Norma M. Riccucci, and Siegrun Fox Freyss

Public Administration in South Asia: India, Bangladesh, and Pakistan, edited by Meghna Sabharwal and Evan M. Berman

Making Multilevel Public Management Work: Stories of Success and Failure from Europe and North America, edited by Denita Cepiku, David K. Jesuit, and Ian Roberge

Public Administration in Africa: Performance and Challenges, edited by Shikha Vyas-Doorgapersad, Lukamba-Muhiya. Tshombe, and Ernest Peprah Ababio

Public Administration in Post-Communist Countries: Former Soviet Union, Central and Eastern Europe, and Mongolia, Saltanat Liebert, Stephen E. Condrey, and Dmitry Goncharov

Hazardous Materials Compliance for Public Research Organizations: A Case Study, Second Edition, Nicolas A. Valcik

Logics of Legitimacy: Three Traditions of Public Administration Praxis, Margaret Stout

The Politics–Administration Dichotomy: Toward a Constitutional Perspective, Second Edition, Patrick Overeem

Managing Development in a Globalized World: Concepts, Processes, Institutions, Habib Zafarullah and Ahmed Shafiqul Huque

Cybersecurity: Public Sector Threats and Responses, Kim J. Andreasson

Reinventing Local and Regional Economies, Gerald L. Gordon

Government Budgeting and Financial Management in Practice: Logics to Make Sense of Ambiguity, Gerald J. Miller

Globalism and Comparative Public Administration, Jamil Jreisat

Energy Policy in the U.S.: Politics, Challenges, and Prospects for Change, Laurance R. Geri and David E. McNabb

Available Electronically
PublicADMINISTRATION*netBASE*
http://www.crcnetbase.com/page/public_administration_ebooks

The Economic Viability of Micropolitan America

Gerald L. Gordon

CRC Press
Taylor & Francis Group
Boca Raton   London   New York

CRC Press is an imprint of the
Taylor & Francis Group, an **informa** business

Cover photo: Alex McVeigh

CRC Press
Taylor & Francis Group
6000 Broken Sound Parkway NW, Suite 300
Boca Raton, FL 33487-2742

Version Date: 20140206

International Standard Book Number-13: 978-1-4665-1368-6 (Hardback)

Library of Congress Cataloging-in-Publication Data

Gordon, Gerald L.
    The economic viability of micropolitan America / Gerald L. Gordon.
        pages cm. -- (Public administration and public policy)
    Summary: "This book addresses the economic history and future of small cities and towns across the country, as they have and will continue to see dramatic shifts in the roles they play in the extant larger economies. The book addresses the difficult questions asked by these communities as they face an uncertain future. Can the small cities and towns of this country survive and, if so, what economic roles can they play? Must they return to the days of being essentially self-sufficient? Or, is it possible that they will become epicenters of progress in the United States? "-- Provided by publisher.
    Includes bibliographical references and index.
    ISBN 978-1-4665-1368-6 (hardback)
    1. United States--Economic policy. 2. Urban economics. 3. Community development--United States. 4. Cities and towns--United States. I. Title.

HC106.84.G668 2014
338.973009173'2--dc23
                                            2013045573

Visit the Taylor & Francis Web site at
http://www.taylorandfrancis.com

and the CRC Press Web site at
http://www.crcpress.com

This book is dedicated to my paternal grandfather, Louis, who at five feet tall, was a giant of a man. He has lent his name to me, to one of my remarkable children, and now to my first grandchild.

Contents

xiv ■ Contents

Preface

Since the early 1980s, I have had the extraordinary privilege of serving as the president and CEO of one of the nation's most progressive and prolific economic development organizations: the Fairfax County Economic Development Authority in northern Virginia. That experience further enabled me to serve as a consultant to a number of communities of various descriptions across the United States and around the world. Over time, a number of adjunct faculty assignments in various universities caused me to consider those experiences and the lessons they taught me in an organized way.

Curiously, those attempts to organize my conclusions so they could be communicated well only led to further questions. It also led, to an extent, to a somewhat growing inability to produce conclusive statements about what cities and regions had learned in regard to growing local economies and bringing communities back from often serious and even devastating economic decline, sometimes over the course of many years, even decades. I began a concerted effort to reach valid conclusions that, at least in a very general sense, could be extracted from previous experiences of community leaders and then be superimposed on similar future situations. Certainly, there are some "givens" that can enable quicker or enhanced success by others who might learn what to try and not to try; what has worked or not worked.

I began to think in terms of a three-part series of published research that would first examine the lessons learned by communities in economic recovery mode, which would then be followed by research that would extract the lessons of the first publication and apply them to specific settings. The locations to be used as case studies would be large US cities and their suburban regions and, most important, their stories would not be told by sitting in a library reading about them or at a desktop Googling them; rather, they would be related through a large number of interviews with the leaders of the case study communities who actually lived through the recovery and "walked the walk." I wished only to be a reporter who would tell the stories and extract the common features and lessons for others to learn. Finally, I envisioned a third component of the series that would apply the same process of interviewing and relating experiences through the eyes of those who lived them, but this time in smaller cities and towns around the country.

I got lucky. CRC Press was publishing books in conjunction with the American Society of Public Administration (ASPA). They called it the Public Administration and Public Policy Series and it fit perfectly with my plans. Happily, they agreed, and in 2009, the first of that three-part series, *The Formula for Economic Growth on Main Street America*, was published. It was followed in 2011 by *Reinventing Local and Regional Economies*. This volume was indeed the result of more than 70 interviews with senior leaders in 35 large cities and metropolitan regions across the United States. I spoke with 11 mayors, college and university presidents, Chamber of Commerce executives, and economic development officials. Their stories contained many commonalities, which I took to be lessons that could be extrapolated onto other communities confronting similar challenges. They also related stories and lessons that were unique to their own settings or possibly to only a relatively few other locales. Still, they were instructive because they conveyed lessons about the intangible components of economic growth: leadership, collaboration, planning, and plain old grit.

This brings us to the final study of this series, and with it the final question: Can lessons be learned from relatively smaller cities and towns about the revitalization of their local economies, including those in the aftermaths of serious and extended decline that can be of benefit to other similarly sized communities that are experiencing like issues? The same approach as was employed in *Reinventing Local and Regional Economies* made the most sense: simple library research would not be adequate to understand fully the impacts of the hardships imposed and the benefits (or lack thereof) of strategies that were implemented.

The best way for me to comprehend the devolution of these local economies, the dislocation of families and communities, and the regrowth that followed was for me to act again as a reporter, interview the leaders who lived through the actual situations and implemented the discussed solutions, then tell their stories and explore the commonalities and distinctions in their tales. With the backing of a supportive publisher, I managed to interview 70 mayors of America's smaller cities and towns. What follows, in *The Economic Viability of Micropolitan America,* is the result. As do the many men and women who agreed to be interviewed and share their stories, my expectation is that it will be of benefit to other cities and towns of their size.

Determining the Size of the Cities to Be Examined

In the initial research and books, the plights of large cities and major metropolitan areas were examined. Their backgrounds—economic and other—were dissected and reconsidered. The causes of their economic declines and the potential benefits of various paths to recovery were detailed. It is an underlying premise of the current phase of the research that the causes of, and recovery from, economic decline in those major cities and metropolitan areas are far, far different from those of smaller cities and towns. It will be interesting to see the extent to which there is a convergence of causes and effects between the larger and smaller communities of America.

Yet, at the other extreme, the very small cities and towns of America also have unique sets of issues and solutions that would probably not be instructive for the communities I want to consider in this book. In 2003, the United States Bureau of the Census, perhaps for similar reasons, created the category of "micropolitan" communities and defined them as "core communities" having between 10,000 and 50,000 inhabitants, sometimes (though not always) existing within a greater region having as many as 100,000 residents. In the census reports of 2010, this definition fit thousands of cities, towns, and regions across the United States.

This is the community size selected for this research. It is felt that communities with fewer than 10,000 or more than 50,000 residents will have different solutions and successes than will the micropolitan communities of the nation. Of course, that is a very general statement that may not always be accurate with great precision, but I believe that it is reasonable as a premise. Thus, this book explores the economic decline and regeneration of the economies of America's micropolitan cities, towns, and regions.

Data on Micropolitan America

The Federal Reserve office in Cleveland (Cleveland Federal Reserve, 2011) issued a review of several macro trends that were revealed in the initial data available from the 2010 decennial census. It concludes that the predominance of the 27.3 million population growth in the United States since the census of 2000 had occurred in major metropolitan regions across the country. That is consistent with existing population trends: nearly two of every three Americans now live in these major metro conurbations. Continuing another trend of the past decade, 48 major metropolitan areas lost population, with many of those areas being located in the Great Lakes region.

Interestingly, the largest states in the country do not necessarily dominate the numbers of micropolitan areas delineated by the Census Department. Of course, some of the most populous states do have many such areas, including North Carolina, Texas, and Ohio. However, there are more in the state of South Dakota than are to be found in California (Brookings Institute, 2010).

The United States Department of Agriculture has further noted that the totality of US micropolitan communities contain nearly two-fifths of all of the American population that is not located in metropolitan areas. Moreover, of significant relevance to this research, the agency also noted that "In general, lack of an urban core and overall population density may place these locations at a disadvantage in efforts to expand and diversify their economic bases" (United States Department of Agriculture, 1999).

Over the same time period noted above (from 2003 on), the areas designated as "micropolitan" also grew in population but at a slower rate than did the nation's major metropolitan areas. Micropolitan regions are defined by the Bureau of the Census as having regional populations of between 12,000 and 200,000 with urban cores of 10,000 to 50,000. Population growth in the 581 micropolitan regions of the United States averaged just over 5% in the decade between 2000 and 2010. However, this statistic masks the average population decline of 28.7% in the subset of micropolitan areas that were losing residents. Unlike the population losses among the nation's major metropolitan areas, the micropolitan areas that experienced population declines were not as concentrated; indeed, although there were several in the Great Lakes region, there was also a significant distribution in the southeastern United States (Cleveland Federal Reserve, 2011), reflecting job losses in steel, overall manufacturing, textiles, and other industries. The report of the Cleveland Federal Reserve states the possible causes in the Great Lakes region as follows:

> The continued after-effects of de-industrialization, older populations, less educated workforces, and the broader trend movement of population to the south, have been associated with low population growth in such areas. Still, many of these factors are "endogenous," as much a result of the slow population growth as a driver of slow growth. (Cleveland Federal Reserve, 2011)

The economic growth of micropolitan regions will, of course, affect the growth of the core areas that reside within; however, for the purpose of this research, the focus is only secondarily on the regions involved, and primarily on the core micropolitan cities and towns. This enables the consideration of possible solutions to economic decline to emphasize geographies over which specific units of local government have direct control. Although regions often have forums for collaboration among neighboring localities, the agreements often do not have sufficient teeth to ensure collaboration at times when intraregional competition for jobs becomes a zero-sum game.

It should be no surprise that economic growth in America's micropolitan communities is no more consistent than it is in the nation's various rural areas or large cities. Some have experienced relative stability while others have grown and contracted and either recovered or not. Some are encountering the first stages of the cycles of economic decline. A 2009 study of small towns in New England focuses on the 18 "forgotten cities" (several of which are included in this study) that face uphill struggles in rebuilding their local economic bases and their communities in general (Leroux, 2009). These are communities that are defined in this way: "... once booming industrial centers dense with population, jobs, shopping, and infrastructure." However, the loss of manufacturing jobs throughout the larger region ultimately prefaced the loss of the most highly skilled to communities where they could find employment, taking with them much of the tax base and leaving behind communities with greater-than-ever public service demands and a markedly reduced tax base from which to provide those services.

The former governor of Michigan observed that "42,000 manufacturing plants throughout the United States closed in the last decade …" (Granholm and Mulhern, 2011). Of course, not all small town economic declines began with the loss of industry to more cost-competitive offshore locations. In some cities, the very waterfront location that had served to provide commerce for so long gave way to more rapid and more efficient modes of transport, including highways and air cargo. Other cities and towns have been eradicated or nearly so as the result of floods, tornadoes, wildfires, earthquakes, and other natural disasters. Some come back slowly and organically and others have recovered more rapidly and strategically. Their recoveries, although variant in origins, can be quite similar in the need for and potential of various solutions. One difference, however, is the influx of federal disaster relief funds and insurance policies to cover some of the physical rebuilding efforts; that does not, of course, repair the psychological damages or all of the economic dislocation.

In addition to the double-edged problem of losses in the tax base coupled with increasing demand for public services, a second double-edged problem surfaces for small towns in these situations. As those who can leave (e.g., those with some resources or some marketable skills) do so, the community loses its primary asset for attracting or creating replacement employment opportunities: the most well-trained of the workforce. As those workers are the most likely to own homes and spend their incomes locally, they may leave behind abandoned homes (i.e., upside-down mortgages) and disproportionately greater declining expenditures in the communities that support local businesses and trade.

Much of the answer to these problems in America's cities (of all sizes) has related to the provision of financial incentives to induce companies to come to, or even to stay in, such locations. These are generally short-term fixes that do not always address the longer-term causes behind the decline. Because they are often short-term solutions, however, they can sometimes be very palatable to local elected officials who don't have the luxury of investing in and then waiting for the longer-term, although potentially greater, return payoffs (defined as those realized after the next election).

A longer-term focus that yields the conditions conducive to business attraction and economic growth may produce greater results in the long run. This may include infrastructure improvements, an enhanced public education system, improvements in other public services, and more. Again, however, these are long-term investments that require extended lengths of development and the management of interim expectations, not at all an easy challenge.

America's small towns and micropolitan communities collectively represent large population bases and great tracts of land. They also are the beneficiaries of much of the revenues generated in the more successful economic centers of their respective states as transfer payments are made to provide essential public services. All of these factors argue for the long-term strengthening of the appeal of small and midsize communities for business attraction, retention, and (organic) growth. Furthermore, the country's small and midsized cities and towns provide lifestyle alternatives for individuals and families who prefer smaller settings or are seeking a lower cost of living. In addition, the lure of living in one of the nation's major metropolises may have lost some of its luster. A poll conducted in 2008 found that "not one of the 30 largest metropolitan areas was judged by a majority of respondents as a place they'd like to live" (Rybczynski, 2010). This may be a contributing factor behind the growth of smaller cities and towns. Yet, even that picture is not always rosy: smaller cities and towns typically have rates of illiteracy and unemployment that are significantly higher than the respective states' averages. Coupled with lower-than-average educational attainments and skill levels, these communities can find it difficult to attract substantial business operations. The resulting brain drain from such areas exacerbates that problem, leaving the community with declining tax bases coupled with increased demands for public support. Frequently, the individuals who remain in place are either those who cannot afford to move away or whose skills do not place them in demand elsewhere. Often, those who stay behind are those who are eking out a retirement living in their hometowns and who do not wish to leave. This latter group does not represent big spenders in the community but do represent relatively high users of public services, thus even further exacerbating municipal budget woes.

As manufacturing facilities close in small and midsized towns, the municipality may only be at the beginning of its challenges. Typically, a large manufacturing facility generates not only tax revenues that provide for public services, but it supports many charitable causes, scout troops, and Little Leagues in communities. That support leaves with the employer. In many situations, the locality has based its water usage and energy consumption planning on forecasts of the facility's demand. In many cases, the costs of those utilities must be borne by the locality after the employer leaves the area.

Even in communities that do retain some or most of their skilled workforce (an asset that can be attractive to replacement employers), the skillsets possessed typically lend themselves largely to the same types of manufacturing functions that departed rather than longer-term employment opportunities that will provide greater resources for the workforce, their families, and their communities.

Acknowledgments

Without the consistent support of my executive assistant, Cheryl Martelli, this research would have taken at least twice as long. I am most grateful for her extraordinary contributions. Vicki Reeve also provided exceptional counsel for which I consider myself most fortunate.

Those who truly deserve my greatest degree of appreciation, and respect, are the many men and women who serve as mayors of the micropolitan cities discussed herein. Unlike many mayors in much larger cities, they are not career politicians; in most cases, they never really entertained the notion of holding elective office. They simply saw a need in their communities and they thought they could help make their cities better places. And these are "their communities." Many of the mayors I interviewed for this book told me how much their cities meant to them: they had grown up there, their parents and even previous generations had lived there, and they often expected their children to live at least a part of their lives in the same cities. There is an emotional attachment to "place" that had caused them to step aside from their normal lives, to take time from their families and their businesses to do what they thought needed to be done. Many couldn't wait to get back to their real lives. To me, they are heroes.

About the Author

Virginia Business Magazine named **Dr. Gerald L. Gordon** as its "2010 Business Person of the Year," and Leadership Fairfax, Inc. named Dr. Gordon the recipient of the 2011 Northern Virginia Regional Leadership Award.

Dr. Gordon is the president and chief executive officer of the Economic Development Authority in Fairfax County, Virginia, one of the largest office space markets in the United States. He has been with the FCEDA since late 1983. In that time, office space in the county grew from 32 million square feet to nearly 120 million square feet and jobs in the county grew from 243,000 to more than 600,000. As a result, the real estate tax rate has decreased from $1.47 to $1.07.

He has also worked for Arlington County, Virginia, and the United States Department of Labor. In 2005, the FCEDA was named by *Site Selection Magazine* as one of the Top Ten Economic Development Organizations in North America. In 2007, *Time* magazine called Fairfax County "one of the great economic success stories of our time." In 2011, the *Washington Post* said that "Fairfax County remains the economic wunderkind of Virginia and in many ways of the Washington area."

Dr. Gordon has taught at the Catholic University of America, the University of Maryland, George Mason University, and Virginia Commonwealth University. He has consulted with numerous city and state governments throughout the United States as well as the governments of the Republic of Poland, the island of Vieques in Puerto Rico, and the Federated States of Micronesia. He has also served as a consultant to various government agencies, the US Navy, businesses, nonprofit organizations, associations, colleges and universities, and the United Nations.

Holding a bachelor's degree from The Citadel, a master's degree from George Washington University, and a doctorate in international economics from the Catholic University of America, he is also the author of 12 books and numerous articles on strategic planning, economic development, leadership styles, and other management topics. His most recent books are *Reinventing Local and Regional Economies* (2011) and *The Formula for Economic Growth on Main Street America* (2009).

Dr. Gordon is the 2003 recipient of the prestigious Israel Freedom Award of the Israel Bonds organization. In 2006, Dr. Gordon became the first American to address the All-Parliamentary Exports Group in the British House of Commons.

In 2007, Dr. Gordon was accepted for inclusion on the roster of Fulbright Senior Scholars. In 2007, Dr. Gordon was named a Fellow of the International Economic Development Council; in 2010 he received the James Rees Award from the Fairfax County Chamber of Commerce; and in 2012 he was named the Trendlines Trendsetter of the Year for the Washington, DC metropolitan area.

Introduction

As the American economy evolved, the contributions of large cities, small towns, and rural areas each evolved in its own unique manner. Over time, the importance of America's largest cities became clear. Typically centered around the most convenient access to natural resources and other product inputs as well as navigable waterways, these cities became the sites of America's manufacturing prowess, drawing upon a density of population that served as the labor pool for businesses.

Over time, cities became overcrowded and riddled with slums, disease, and crime. Those who could not afford to move their families to more pleasant environs remained in steadily worsening neighborhoods with steadily declining conditions. The cities became home to low-income residents who required a great deal of public support. Employers observed that the more employable of the urban populations were moving and they followed suit by taking their manufacturing functions from the inner cities to suburban areas. There they were able to retain close proximity to the workers who had previously moved outward to realize the American dream: a house with a yard, fresh air, and still relatively easy access to jobs. The cities were left with the challenges associated with low incomes, reduced tax revenues, no jobs, and increasing demands for public support. Later, as many of the manufacturing jobs began to move overseas, the cities suffered even more, whereas suburban business locations that had attracted the best and brightest began to see the emergence of the service economy that drew upon their greater skill levels and technical educations.

Although America's major cities and their suburban neighbors saw their respective economic roles defined and redefined, the economic roles of small towns and smaller cities across the United States began to evolve as well. In the initial phase, these cities and towns served to provide essential services strictly for those who lived there. This normally entailed the collection and milling of crops, the establishment of marketplaces for the sale and purchase of livestock or produce, and the distribution of other essential materials throughout the community. Exportation of goods was atypical, meaning that income from outside sources was not generally the currency of local commerce. Rather, goods and services were bartered within the community for other goods and services, and small towns remained largely self-sufficient.

Those small cities and towns that were fortunate to be located near navigable waterways, train lines, or major highways were able to generate revenues by serving as waystations and distribution centers for the people and goods that passed through. Other small cities and towns grew as they began to specialize in the manufacture of different products. To the extent that a locally produced item could be manufactured more efficiently, that process created a competitive advantage over others producing the same or similar goods. The result was an opportunity to develop an export trade that generated more jobs, an income stream, and the beginnings of the infrastructure needed to support that trade.

Another consequence of the growth of these more efficient markets was the decline, and even the demise, of the less efficient markets that could no longer compete. These cities and towns either reverted back to being self-contained communities, discovered other production possibilities for which they did have a sufficient competitive advantage (e.g., part of the supply chain or storage and distribution points), or simply went away. For those that became primarily residential areas (and depending upon how state tax structures were established), many of these communities were faced with providing services to a largely residential population without the benefit of tax revenues generated from businesses. The combination of lower incomes and a residentially grounded tax base with a growing demand for public education and other public services often spelled financial difficulties for these smaller towns. The resultant poor public services made these locations even less attractive to prospective businesses, and the brightest young people departed for employment in the more efficient areas.

Ultimately, the evolution of the more efficient meant the expansion of local populations and the emergence of the institutions normally found in larger cities and regions. Although this generated some revenues for some locations, most small cities and towns really continued to be largely self-contained economies. This all changed with the advent of global competition and the advance of technology, most especially information and communications technologies.

As global competition resulted in the production of products for lower costs, both big cities and small towns saw the departure of businesses and industries from their economies. One after another, US cities and towns lost market share to developing countries in a wide range of industries including steel, textiles, electronic goods, automobiles, and more. Any production function that was labor intensive could be performed elsewhere more cheaply due to the significantly lower labor costs overseas. If it needed to be made more cheaply or made repetitively or reduced in size, American manufacturers lost out.

The rapid and growing advance of information and communications technologies also had an impact on the ability of overseas competitors to wrest industries from American communities. These technologies, however, also had the effect of creating new markets and new production functions, including manufacturing functions, for small cities and towns in the United States because they were not labor intensive; rather, they were capital intensive. Moreover, they were *knowledge* intensive, and that capacity, although growing quickly worldwide, was largely to be found in the United States.

The relative impact of technology development and enhancements on major markets around the United States has, to date, varied. Large cities became home to the development of the new technologies because they required a density of professionals trained in the latest techniques, universities, research laboratories, and investment capital. Small-town America had little or no role to play in the advance of technology and attempted merely to perform production and back-office functions. The hope was that the global markets which had taken on the merely labor-intensive mass production functions did not possess the knowledge or sufficient English language skills to perform the needed back-office tasks required by the new technology service providers and that the smaller cities and towns across America could attract those jobs.

The approach did not succeed, however, as overseas workforces became better trained and more adept at various technologies, yet their markets remained substantially lower-wage environments. American employers began to remove a variety of production jobs and back-office operations to India and other overseas locations. As the global recession of 2008 and beyond took hold of the American economy, these smaller markets were disproportionately affected by job losses as well as the resultant brain drains, tax base reductions, diminished housing values, and diminishment of their overall quality of life.

So, where do the small towns of America go from here? Can they grow local economies that are sustainable or must they, of necessity, revert to being largely self-contained once again in order to survive? Or, perhaps, can the small towns of America become the homes of tomorrow's economic growth and become even more viable than ever before?

To understand the potential for America's small-town economies to thrive in the future, one must first understand the historical context in which America's small-town economic structures emerged and evolved as well as what the businesses of the future will need in terms of assets and amenities for both the businesses and for the kinds of people they will wish to employ. Today's small towns must be analyzed to see which of those assets presently exist and what is missing. Finally, it will be necessary to determine the likelihood of those asset gaps being closed by communities going forward and the means by which this can be accomplished.

Chapter 2 considers this 300-year history of America's economic structures in substantial detail and with an eye toward the effects of that ever-changing context on the development and growth of, and the changes to, the economic geography of the United States. Moving on from that context, Chapter 4 explores the fate of the small cities and towns in America. How have they emerged over time? And, more important, what will be their economic fate in the future? We first consider what constitutes a small city or town. Who lives there and how do they support their families and their communities? As the communications and information technologies evolve and become readily available everywhere, what new roles can these communities play in the larger economic picture? Is it possible that small cities and towns can offer enough in the way of assets and amenities to become economic hubs in the future? And if so, will that evolution create such growth that it will override and eliminate the very qualities from which they derived their initial appeal?

Chapter 1

What Is a Small City/Town?

Dictionary definitions of "small towns" invariably include descriptions such as "provincial" and "unsophisticated." This is such a gross generalization that it is hardly worthy of review; however, perceptions often being the same as or greater than reality, there must be comment. Of course, small towns may, at one time in their respective histories, have been unsophisticated because they were isolated. Larger cities and towns create sufficient demand to attract events, build museums, libraries, and other cultural centers. Such intercourse provides greater opportunities for the growth of culture and sophistication. However, that does not mean that those who live in less-populated areas are somehow less sophisticated than their big city counterparts. In short, urban environments do not necessarily yield more urbane residents.

What smaller cities lack is not sophistication but scale. Although their larger counterparts have greater needs that accompany their larger budgets, the fact remains that small cities do not have the human and capital resources to diversify their local economic bases greatly. They must therefore rely on selected assets to attract and support selected industries. They are much more susceptible to corporate out-migrations, corporate deaths, and the negative consequences of macroeconomic forces; furthermore, those forces tend to be further out of their control than in larger communities.

One thing that the smaller cities in this study do not lack is pride. For many of the elected officials interviewed and for many of their constituents, the micropolitan city in question is their lifelong home. Their parents and their children may also live there. This seems to be much more typical in these smaller towns and the result is a drive to make the community succeed well into the future. There also seems to be less of a sentiment to the effect that, if the jobs do not come back, the residents will move away. The attitudes seem to be much more geared to doing whatever is necessary to avoid having to move away, including scraping to make ends meet and working several jobs to do so.

America's micropolitan cities and regions cannot easily be defined. There are more than 100 communities included in the initial phase of this research and they are all quite different. However, there are numerous interesting commonalities, and many suggest that these cities will figure out ways to rebuild and sustain their economies for the succeeding generations.

In purely technical terms, a small city or town is a quantitative designation. Micropolitan cities are so designated because they have between 10,000 and 50,000 residents. Populations of 9,000 are too few; 51,000 are too many. It is all very cut and dried. But is that how we define a small town? Is it really all just about the numbers?

Of course it is not; when we think about a "small town," we presume that a certain *culture* exists that is lost in a larger city. In major metropolitan areas, one can find the same culture in some (although not many) neighborhoods. Jane Jacobs (1969) wrote about how certain neighborhoods in New York City and elsewhere could achieve the kind of culture that one finds in many small cities.

Of course, there is no guarantee. A city of 30,000 residents may not have such a culture, or may have lost it. Larger cities can possibly achieve something like it. It is indeed a generality, one about which many of the mayors of micropolitan cities interviewed for this book spoke. They refer to that culture as being their cities' very essence, the quality of life that brings people and residents to, and back to, their communities.

Indeed, these are the reasons that many residents of micropolitan communities live there: pride, determination, the ability to pull together in times of need, and the presence of a lifestyle that those who grew up there want their children to experience as well. These are small town "values" that their residents do not believe they can find elsewhere. A few of the mayors who were interviewed stated up front that they were not natives of the cities they now lead; some even said it wistfully. But, in each of those cases, they related the stories of their arrivals and their accession to the city council and to the mayor's office with such pride that it is clear that cities of this size have a certain quality of life that captures many people and will not release them. This is why they will survive and build or rebuild local economies that will be sustainable over the long term. The next step is knowing how.

Chapter 2

Economic History of American Cities and Towns

The original 13 colonies were founded and populated by farmers. Communities grew initially as the farms, which were designed to be essentially self-sufficient, abutted one another and interaction necessarily occurred. The need for general safety from both the indigenous population and the elements promoted increasing collectivity and enabled the earliest interdependence to evolve. Over time, agricultural and industrial specialization would help create economic efficiency and the beginnings of urbanizing trends, but, in the earliest years, even small rural towns were quite few and located far between. Even when such growth did occur, most of it took place in proximity to the navigable rivers that provided the most effective transportation available.

In 1790, the very first US census to be taken showed only 24 locations with populations of at least 25,000 residents. In those small towns were located just over 200,000 humans, a mere 5% of the total US population, which numbered nearly four million that year (Hughes and Cain, 2007). At this early stage, the smallest of towns had no real economy beyond the self-sufficiency of its residents. Crops were raised by families, and prior to 1800, according to Cochran, each house "averaged a spinning wheel for every adult female ... itinerant shoe, hat, and candle makers, iron workers, and other artisans moved from place to place satisfying local demands" (Cochran and Brewer, 1966).

All of the more populous locations that were inland could be found on navigable rivers and all of those that were coastal could be found near natural seaports. None less than Henry Clay saw the advantages of developing the new "internal improvements." The Heidlers wrote in his biography that he believed strongly that internal improvements "could speed American commerce, bolster American security, refine life on rough farmsteads, and transform remote villages into thriving townships (Heidler and Heidler, 2011).

From that time forward, America's urban areas grew and the nature of technology began to enable more efficient agricultural production and industrial growth. Over time, the labor force would learn that many of these advances would cost them their jobs and sources of livelihood. Cochran wrote that the initial growth of New England cities and towns was really found in two distinct patterns. The first, coastal locations, were connected by oceangoing vessels. The proximity of four deepwater ports (Boston, New York, Philadelphia, and Charleston) enabled the rapid growth of each by encouraging not only trade but an inherent specialization of goods. The backwoods locations where people gathered of social necessity lagged behind the development of larger areas or the structure and institutions that could be found in the coastal locations (Cochran and Brewer, 1966).

To some extent, efforts to extend the reach of the inland areas with the larger coastal cities and towns was the result of the foreign wars that curtailed international trade and led to the search for other markets. As intra-American trade increased, the demand for structure and infrastructure also increased, resulting in the development of roads, canals, and waystations. But it was technology that played the key role in the development of inland trade, westward expansion, and inland city and economic development. One technological advancement that hastened the growth of new economies was rail travel and rail shipment. As mileage grew, communities could be connected and travel and shipments were no longer overly dependent upon waterways. Rail mileage developed quickly: in 1840, the total mileage was about 3,300 miles; by 1850, 8,900; and by the beginning of the Civil War in 1860, more than 30,000 miles of track connected cities and rural areas up and down the eastern seaboard as well as to inland destinations (Hindle and Lubar, 1986). Thus, the growth of communities could take place anywhere along the rail lines moving north and south or east and west. Even these would one day give way to primary roads, networks, and interstate highways. In the meanwhile, however, it gave inland farmers an opportunity to produce food for sale in the urban areas.

The rail lines did bring challenges for the economies of seacoast and riverside areas. Furthermore, the advent of steam engine applications to various production processes led to the realization that smaller shops could be combined to find greater efficiencies in larger workforces. Thus, the small shops merged into larger factories. This generally meant that machines were used to perform much of the work previously performed by humans, leaving for the latter only the most difficult, often dangerous, and low-paying jobs with little reward and little future.

Through the first years of the Civil War, the economic foundations of the northern colonies/states and those in the south, and later those to the west, remained poorly connected. The growing demand for the cotton and tobacco crops of the south began to cause shifts in that interconnectedness; but the years and issues leading to the Civil War, of course, did great damage to the development of any overall national economic structure.

Between the date of that first census (1790) and the beginning of the Civil War (1860), the number of urban places in the United States grew at twice the rate (sixteenfold versus eightfold) of the national population (Hughes and Cain, 2007). Because these areas began to represent increased buying power, manufacturers and other providers of goods were able to produce their wares locally rather than residents having to import them from other larger areas. This meant that the limited resources of the local consumers stayed in the community and that the manufacturers were able to become increasingly efficient in the production and delivery of goods.

The resultant specialization of each small town led to mutually beneficial trade between them, thereby creating nascent marketplaces. Consumers were thus able to travel somewhat greater distances to satisfy their purchasing needs because they could now satisfy all of those needs in one location. As these markets continued to flourish, and their operations began to support a customer base of greater distances, the towns grew and the urbanization process became ever more entrenched.

Nonetheless, by the onset of the Civil War, 80% of the country's population could still be classified as rural (Hughes and Cain, 2007) and the proportion of rural to urban was even greater in the largely agriculturally based southern states. However, as the best of the farmland in the existing states was exhausted, farmers turned their sights westward and began to seek new opportunities in that direction. As the population began to expand toward the west, several strategically located places began to expand not only their residential base, but also their economic opportunities. Pittsburgh, Chicago, and other areas that were located near rivers and lakes provided staging points for both people and products to move about. Jane Jacobs referred to them as "depots" (Jacobs, 1969). These depot locations served as collection points as well as production points and grew entirely new businesses (what we today would call logistics) around the processes of gathering, storing, selling, and transporting goods.

Many of these depot locations experienced exponential growth as their marketplaces and transportation connections fostered even greater efficiencies and thus attracted more people, more manufacturers, and more trade. As these small cities and towns grew to become midsize and (relatively) large cities, their populations exhibited needs for, and an adequate size to provide, a variety of services that one had previously either had to provide for one's self or obtain from a variety of sources in a range of locations. Thus, such services became more efficient by being in cities in the same way that manufacturing had become more efficient. These initially included personal services such as barbers, medical care, general and specific types of retail, schools, banks, legal services, printing, newspapers, and more.

The next phase in the city's evolution was, according to Jane Jacobs, realized when it gained a "greatly enlarged and greatly diversified local economy" and "becomes a potential source of numerous and diversified exports, built upon local goods and services" (Jacobs, 1969). That enabled the growth of local suppliers and artisans which, in turn, generated additional local economic and governing structures as well as marginal increases in expendable income which, again, generated growing demand for new and higher-value imports. Thus it was that, as Cochran stated, "... the old order was being inevitably ended by hammers, drills, and lathes in small metalworking shops that produced everything from hay rakes to steam engines. The change to new occupations was facilitated by increasingly efficient farms that fed the workers in the rapidly growing cities" (Cochran, 1966).

In the postbellum era, urban life dominated the growth patterns of the nation as well as its politics. As Singer was later to note, "The United States was born in the country and has moved to the city" (Heilbroner and Singer, 1994). By 1870, there were 14 US cities with populations greater than 100,000, and 26% of all Americans lived in places with at least 2,500 residents. That trend was increasing as well: by 1910, there were 50 places in the United States with more than 100,000 residents and 46% of all Americans lived in places with at least 2,500 residents (Hughes and Cain, 2007).

Major US cities began to grow following the Civil War. The population of the city of Chicago grew between 1860 and 1900 from 109,000 to nearly 1.75 million residents. By 1929, there were five American cities with more than one million inhabitants (Heilbroner and Singer, 1994).

Following the cessation of slavery, southern plantations gave way to the system of sharecropping, which proved the undoing of the southern agricultural economy. By 1900, more than one-third of all US farms were being operated by tenants who were hoping, under a series of schemes, ultimately to own the land on which they had been working. The system, however, did not seem to work and ownership remained a dream for most (Gardner, 2002).

Furthermore, most of the arable land throughout the United States was taken, thus causing further migration westward. The Homestead Act was an attempt to allow the growth of farming in support of those migration patterns, however, that mechanism allowed the establishment of farms that were too small to be efficient and competitive. Indeed, it was not until the onset of World War I that efforts were made to address this issue through a series of measures aimed at farm consolidation. Until that time, small farm ownership was inefficient and often devoted primarily to sustaining the individual families. Additional sources of income were sought by those living on farms and off-farm employment grew to the point that, in 1929, more than 6% of US farm families reported at least 200 workdays away from the farm. By 1949, that percentage had nearly tripled, to more than 17%. And, in 1997, the United States Department of Agriculture reported that the average farm family derived about 85% of its total family income from off-farm sources (Gardner, 2002).

Ultimately, the consolidation of farms and the need for external sources of income, as well as the perceived higher (and easier) quality of life in the cities, spelled a precipitous decline in the population on farms. In 1900, 61% of the nation's total population of 76 million lived in rural areas; and 30 million people, or nearly 40% of the nation's total population, lived on farms. By 1990, only 7% of all Americans lived in rural areas and only 2% on farms (Gardner, 2002).

Yet American agricultural productivity continued to increase impressively, in large measure driven by new methods and equipment as well as greater knowledge of the benefits of crop rotations and fertilization. By the middle of the twentieth century, many of the improvements were coming from biochemistry and machinery. New reapers, threshers, and other implements—and the resultant increases in yields per acre—meant that fewer laborers would be required. Improvements in transportation and the refrigeration of produce during transport meant that more distant markets could be reached. This in turn meant that producers could translate the greater efficiencies of production and transportation into greater profits, thereby enabling even further growth and distribution. Farm production was booming but it did not represent a stable source of employment for rural Americans.

Other technological improvements resulted in the irrigation of large tracts in the American southwest. This meant that overall agricultural production was increased even more. The increase in irrigated farmland was dramatic: 1 million acres in 1880; 3.5 million acres by 1890; and 19 million acres by the end of World War I in 1919 (Hughes and Cain, 2007).

American productivity was to be further increased due to the trends of in-migration that had begun prior to the Civil War. Between 1840 and 1914, 24 million people came to the United States. Nearly 13 million of those immigrants arrived on these shores in just the two decades leading up to the First World War.

The US population began increasingly to show its foreign-born roots. In 1860, 13.2% of the population was foreign-born; over the next 50 years that percentage grew to 14.7% (Hughes and Cain, 2007). The impacts of this in-migration were felt most strongly in the cities, which is surprising inasmuch as many of the immigrants had come from rural areas in their old countries. Still, by 1890, the majority of America's urban populations were comprised of foreign-born individuals while three-fourths of the white natives lived in rural areas (Hughes and Cain, 2007). Between 1895 and 1907, more than one million immigrants had arrived in the United States (Hughes and Cain, 2007).

The dramatic growth of US cities is evident in Table 2.1, which illustrates the growth of the number of tenements in the primary point of debarkation, New York City, between 1869 and 1900. The black line represents the number of tenements in the city and is measured against the right vertical axis, whereas the number of residents in those projects is represented by the gray line, which is measured against the left vertical axis. Cities were becoming the sites of the growing

Table 2.1 Population Growth of New York City Tenements, 1869 to 1900

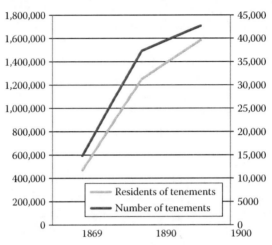

Source: Heilbroner and Singer, 1994. *The Economic Transformation of America since 1865.* Orlando, FL: Harcourt Brace. With permission.

manufacturing employment base that was more than offsetting the loss of farming jobs to technological improvements.

The wave of immigration was useful as the cities required increasing amounts of laborers to work in the growing manufacturing businesses. They provided a steady source of laborers who were happy (at first, at least) to receive low wages and work long hours. The nation was growing and was becoming increasingly urban in the 1920s. The US Census Bureau data show that "… for the first time in history, half of America's 105 million residents were living in urban areas rather than on farms" (Fleming, 2007).

The Great Depression, finally resulting from the collapse of the stock market, had, as its ultimate causes, the following events and issues. The decade that had led up to the 1929 crash had been one of high living, new social mores, rising production, stable employment, and growing wages. Accelerating automobile production meant lower costs and greater demand from average consumers. It was, wrote one author, "A grand time, one of frenzied metamorphosis, endless optimism, and wild experimentation" (Fleming, 2007).

But, by the end of the fall in 1929, the values of stocks bore no direct relationship either to current earnings or to potential earnings. Thus, when the crash occurred, there was no value to support the demands for payouts. Holders of the stocks viewed them as worthless and because many of the purchases had been made on margin, tried unsuccessfully to liquidate their portfolios. The companies that had issued the stocks were forced to pay off what they could and then go out of business, exacerbating the situation by dramatically increasing the unemployment rates as shown in Table 2.2.

Table 2.2 US Unemployment During the Great Depression

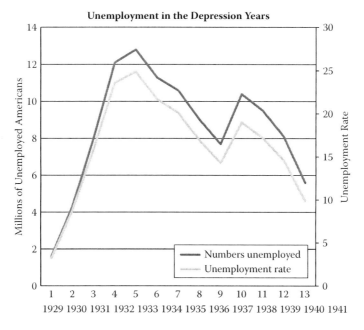

Source: Heilbroner and Singer, 1994. *The Economic Transformation of America since 1865.* Orlando, FL: Harcourt Brace. With permission.

Following the crash in late October, the situation continued to worsen with alarming speed. The stock market had lost about one-third of its total value within a few short weeks. Consumer spending stopped immediately, driving companies out of business as banks called their loans. The growing levels of unemployment created panic, fueled by the inability of the nation's banks to provide the cash to depositors upon demand. Banks followed consumers into failure and the cycle of decline, one element feeding on the demise of another, accelerated.

Cities and towns, with rapidly diminishing tax bases, found themselves unable to cope with the human services needs of their residents. National leaders, including President Hoover, were slow to acknowledge the instability of the entire banking system, attributing the failures to a few banks, but remaining steadfast in their belief that the system generally remained sound. The need for cash drove the remaining financial institutions to call the loans from the nation's farmers who, although consistent in the repayment of their loans before, could not sell enough food because there were not enough buyers, now were forced to fall into arrears and ultimately lose their lands and their homes.

Two major technological advances caused major changes in the next generation's economic structure: the provision of electrification to rural areas and the advent of assembly line production methods. The former—the ability to have electrical power on farms and in rural communities—meant that cities and towns could be located anywhere. This meant that small communities could be established not simply near navigable waterways and other transportation hubs, but closer to the sources of supplies and natural resources or anywhere one could find arable land or a pleasant setting.

The more important changes resulted from the application of the concepts of assembly line production. Through this means, the Ford Motor Company was able, as early as 1914, to produce and ship as many as eight cars per day. This meant that production times were not only accelerated but were increasingly efficient as well, so it meant enhanced profits, but it also meant that fewer employees would be needed than when production was essentially piecework.

Over time, Asian automobile manufacturers and producers of steel chipped away at US dominance in those industries. Although much can be said of the comparably lower wage rates in Japan and other Asian countries, US manufacturers were slow to respond and delinquent in the conversion of their plants to new technologies that might have offset the wage comparisons. Furthermore, the arrogance and obstinacy of the US automobile makers, notably the Big Three, meant that there was little or no responsiveness to the demands of the American consumers. The impacts on the economies of areas such as Pittsburgh, Detroit, Youngstown, Allentown, Bethlehem, and other Rust Belt cities was enormous and enduring. Hughes and Cain state the belief that US industry became less adept at competing effectively and openly and more adept at mergers and price-fixing. In the 70 years between 1937 and 2007, the US manufacturers' collective share of the American automobile market declined precipitously. This is illustrated in Table 2.3, where the black line represents the decline of the US manufacturers' share of the domestic market and the gray line shows the corresponding share of all foreign manufacturers.

Table 2.3   US versus Overseas Manufacturing from the Depression to 2005

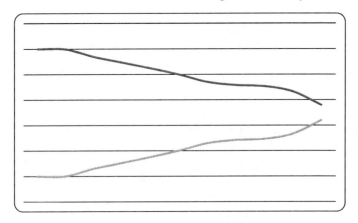

Source: J. Hughes and L. Cain, *American Economic History*, 8th ed. New York: Addison-Wesley, 2007. With permission.

Thus, as American agricultural output was increasing due to the application of various forms of technology, automobile and steel production were consistently declining due to the ignorance of the technological advances in those industries. Two changes to American farm life had an impact on how farmers and their families worked and lived. Jane Jacobs reported that, as late as 1935, fewer than 5% of America's farms had electrical power (Jacobs, 1969).

Electrical power was difficult to provide to rural areas and was not a profitable endeavor simply because the demand was so much less than in denser population bases. For this reason, during the Depression, President Roosevelt saw the need to provide public support for the electrification of America's farms and rural communities. The Rural Electrification Act (REA) increased the percentage of US farms with access to electrical power from 20% in 1935 to more than 80% a decade later (REA, 1936; Gordon, 2011). In addition to enhancing the quality of life in those areas, the REA also enabled a greater production facility from the agricultural sector generally.

However, it was the mass production of the automobile that may have had the widest range of impacts on farm and rural life. By 1920, American automobile manufacturers were using 20% of all US steel, 80% of its rubber, and three-fourths of all plate glass (Gordon, 2011). The growing numbers of cars in use meant that more roads needed to be built. This generated jobs, revenue, the growth of small businesses, and a new interconnectivity between US markets. The total mileage of paved roads in the United States increased from 370,000 miles in 1920 to more than 662,000 by that decade's end (Gordon, 2011).

The automobile had a number of other effects as well. It ended the isolation of farming and rural lifestyles. It fostered the growth of bigger cities and enabled the growth of suburbs because people could live outside the city limits, enjoy a different quality of life for their families, and still reach the employment centers in the downtowns. Heilbroner and Singer noted that cities were not generally pleasant places to live: "Police and fire protection was inadequate. Garbage collection was haphazard at best. City water was often impure. Sewers were smelly and often clogged. Disease could spread quickly under such conditions. In 1882, half the children in Chicago died before reaching the age of five" (Heilbroner and Singer, 1994).

By contrast, suburban neighborhoods, according to Teaford (1997), "combined flowers, fresh air, and neighborliness with transportation links to the big city. What suburbanites wanted was the village of the past with the convenience of the present."

When the Second World War ended, and the troops returned home, a pent-up demand for the good things associated with a "normal" life began to exhibit itself. The American people had suffered through a great deal in less than 30 years, the period from the outset of the First World War through the Great Depression and the Second World War. When the armistices were declared, the returning servicemen and their families wanted a quiet home, a small yard, a secure job, a car, and the appliances that were becoming available, including radios, washing machines, and more. As a result, manufacturing boomed and the suburbs expanded. As the best of the workforce moved outward from the city centers, the businesses of America moved with them, and the populations of the urban cores declined precipitously.

One of the trends that affected small city economies occurred concurrently with the recession of the early 1980s. By the end of 1982, factory utilization in the United States had reached a low of 68% of total capacity. This was the lowest level since that metric had been measured in 1948. The same year also saw the failure of more than 25,000 businesses across the United States, representing the highest such count since the Depression year of 1933. Key for the nation's smaller cities was that more than 2.25 million jobs were lost from the country's manufacturing sector and, when the economy began to grow again, those jobs were replaced by opportunities that were largely in the services sector, which did not benefit the rebound of the country's smaller cities and towns. The impact on urban and suburban areas was clear: in the decade of the 1980s, about three million square feet of office space was constructed nationwide, little of which was in small cities and towns. Over the same time, the services sector added more than 19 million jobs, primarily to urban and suburban locations (Sloan, 1999).

What really damaged the cities of America, however, was not just the overall decline in population. The effect of the best workers moving out, and the companies following them, was that the cities were left with fewer jobs and the least qualified of the potential workforce that could be used to attract or develop new businesses. Furthermore, with the loss of the companies and the highest wage earners, the cities were left with greatly diminished tax bases from which to provide the public services that also typically serve as attractions to businesses to relocate.

As the best jobs went elsewhere, the cities were left with populations that were more likely than their suburban counterparts to demand a range of public services and public support at the same time that the cities' tax bases were diminished by the departure of businesses.

Over the course of the post-World War II period, this decline of cities' fortunes continued and even accelerated, leading to myriad problems ranging from race relations to infrastructure. As the information age began, the "business of business" in America and around the world changed. The use of personal computers and the advent of the Internet changed everyone's fortunes, including those of municipalities. Cities, suburbs, exurbs, and rural areas had an equalizing force in this new age if one acknowledges that the new technologies allow much work to be done from a distance. "The steam engine brought down the price of work-doing energy; the computer brought down the price of storing, retrieving, and manipulating information" (Gordon, 2011). The Internet had the effect of making it easier for buyers and sellers to interact without the cost of an intermediary, thus reducing not only the timing, but the costs of transactions.

The question for economic development must, to some extent, come to this: if people can work from any location, what would attract them to our community? The awareness of this change initially enabled many cities to grow a small or midsized, technology-based service economy to complement and diversify from other more traditional employment. "City size is not bad, but simply irrelevant" (Neal, 2010).

At first, this appeared to be a sound solution to the future sustainability and growth of small and midsized cities and towns. Until, that is, the recession began. As the recession began and jobs were lost, tax bases were eroded to the extent that many small and midsized cities and towns faced an inability to provide adequate services. Some have contemplated, and some have actually begun, sacrificing their charters and yielding their incorporations. In Minnesota, for example, there are an estimated 300 to 700 "ghost towns." In addition, there are another 324 cities and towns of fewer than 1,000 residents, many of which are in difficult, even desperate, financial straits, and another 150 unincorporated places. The total population of all of these Minnesota locations exceeds 170,000 people, so the issue is not insignificant (Egerstrom, 2007).

As these locations struggle to survive or succumb to mounting financial pressures, they place enormous additional stress points on the state budgets that are expected to assume the responsibilities of providing basic public services to their residents. The cuts that must be made and the vital services that are unable to be made available can lead to citizen outrage and pushback as has been seen in Wisconsin, California, and elsewhere. Says a local observer of the Minnesota quandary: "Reinvention of small towns is not an impossible task" (Egerstrom, 2007).

Against this background, economists have begun to look at the consolidation of relatively contiguous economies into regional economies that have greater mass and can create greater demand, but can also level out intraregional inequities. This type of approach may have merit in some places but not others. Where it does have merit is in states that permit local income taxes. In such cases, a new employer creates jobs for everyone and opportunities for small businesses regardless of which specific jurisdiction they call home. However, in states that do not permit local income taxes—such as the Commonwealth of Virginia—that kind of regional approach can be effective only to a point.

Fairfax County, for example, is the source of fully one-fourth of all income taxes in Virginia. Yet, the county receives back in the form of goods and services less than 19 cents on every income tax dollar that goes to the state coffers. Thus, about two-thirds of the county's $3 billion plus general fund is derived from real estate taxes. Hence, although a company that might locate in a neighboring jurisdiction may still represent jobs and small business opportunities, only one jurisdiction will win the real objective: a tax base. Complete regionalism in this setting is unlikely to be very effective.

Seigel and Waxman (2001) concur and note that this is particularly severe throughout New England. There, limited county government and a "… fiscal structure with a heavy dependence on the property tax are major deterrents to regional action." As long as property taxes remain the major revenue source for these cities to provide public services to their residents, "… competition for economic activity amongst municipalities constrains regional cooperation." When one locality wins a prospect decision, it receives the beneficial tax base impacts. "There is little incentive for communities to work together to promote economic development."

There are, of course, other tax structures and other environments in which regional approaches to economic sustainability can be very effective. Some small and midsized cities and towns have grown over time into truly integrated regional economies in order to constitute sufficient demand to be competitive with other larger cities and regions, and to attract the amenities that are important in building a nice lifestyle. These amenities might include personal services, advanced medical care, retail outlets, parks, libraries, entertainment, and more. In short, many places have had to adjust a long-standing way of life in order to thrive. Cities that grew around navigable waterways as described earlier now may find that their advantage for traffic has moved to the nearest interstate highway. In such locations, cities have begun to redevelop these locations for upscale housing, parks, river walks, and other assets. But, these transitions are expensive.

Small cities are getting smaller. In this reverse process, the reason behind their initial growth now bedevils their shrinking. They become less efficient and have smaller customer bases. Lower demand for retail means that the costs will increase, and service businesses will tend to seek locations where the demand is, at a minimum, more stable. Over the years, federal policies of urban renewal and support have focused largely on America's larger inner cities and the plight of farming communities.

Small cities and towns today face a variety of challenges as their leaders attempt to develop the economic foundations that will sustain their communities over time. As has been noted, small cities may find themselves in an economic competition with larger cities and regions that represent larger workforces, greater demand for products and services, and potentially more attractive lifestyles. The communications infrastructure in larger cities tends, for reasons of the aggregate demand, to be more modern and more comprehensive. This fact alone places rural areas at an extreme competitive disadvantage. Other lifestyle and business amenities may also be lacking in smaller cities, including limited access to investment capital for business growth, the presence of an inadequate workforce with mismatched skills, and fewer entertainment options for leisure time.

In terms of the locations available for employers, land may be available in greater abundance (an advantage for some smaller cities) but office space is likely not as available as it is in larger areas. Furthermore, some of the land may have had prior industrial uses from a time when environmental concerns were not apparent, meaning that some of the land may require remediation before it can site more modern industrial companies. On the other hand, in many smaller cities, land is not available. These cities have finite borders and development may have reached its limits. Although some of them may be able to annex adjacent lands for new growth, it may be brownfield sites or farming areas. These cities then have to face the costs of infrastructure development to prepare such sites for the market. They may also have to face debates about the changing nature of their communities.

Another, sometimes overlooked asset that is possessed by larger cities and regions is the availability of air service for both passengers and cargo to a greater share of domestic and global markets. Employers who need to transport their product from the plant to the airport will calculate the additional costs as a negative to doing business outside a given radius from the airport. Similar cost estimates are assigned to sites from which products can be shipped by rail but from which a spur to the main line does not yet exist.

All of these factors affect the ability of the community to attract employers and thus retain their best and brightest students and young people. Much has been written about the impacts of the brain drains from these communities; it is clear that, to rebuild a local economy, cities and towns will need the young workforce that is so attractive to employers across all sectors of business today. Communities that lose employers and then lose their young workers must try to attract employers without being able to assure them of the employees they will need. Young people, especially those whose skills give them greater options, will not return to cities that cannot provide them with jobs and careers.

The critical lesson to be learned here is that in such situations efforts to attract employers and to diversify local economies absolutely must begin long before the loss of jobs is announced. At best, the reaction (to replace departing companies and job opportunities) to such situations must be immediate and consistent over time. At the other end of the employment spectrum, the loss of companies also results in the loss of the senior managers of the departing companies, another asset that will be needed to rebuild the economic base.

Where does this leave America's smaller cities and towns as they struggle to sustain their local economic growth and perhaps even survive as communities? Can they survive? Must there be state and federal subsidies to ensure their survival? Are there unique advantages of not being large cities that are sufficient competitive advantages to attract and retain businesses? Are there economic development strategies that are more effective in this setting or that have proven successful for some and thus may be transferable to others? And is there a way to rebuild smaller city and town economies such that they can be where the economic action takes places in future America?

Chapter 3

What We Know Now

My previous book (*Reinventing Regional and Local Economies*, 2011, Boca Raton, FL: CRC Press) cited numerous lessons learned in the course of speaking to 70 mayors and other local officials—elected, appointed, and otherwise—in major cities and metropolitan areas around the United States. The lessons learned from that exercise are summarized below:

1. State of Mind/Advance in the Worst of Times
   Seventy leaders were interviewed from more than 120 American cities. At the height of this nation's worst recession in 80 years, they were overwhelmingly enthusiastic and proud of their cities, their regions, and the response of their citizenry to the economic hardship.

   Of course, not all was sunshine; many of the leaders interviewed laid out their concerns and objections to city or state policies and some of the other barriers that were affecting the ability to grow a stronger, more future-oriented economic base. There was also a general recognition throughout that there would need to be resources invested in the effort to develop the economy, and that those resources are both human and financial, and that they are both public and private.

2. Static Economies/Laissez Faire
   The interviews revealed a strong sentiment that cities can no longer sustain their economies without making an effort. In some regions, it was considered possible that the economy could essentially sustain itself over time, providing they could generate the necessary tax base to support the provision of some vital public services. Cities and regions that earlier had taken this kind of laissez faire approach to their economic future have been unable to weather the fluctuations that inevitably occur within the larger economy or

the industries and companies to which they are home. They have reached the inescapable conclusion that a lack of attention to the needs of businesses will cause them to move and that, as the world's economy passes by, those cities and regional economies will first stagnate and then decay. Companies will leave, taxes will be lost, and public services will decline in both quantity and quality. Total income will decline, the physical city will decline with it, and a downward spiral that includes dramatic shifts in public safety and the general public welfare will begin that can only be reversed when the policy of economic ignorance and inattention is abandoned.

No economy is static because there are too many external forces that cannot be controlled by local leadership and there are simply too many competitor cities rising and falling all around. Cities must advance their economic development or fall behind. In today's world, those are the only two options. Thus, complacency is not an option for the community seeking economic development. Neither is it an option for the community that has achieved significant economic development. The interrelationship of the nation's and the world's local economies is moving forward at an accelerating rate.

3. Taking the Long-Term View

Any economic development professional will tell you that the process of reinventing a community's economic position is a long-term endeavor. There will typically be little in the way of significant positive results in the short term. Cities must be prepared to stay the course for years in order to generate results. Company outreach is a relationship building exercise, and relationships need time to mature before they begin to bear fruit. In some cases, this has been inconsistent with the short-term views of some elected officials who feel the need to demonstrate immediate results (read "during their term in office") and less of a need to benefit their successors. Fortunately, this has been the exception rather than the rule; however, when it occurs, it is extremely harmful to economic development. Business executives expect not only a pro-business environment, but a consistently pro-business environment.

4. Closing the Asset Gaps

Many US communities have pursued business attraction (and, to a lesser extent, retention) through the provision of cash grants, tax abatements, or other incentives. Arguments have been made on both sides of that debate, but however a community elects to use such incentives, it must, at a minimum, also be mindful of the other factors that cause businesses to select given locations. The successful community is the one that will start with the identification and provision of the assets and amenities that are of greatest benefit to the types of industries being pursued. If the workforce is weak, training must be provided; if the business areas or the downtowns are unsafe or need updated infrastructure, it must be provided. If these things are not done, declining economies do not seem to continue on straight-line declines but rather on an accelerating trend-line of decline. The loss of the best and brightest from an area, the so-called brain drain, results in the loss of what is perhaps the primary asset needed to attract new employers to a city, county, or region. Incentives are often useful in "closing deals" but a community without the essential components businesses require is unlikely even to make it to that point in the process.

5. Public Leadership Redefined

   To ameliorate, reverse, or even avoid economic decline requires exceptional leadership from all sectors concerned: public, private, residential, and institutional. Local and regional economic growth and stability cannot be seen as solely a public responsibility. Leadership is the capacity to cause change through vision and insight. It is the ability to get others to follow because they have confidence in the directions being espoused. In the civic arena, it does not have to be just the mayor, although it will likely be extremely difficult without the support of the mayor or board chair.

   Strong leadership for economic development requires a willingness to stand in front of audiences and explain why expenditures are being used to market, advertise, and bring new people into the community. And it requires an ability to keep people focused on the long-term possibilities rather than the short-term sacrifices inherent in the allocation of funds for economic development. In short, the practice must be seen as an investment rather than a cost.

6. Planning and Implementation across Traditional Lines

   The wise community leadership seeks to collaborate in its economic development efforts with all of the relevant stakeholders in the community and to do so in such a way as to find and to further their mutual interests. Yet, there remain in some cities and regions unproductive relationships that can only be identified as "we–them" situations. That is, the business community and the residential communities are seen as being on opposite sides, somehow forgetting that businesses are comprised essentially of the area's residents and that economic reinvention will be to the long-term benefit of all segments of the community. As the cartoon character, Pogo, was fond of saying, "We have met the enemy and it is us!"

   New technologies and companies based on new technologies have a number of sources, including businesses attracted from elsewhere. But new companies can also be generated from within. This means that local colleges and universities, hospitals, research and development (R&D) facilities, and other community institutions are integral to an area's economic development. Furthermore, there is a growing recognition by businesses that, when one speaks of the economic development–higher education nexus, America's community colleges can be a vital partner in revitalizing local economies. A qualified labor force across a wide range of specialties is critical to an evolving economy.

7. Managing Expectations

A community that sets out on a course of deliberate economic reinvention needs to understand the time frame required for results. This will involve the deft management of expectations among local residents who must sacrifice other, often critical, services in order to allocate funds to business attraction programs. Managing such potentially unrealistic expectations generally requires the responsible agencies to conduct the necessary planning in a publicly transparent process, to ensure opportunities for citizen input, to coordinate the various forms of planning throughout the community, to agree upon and advertise proposed metrics of performance, and to regularize and report the measurements of progress toward the stated outcomes.

One successful way to sustain the effort is to report successes as they occur and to translate the immediate results into items that the community can appreciate. This means that a company relocation or expansion does not just yield 100 new jobs or generate a quarter million dollars in taxes annually. It also means that the new tax revenues can support three new teachers or three new police officers. Citizens may be more willing to accept services that are important to them as the basis for their ongoing sacrifices.

8. Return-on-Investment

The costs of business attraction and retention as well as the costs of business asset development are too often viewed solely as expenses. A greater acceptance of these expenditures can be gained by measuring and reporting the returns on such public investments. However, those returns are all too often measured in terms of the positive deliverables such as jobs, tax base, and wealth generation. Other returns should also be reported to the community; these include the elimination of urban negatives, including crime, high welfare payments, poor school achievement scores, and dilapidated structures.

9. Growing City–Suburban Tensions

Economic development is a highly competitive endeavor for cities, counties, and regions. That competition exists not only between various regions across the country, but within many regions as well and can be the source of significant intraregional tensions as inner cities can be pitted against their suburban neighbors. Often that tension is exacerbated by those who can afford to move to the suburbs in pursuit of the American dream. This typically results in the cities disproportionately becoming the home of lower-income families with higher demands for public services while the best jobs and the tax base move to suburban jurisdictions. Cities then face the need to provide increasingly more with increasingly less.

The resulting impact on the inner cities of this country has been that they have become even less hospitable to new businesses and less attractive to the existing businesses who quickly become overtaxed to make up for the losses. If the inner city deteriorates, no one benefits and the entire region has an even more difficult task in attracting and retaining businesses.

Beyond the lessons learned in the research and interviews that resulted in *Reinventing Regional and Local Economies*, the existing literature highlights several key factors essential for economic growth in micropolitan cities. These components of growth are felt to have validity in explaining why some communities are successful while others continue to falter, or, as Schultz (2004) wrote, "Prosperous small towns abound in every region of the country and in every state; oddly enough, they are often a stone's throw away from a town that is dying on the vine." Those that are successful are the ones that have solid, aggressive, and consistent leadership that plans for the future in conjunction with the entire community: public, private, residential, business, and institutional. However, that will not, of itself, be sufficient.

Midsized cities and regions do indeed offer much that cannot be found in the major metropolitan areas of the country. Schultz argues that one merit of micropolitan communities is that they allow relatively more people to become involved in the affairs of the community and the public. Individuals who are either successful or who get involved in activities can make a greater impact on the life of the community and its people (Schultz, 2004). Knox and Mayer (2009), as well as others, have argued that quality of life issues have drawn significant numbers of individuals and families away from larger cities to the smaller and midsized cities.

This leads one to consider what the literature reveals about the critical components of micropolitan life that can be attractive enough to outsiders to draw them to those communities. Generally, the following factors (listed in no particular order) are given the greatest attention in the literature:

- Community development as a prerequisite to economic development
- A solid vision and strategies for economic growth that enjoy general consensus
- Leadership that embraces change and innovation
- Awareness and use of the community's competitive economic advantages
- The presence throughout the community of hope and optimism
- Local institutions that support economic growth
- Local retail establishments that survive the entrance of national chains
- Local residents making purchases locally, recirculating dollars throughout the community
- Local businesses that attract outside expenditures, thereby importing capital into the community
- An existing business base with a generally and demonstrably lower overall cost of doing business than in accessible larger cities and markets
- Local banks and private investors to finance business development and growth
- Opportunities for industrial and commercial uses of existing buildings and land for economic development and public policies supportive of such uses
- Effective and efficient multimodal transportation networks
- A skilled and available workforce that serves as an asset for business attraction and retention
- A desirable quality of life, including cultural, recreational, and other non-work activities

Much of the literature also warns communities about the potential for economic growth to change the very nature of the community, that which made it so attractive for growth in the first place. Knox and Mayer wrote that "... suburban residential development is spoiling the character (of the community), chain stores moving to the edge of town force local businesses on Main Street to close, ... and their unfettered growth may mean loss of identity and heritage" (Knox and Mayer, 2009). Other writers have recognized the concurrent evils of some growth, with communities beginning to encounter increases in crime and cost of living, the same factors that cause many to leave the nation's major cities in favor of the micropolitan cities and regions.

The consensus seems to be that as communities grow and begin to encounter these related issues they are better served through longer-term growth strategies that allow the cities and their economic foundations to expand at a rate that enables the local governments to acquire the resources and knowledge to address and control those factors rather than encountering them all at the same time and becoming overwhelmed by the changes in their communities.

This consideration of the factors essential for economic growth will be maximally instructive if the reader keeps them in mind while reading the case studies of micropolitan experiences and lessons.

Chapter 4

Case Studies

Interviewing the Experts: Small City Leadership

A great deal can be learned by conducting library research into the experiences of local economies and the leadership, both public and private, of the communities in which they are located. Much can also be learned by talking to the men and women who led those communities through the evolutionary phases of the local economic condition. Most often, those who write about their individual experiences do so within the context of their native communities. This can yield a wealth of lessons about what does or does not work in given sets of circumstances and can then be compared with the conclusions of other leaders in other communities undergoing similar events and conditions. Over time, the cumulative knowledge of these histories can yield some understanding about trends and the effectiveness of various strategies that have been employed.

When looking at micropolitan communities (those with populations between 10,000 and 50,000) there is far less research available to draw from than exists relative to the nation's major metropolitan marketplaces. There seems to be greater interest in what has happened and what responses have been tried in New York, Chicago, and Los Angeles than in Danville, Virginia; Ponca City, Oklahoma; or Winona, Minnesota.

Nonetheless, these micropolitan communities are home to many families and individuals, businesses, and institutions, and a different standard of living than that which exists in the larger economies of the major cities. When viewed from the national perspective, the numbers are both impressive and important. Their stories must also be told, their lessons learned. Other micropolitan communities are experiencing similar economic challenges today to those that others have already lived through, thought about, acted upon, and from which lessons were learned. Others can benefit.

But, from what can other communities learn? They can read about or talk to one colleague in a micropolitan city's leadership at a time and begin to draw conclusions across their discussions that may be applicable to their situations. Or, they can draw upon the resources of a collection of cumulative knowledge, expressed not from library research, but rather from discussions held between an author/practitioner who complements not his or her own experiences alone, but also those of numerous leaders from many jurisdictions around the country. That is what this book purports to provide. As such, it is based on no fewer than 70 interviews with the mayors of micropolitan cities who relate their personal experiences and conclusions about what can be or not be effective in given sets of circumstances. This book does the legwork; the research will enable others to observe the experiences and lessons of their colleagues in other communities as they confront their own challenges.

In *Reinventing Regional and Local Economies*, a similar examination of America's larger cities was undertaken. The interviews were conducted with mayors, university presidents, business executives, chamber of commerce and economic development officials, and others. The data were rich and revealing, and numerous trends emerged upon an across-the-board examination of about 35 cities. Although much of the information was provided by others, I felt that the richest data came from the 11 mayors I interviewed. They pulled no punches and were equally obliging when asked to discuss their successes and their failures, what they did right, and what they accept now as mistakes. I take their conclusions and combine them with my personal hypothesis that, in the micropolitan cities under study in this research, the senior elected officials play a relatively greater role in directing the local economic evolution than their big-city counterparts. As such, the intent of this book is to relate the stories and conclusions of 70 mayors, and only mayors, from 70 of America's micropolitan cities.

The men and women who agreed to be interviewed for this book are often unsung heroes. Communities are sometimes quick to criticize elected officials for an inability to manage external forces that are actually beyond their control. Yet, time and again, we are reminded that success has many mothers and fathers. There was no real surprise in this for the mayors who talked to me; they are not mayors for the glory or recognition. Without exception, I had the distinct impression that these were people with sincere interest in doing good things for places they love and the people they know, live with, and represent. As a group, they are among the most impressive and most dedicated people I have "met" and their time, energies, and stories are greatly appreciated. The mayors who participated in this study are shown in Table 4.1.

Table 4.1 Micropolitan Mayors

City/State	Mayor	Region
Aberdeen, South Dakota	Mike Levson	Central
Adrian, Michigan	Greg Dumars	Central
Bangor, Maine	Cary Weston	Northeast
Baraboo, Wisconsin	Mike Palm	Central
Beckley, West Virginia	Emmitt Pugh	Southeast
Blackfoot, Idaho	Mike Virtue	Northwest
Bowling Green, Ohio	Richard Edwards	Central
Bozeman, Montana	Sean Becker	Northwest
Brigham City, Utah	Dennis Fife	Northwest
Brookings, South Dakota	Tim Reed	Central
Chambersburg, Pennsylvania	Pete Lagiovane	Northeast
Chelsea, Massachusetts	Jay Ash	Northeast
Couer d'Alene, Iowa	Sandi Bloem	Central
Danville, Virginia	Sherman Saunders	Southeast
Doral, Florida	J. C. Bermudez	Southeast
Durango, Colorado	Doug Lyon	Southwest
Elk Grove, Illinois	Craig Johnson	Central
Elko, Nevada	Chris Johnson	Northwest
Elmira, New York	Sue Skidmore	Northeast
Enid, Oklahoma	Eric Benson	Central
Eureka, California	Frank Jager	Northwest
Farmers Branch, Texas	Bill Glancy	Central
Findlay, Ohio	Lydia Mihalik	Central
Fremont, Nebraska	Scott Getzschman	Central
Galesburg, Illinois	Sal Garza	Central
Gillette, Wyoming	Tom Murphy	Northwest

Continued

Table 4.1 (*Continued*)   Micropolitan Mayors

City/State	Mayor	Region
Hobbs, New Mexico	Sam Cobb	Southwest
Holyoke, Massachusetts	Alex Morse	Northeast
Jamestown, New York	Sam Teresi	Northeast
Jasper, Indiana	Terry Seitz	Central
Kinston, North Carolina	B. J. Murphy	Southeast
Kokomo, Indiana	Gregory Goodnight	Central
Lagrange, Georgia	Jeff Lukken	Southeast
Lewiston, Maine	Robert Macdonald	Northeast
Littleton, Colorado	Debbie Brinkman	Southwest
Marquette, Michigan	John Kivela	Central
Martinsville, Virginia	Kim Adkins	Southeast
Maryland Heights, Missouri	Mike Moeller	Central
Mason City, Iowa	Eric Bookmeyer	Central
Menomonie, Wisconsin	Randy K'naack	Central
Moline, Illinois	Don Waelvert	Central
Murray, Kentucky	Bill Wells	Central
Naples, Florida	John Storey	Southeast
Natchitoches, Louisiana	Lee Posey	Southeast
New Bern, North Carolina	Lee Bettis	Southeast
Newberry, South Carolina	Foster Senn	Southeast
Ossining, New York	William Hanauer	Northeast
Owatonna, Minnesota	Thomas Kuntz	Central
Paducah, Kentucky	Bill Paxton	Central
Picayune, Mississippi	Ed Pinero	Southeast
Pottsville, Pennsylvania	John Reiley	Northeast
Pullman, Washington	Glenn Johnson	Northwest
Quincy, Illinois	John Spring	Central

Table 4.1 (*Continued*) Micropolitan Mayors

City/State	Mayor	Region
Rolla, Missouri	Bill Jenks	Central
Ruston, Louisiana	Dan Hollingsworth	Southeast
San Luis Obispo, California	Jan Marx	Southwest
Sedalia, Missouri	Elaine Horn	Central
Selma, Alabama	George Evans	Southeast
Starkville, Mississippi	Parker Wiseman	Southeast
Tifton, Georgia	Jamie Carter	Southeast
Tupelo, Mississippi	Jack Reed	Southeast
Tuskegee, Alabama	Omar Neal	Southeast
Twin Falls, Idaho	Don Hall	Northwest
Uvalde, Texas	J. Allen Carnes	Central
Valparaiso, Indiana	Jon Costas	Central
Walla Walla, Washington	Jim Barrow	Northwest
Watertown, Wisconsin	Ron Krueger	Central
Winona, Minnesota	Jerry Miller	Central
Winter Haven, Florida	Jeff Powell	Southeast
Zanesville, Ohio	Jeff Tilton	Central

Selecting the Micropolitan Cities for Inclusion in the Research

In 2003, the United States Department of the Census reported that America had more than 1,600 micropolitan cities. The selection of the cities to be included in this research was the result of passing that list through several "filters." The primary consideration was the diversity of the communities. I wanted to ensure that all parts of the United States were represented and that the universe involved cities that had experienced economic decline and were recovering (or had recovered) as well as those that had only declined thus far, and those that had experienced only growth or relatively stable economic foundations. As a consequence, there are various settings included herein and a wide range of conclusions about what may or may not be effective. There are cities of which many people—beyond several hundred miles—have never heard of, and there are some that are well known for various reasons, some good, some not so good.

As I heard the stories of these cities and their respective economic evolutions, I had a variety of immediate personal reactions. Often I thought I might enjoy experiencing life in those places and knowing the people and being part of the effort to grow or revitalize their declining economies. The most attractive places seemed to me to be those in which the problems were regarded as challenges to be overcome; less attractive were the cities where all that could be seen were the challenge and the impending struggle. There is something very invigorating about cities and leaders who are aggressive about improving their collective lots. It strikes me as the "American way," writ large.

The selection of the cities was less than scientific but was designed to incorporate the following overall characteristics among the sample cities:

- Diversity of regions across the United States
- Diverse rates of success/difficulties in growing/sustaining/re-establishing the local economies
- Variation of city population bases within the allowable range for micropolitan cities (10,000 to 50,000)
- Variation of cities with increasing and declining population bases
- Wide representation of the three types of micropolitan cities (i.e., subsets of major metropolitan areas, somewhat isolated regional hubs for various services, and completely isolated cities that need to be nearly totally self-sufficient)

Chapter 5

Economic Development Issues of America's Micropolitan Cities

All cities, like all people, are very different. And all cities, like all people, have some things in common. So it is for the micropolitan cities in this study. The following lists include the key issues for future economic development cited by the 70 mayors of the 130+ cities in this research who responded. Each city is listed first with the issues cited by their respective mayors. Following that are the various issues cited with a list of each city whose mayor made reference to it.

Issues by City

Aberdeen, South Dakota

- An isolated micro (micropolitan city) can fuel growth for an entire region
- So can economic decline affect the entire region in a negative way
- Mismatch of jobs and skills sets
- Importance of aesthetics and appearance
- One announcement can change everything
- Growth of jobs in the secondary economy (e.g., construction, shipping, distribution)
- Growth creates new challenges as well (e.g., housing, retail)

Adrian, Michigan

- Effectiveness of incentives
- Use of higher education

Albany, Oregon

- The housing–jobs balance
- Downtown issues
- Utility requirements for growth
- Aesthetics

Ardmore, Oklahoma

- Economic diversification
- "Build it and they will come" (chicken and egg)

Athens, Ohio

- Use of higher education
- Economic diversification
- Social impacts of job loss (e.g., hunger, poverty, crime)
- Tax cuts versus federal giveaways

Bangor, Maine

- Events and festivals as economic development
- Reputation as the worst state for doing business (forbes.com)
- Use of higher education
- Overdependence on government spending
- Growth in recreation, arts, and retail as economic development

Baraboo, Wisconsin

- Riverfront development
- Tourism as economic development

Bartlesville, Oklahoma

- The arts as economic development
- Use of higher education

Beckley, West Virginia

- Economic diversification
- Regionalism

Blackfoot, Idaho

- Economic diversification
- Use of higher education
- Physical growth constrained by neighboring federal labs and a Native American reservation
- Secondary economic impacts/clusters
- Regionalism/collaboration

Blytheville, Arkansas

- Economic diversification

Bowling Green, Ohio

- Use of higher education
- Capital formation as a growth strategy

Bozeman, Montana

- Tourism as economic development
- Retail growth as economic development
- Use of higher education

Brigham City, Utah

- Tourism as economic development
- Brain drain

Brookings, South Dakota

- Use of higher education
- Economic diversification
- Retail spending leakage

Burlington, Vermont

- Airport growth

■ Economic diversification
■ Tax base issues

Carbondale, Illinois

■ Use of higher education
■ Economic diversification

Chambersburg, Pennsylvania

■ Tax base issues
■ State policies

Chelsea, Massachusetts

■ Economic diversification (i.e., casinos)
■ Aesthetic considerations

Chillicothe, Ohio

■ Economic diversification

Clarksburg, West Virginia

■ Job losses
■ Brain drain
■ Population losses

Clinton, Iowa

■ Cultural and recreational improvements as economic development
■ Tourism as economic development

Clovis, New Mexico

■ Impacts of military base
■ An insufficient and skilled labor force

Coeur d'Alene, Idaho

■ Some population subgroups (e.g., Hispanics) more affected than others by recession
■ The small work force will slow economic growth

Concord, New Hampshire

- Tourism as economic development

Cookeville, Tennessee

- Use of higher education
- Regionalism
- Psyche/attitude

Covina, California

- Economic diversity
- Community problems related to economic decline

Culver City, California

- Is a high transient occupancy tax (14%) a source of revenues or a deterrent to business attraction (visitors)?
- Economic diversification
- Retail growth as economic development
- Tourism as economic development

Danville, Virginia

- Regionalism
- Workforce issues
- Economic diversification

Denison, Texas

- The long-term return on investment for aggressive tax incentives
- Regionalism

Dodge City, Kansas

- Economic diversification

Doral, Florida

- Tax policies
- Tourism as economic development
- Retail

Douglas, Georgia

- Alignment of stakeholders (public, private, academic, institutional, state, local)
- Economic impact of colleges (Georgia College)
- The importance of fostering entrepreneurialism to grow start-up businesses
- Strip malls outside of town are hurting downtown retailers
- Very high rates of home foreclosures
- Infrastructure improvements to help drive economic development

Durango, Colorado

- Use of higher education
- Tourism as economic development

Elk Grove, Illinois

- Economic diversity
- Issues related to the state

Elko, Nevada

- Economic diversification
- Tax base issues

Elmira, New York

- Declining population hurts job attraction
- Relatively high taxes hurt job attraction
- Loss of an industry
- Economic diversification

Enid, Oklahoma

- Impacts of military bases (Vance AFB)
- Importance of the residents' psyche for economic development

Eureka, California

- Importance of in-migration to help stabilize the population base
- Use of higher education

Farmers Branch, Texas

- Infrastructure issues

Findlay, Ohio

- Economic diversification
- Public-private collaboration
- Downtown issues

Frankfurt, Kentucky

- Regionalism
- Economic diversification

Fremont, Nebraska

- Do those who live in Fremont and commute to Omaha create problems for how Fremont pays for public services?
- Tourism as economic development

Galesburg, Illinois

- Aesthetics, downtown issues
- Poverty
- Brain drain
- Use of incentives
- Managing expectations

Gallup, New Mexico

- Economic development with a negative image (reservation alcoholism)
- Economic diversification

Gillette, Wyoming

- Federal policies
- Natural resource assets
- Infrastructure issues (i.e., water)

Grand Junction, Colorado

- Dependence on a single industry (energy)
- Economic diversification

Greenburg, Kansas

- Recovering from natural disaster (2007 tornado)

Greenwood, South Carolina

- Use of higher education

Hannibal, Missouri

- Riverfront development
- Tourism as economic development

Hays, Kansas

- Use of higher education

Helena, Montana

- Population loss

Hobbs, New Mexico

- Economic diversification
- Downtown issues

Holyoke, Massachusetts

- Poverty
- Use of higher education
- Workforce issues
- Downtown issues
- The arts as economic development

Hutchinson, Kansas

- Immigration issues
- One major announcement can change everything; incentives and return on investment

Jamestown, New York

- Public–private collaboration
- Managing expectations
- State policies
- Loss of an industry

Jasper, Indiana

- Incentives and return on investment
- Managing expectations
- Brain drain

Jesup, Georgia

- Economic diversification

Kearney, Nebraska

- Use of higher education

Kerrville, Texas

- Poverty
- Incentives and return on investment

Kinston, North Carolina

- Poverty
- Economic decline creates social issues (i.e., condemned housing, crime, physical decline)
- Economic development incentives and return on investment

Kokomo, Indiana

- Overdependence on single industry
- Impacts of decline are long-term
- Incentives and return on investment
- Brain drain
- Use of higher education

LaGrange, Georgia

- Economic diversity
- Industry clusters
- Poverty
- Use of higher education
- Military base and relation to economic development

Laramie, Wyoming

- Tourism as economic development
- Use of higher education

Lewiston, Maine

- Use of higher education
- Poverty
- Aesthetics, downtown issues

Littleton, Colorado

- Innovation/entrepreneurialism/"economic gardening"
- Regionalism

Lompoc, California

- Relation of economic development to military base (Vandenberg Air Force Base)
- From traditional agricultural products to value-added components and clusters (i.e., seed research, boutique wineries)

Lufkin, Texas

- Overdependence on a single industry
- Economic diversification

Marquette, Michigan

- High taxes impede growth
- Use of higher education
- Tourism as economic development

Marshall, Texas

- Use of higher education

Marshalltown, Iowa

- State taxes impede local economic growth
- State/local environmental legislation and regulatory issues (e.g., mixed coal plant plans for Alliant)

Martinsville, Virginia

- Loss of dominant industries
- Use of higher education
- Poverty

Maryland Heights, Missouri

- Infrastructure issues
- Poverty
- Tax base issues
- Managing expectations

Mason City, Iowa

- Incentives, return on investment
- Brain drain

Menomonie, Wisconsin

- Regionalism
- Incentives, return on investment
- Use of higher education

Meridian, Mississippi

- Tax base issues

Minot, North Dakota

- Relation of military bases to economic development (Minot Air Force Base)
- Recovering from natural disasters (flood)
- Overdependence on a single industry (oil)

Moline, Illinois

- Economic diversification
- Impacts of state policies
- Riverfront issues

Mount Pleasant, Michigan

- Use of higher education
- Waterfront issues

Murray, Kentucky

- Tourism as economic development
- Use of higher education

Muskegon, Michigan

- Building on the area's historic skillsets
- Economic diversification

Muskogee, Oklahoma

- Incentives and return on investment

Naples, Florida

- Tourism as economic development
- Tax base issues

Natchitoches, Louisiana

- Use of higher education
- Tax base issues
- Infrastructure issues

New Bern, North Carolina

- City administration
- Poverty

Newberry, South Carolina

- Downtown issues
- Use of higher education

New Castle, Pennsylvania

- Poverty
- Tax base issues

Nogales, Arizona

- Regionalism (including Mexico)

- Immigration issues
- Tourism as economic development

Ossining, New York

- Are state taxes impeding local growth?
- Downtown redevelopment and historic preservation
- Riverfront issues
- Residential growth issues

Ottumwa, Iowa

- State laws relative to local needs create tensions between the environment and economic development
- Need for the manufacturing base to return

Owatonna, Minnesota

- Incentives and return on investment
- Economic diversification
- Tax base issues

Paducah, Kentucky

- Integrating land use and economic development
- Economic diversification
- Incentives and return on investment
- Riverfront issues
- Use of higher education

Paramus, New Jersey

- Environmental issues impede growth potential

Picayune, Mississippi

- Infrastructure issues
- Tourism as economic development

Placentia, California

- Tax base issues

Plainfield, New Jersey

- Economic diversification
- Tax base issues

Plattsburgh, New York

- Loss of an industry
- Use of higher education

Ponca City, Oklahoma

- Technology jobs (the new economy) or manufacturing (the way of life we've always known)
- Loss of a primary employer (Conoco Phillips)

Portsmouth, Ohio

- Decline of the primary industry
- Riverfront issues
- Tourism as economic development

Pottsville, Pennsylvania

- Infrastructure issues
- Tax base issues

Poughkeepsie, New York

- Brain drain
- Use of higher education

Pullman, Washington

- Use of higher education
- Economic diversification

Quincy, Illinois

- Local economic growth impeded by high state taxes
- Regionalism
- Economic diversification

Roanoke Rapids, North Carolina

- Sprawl is not an issue just in metropolitan cities

Rolla, Missouri

- Use of higher education
- Tax base issues
- Economic diversification

Ruston, Louisiana

- Use of higher education
- Creating the right environment for economic growth
- Regionalism

Salina, Kansas

- Loss of a primary industry
- Economic diversification
- Incentives and return on investment
- Value of air service for economic development

San Luis Obispo, California

- High cost of living
- Need more workers
- Downsizing the local government: what happens to public services?
- Aesthetics
- Regionalism/collaboration

Sedalia, Missouri

- Economic development incentives, return on investment
- Be aggressive in the good times

Selma, Alabama

- Economic diversification
- Air service as a driver of economic development
- Aesthetics, downtown issues

Shelby, North Carolina

- Loss of two major projects due to lower incentives than competitors
- Loss of primary industries (i.e., textiles/apparel)
- Immigration issues
- Use of higher education

Shelbyville, Tennessee

- Reduced city spending hurts public services
- Aesthetics/Main Street

Sierra Vista, Arizona

- Relation of military bases to economic development (Fort Huachuca)
- Image issues (i.e., immigration and drugs from Mexico)

Starkville, Mississippi

- Economic diversification
- Use of higher education
- Regionalism

Staunton-Waynesboro, Virginia

- Regionalism: competitors or collaborators?
- Downtown issues

Stevens Point, Wisconsin

- Air service as a driver of economic development
- Use of higher education
- Economic diversification
- Tax base issues

Stillwater, Oklahoma

- Incentives for economic development and return on investment
- Use of higher education
- Economic diversification

Texarkana, Texas

- Growth of hotels, convention center, a sportsplex as economic development

- Use of higher education
- Regionalism; cross-border issues

Tifton, Georgia

- Use of higher education
- Loss of a primary industry

Tupelo, Mississippi

- Preparing for economic growth in the good times
- Regionalism

Tuskegee, Alabama

- Managing expectations
- Tourism as economic development
- Use of higher education

Twin Falls, Idaho

- In-migration of businesses from California
- Use of incentives (alternative energies)
- Economic diversification

Uvalde, Texas

- Infrastructure issues
- Downtown issues
- Brain drain

Valparaiso, Indiana

- Use of higher education
- Is the local psyche for growth gone?
- Relatively low state taxes help drive economic development

Vicksburg, Mississippi

- Casino as economic development
- Relation of military installations to economic development (the US Army Corps of Engineers)

Walla Walla, Washington

- Use of higher education
- Economic diversification
- Clusters

Warren, Ohio

- Labor force issues
- Use of higher education
- Economic diversification

Watertown, Wisconsin

- Downtown issues
- Infrastructure issues
- Economic diversification
- Regionalism
- Industry clusters
- Micropolitan cities must not just attract, but retain, companies
- Local confidence and managing expectations

Wilson, North Carolina

- Use of higher education
- Economic diversification

Winona, Minnesota

- Economic diversification
- Industry clusters
- Use of higher education

Winter Haven, Florida

- Economic diversification
- Labor force issues
- Use of higher education
- Tax base issues
- One announcement can have a disproportionate impact

Wooster, Ohio

- Use of higher education

Zanesville, Ohio

■ Poverty
■ Economic diversification
■ Use of higher education

The obverse of this listing is to attach each of the micropolitan cities in this research to the issues cited by their respective mayors as being key as economic development proceeds in their communities. Such a view of these issues follows.

Cities by Issue

Issues related to residential growth
> Clarksburg, West Virginia; Helena, Montana; Ossining, New York

One announcement can change everything in an entire region
> Aberdeen, South Dakota; Clarksburg, West Virginia; Hutchinson, Kansas; Ponca City, Oklahoma; Winter Haven, Florida

Aesthetic/appearance/downtown/environmental issues/riverfront uses
> Aberdeen, South Dakota; Albany, Oregon; Baraboo, Wisconsin; Chelsea, Massachusetts; Findlay, Ohio; Hannibal, Missouri; Hobbs, New Mexico; Holyoke, Massachusetts; Lewiston, Maine; Marshalltown, Iowa; Moline, Illinois; Mount Pleasant, Michigan; Ossining, New York; Ottumwa, Iowa; Paducah, Kentucky; Paramus, New Jersey; Portsmouth, Ohio; Roanoke Rapids, North Carolina; San Luis Obispo, California; Selma, Alabama; Shelbyville, Tennessee; Staunton-Waynesboro, Virginia; Uvalde, Texas; Watertown, Wisconsin

Secondary economic impacts/clusters
> Aberdeen, South Dakota; Blackfoot, Idaho; Elko, Nevada; Lompoc, California; Twin Falls, Idaho; Walla Walla, Washington; Watertown, Wisconsin; Winona; Minnesota

Growth creates new needs (before or after) infrastructure issues
> Aberdeen, South Dakota; Albany, Oregon; Douglas, Georgia; Eureka, California; Farmers Branch, Texas; Gillette, Wyoming; Maryland Heights, Missouri; Minot, North Dakota; Natchitoches, Louisiana; Picayune, Mississippi; Pottsville, Pennsylvania; Texarkana, Texas; Uvalde, Texas; Watertown, Wisconsin

Loss of an industry
> Elmira, New York; Jamestown, New York; Martinsville, Virginia; Menomonie, Wisconsin; Tifton, Georgia; Plattsburgh, New York; Portsmouth, Ohio

Incentives/questions of ROI/"must" use incentives
> Adrian, Michigan; Denison, Texas; Hutchinson, Kansas; Jasper, Indiana; Kerrville, Texas; Kinston, North Carolina; Kokomo, Indiana; Mason

City, Iowa; Menomonie, Wisconsin; Muskogee, Oklahoma; Paducah, Kentucky; Salina, Kansas; Sedalia, Missouri; Twin Falls, Idaho; Shelby, North Carolina

Social impacts of economic decline, poverty

Athens, Ohio; Covina, California; Galesburg, Illinois; Holyoke, Massachusetts; Kinston, North Carolina; LaGrange, Georgia; Lewiston, Maine; Martinsville, Virginia; Maryland Heights, Missouri; New Castle, Pennsylvania; New Bern, North Carolina; Zanesville, Ohio

Tax cuts/public services

Athens, Ohio; Burlington, Vermont; Chambersburg, Pennsylvania; Doral, Florida; Elko, Nevada; Meridian, Mississippi; Maryland Heights, Missouri; New Castle, Pennsylvania; Naples, Florida; Natchitoches, Louisiana; Owatonna, Minnesota; Placentia, California; Plainfield, New Jersey; Pottsville, Pennsylvania; Quincy, Illinois; Rolla, Missouri; San Luis Obispo, California; Walla Walla, Washington

Insufficient workforce/jobs-skills mismatch/immigration issues

Aberdeen, South Dakota; Albany, Oregon; Clovis, New Mexico; Cookeville, Tennessee; Couer d'Alene, Idaho; Danville, Virginia; Elmira, New York; Eureka, California; Holyoke, Massachusetts; Hutchinson, Kansas; Nogales, Arizona; San Luis Obispo, California; Shelby, North Carolina; Twin Falls, Idaho; Warren, Ohio; Winter Haven, Florida

Entrepreneurialism

Cookeville, Tennessee; Douglas, Georgia; Littleton, Colorado

"Build it and they will come"/chicken and egg?

Ardmore, Oklahoma; Ruston, Louisiana, Tupelo, Mississippi

Negative image issues

Bangor, Maine; Gallup, New Mexico; Selma, Alabama; Sierra Vista, Arizona

Events and festivals, tourism

Bangor, Maine; Baraboo, Wisconsin; Bozeman, Montana; Brigham City, Utah; Clinton, Iowa; Concord, New Hampshire; Doral, Florida; Durango, Colorado; Fremont, Nebraska; Hannibal, Missouri; Holyoke, Massachusetts; Laramie, Wyoming; Marquette, Michigan; Murray, Kentucky; Naples, Florida; Nogales, Arizona; Picayune, Mississippi; Tuskegee, Alabama

Use of higher education

Adrian, Michigan; Athens, Ohio; Bartlesville, Oklahoma; Bangor, Maine; Blackfoot, Idaho; Bowling Green, Ohio; Bozeman, Montana; Brookings, South Dakota; Carbondale, Illinois; Cookeville, Tennessee; Douglas, Georgia; Durango, Colorado; Eureka, California; Greenwood, South Carolina; Hays, Kansas; Holyoke, Massachusetts; Kearney, Nebraska; Kokomo, Indiana; LaGrange, Georgia; Laramie, Wyoming; Lewiston, Maine; Marquette, Michigan; Martinsville, Virginia; Menomonie,

Wisconsin; Murray, Kentucky; Natchitoches, Louisiana; Newberry, South Carolina; Paducah, Kentucky; Plattsburgh, New York; Poughkeepsie, New York; Pullman, Washington; Rolla, Missouri, Ruston, Louisiana; Shelby, North Carolina; Starkville, Mississippi; Stevens Point, Wisconsin; Stillwater, Oklahoma; Texarkana, Texas; Tuskegee, Alabama; Valparaiso, Indiana; Walla Walla, Washington; Warren, Ohio; Winona, Minnesota; Winter Haven, Florida

Military bases

Clovis, New Mexico; Enid, Oklahoma; Lompoc, California; Minot, North Dakota; Sierra Vista, Arizona; Vicksburg, Mississippi

Brain drain

Bangor, Maine; Brigham City, Utah; Jasper, Indiana; Kokomo, Indiana; Mason City, Iowa; Poughkeepsie, New York; Uvalde, Texas; Vicksburg, Mississippi

Growth based on recreation, retail, the arts: is the tax generation sufficient?

Bangor, Maine; Bartlesville, Oklahoma; Bozeman, Montana; Brookings, South Dakota; Clinton, Iowa; Doral, Florida

If higher taxes impede growth, how to pay for public services?

Culver City, California; Elmira, New York; Marquette, Michigan; Marshalltown, Iowa; Quincy, Illinois; San Luis Obispo, California; Stevens Point, Wisconsin; Valparaiso, Indiana

Regionalism/collaboration

Beckley, West Virginia; Blackfoot, Idaho; Danville, Virginia; Denison, Texas; Douglas, Georgia; Findlay, Ohio; Frankfurt, Kentucky; Fremont, Nebraska; Jamestown, New York; Littleton, Colorado; Menomonie, Wisconsin, Nogales, Arizona; Quincy, Illinois; Ruston, Louisiana; San Luis Obispo, California; Starkville, Mississippi; Staunton-Waynesboro, Virginia; Texarkana, Texas; Tupelo, Mississippi; Watertown, Wisconsin

Disaster recovery

Minot, North Dakota; Natchitoches, Louisiana

Airport impacts

Burlington, Vermont; Salina, Kansas; Selma, Alabama; Stevens Point, Wisconsin

Attitudes/psyche/managing expectations

Enid, Oklahoma; Galesburg, Illinois; Jamestown, New York; Jasper, Indiana; Maryland Heights, Missouri; Tuskegee, Alabama; Valparaiso, Indiana; Watertown, Wisconsin

Impacts of state or federal policies

Chambersburg, Pennsylvania; Elk Grove, Illinois; Gillette, Wyoming; Moline, Illinois

Long-term nature of process

Kokomo, Indiana

■ Role of higher education
▩ Catastrophes loss of industry social impacts image
■ Tax issues
■ Regionalism and collaboration
▩ Workforce issues
▩ Aesthetics downtown and riverfront
▩ Infrastructure issues
▩ Events and festivals

Figure 5.1   Relative frequency of mayoral reference to individual cities' issues.

These issues are common themes in many of the micropolitan cities studied in this book and can be tallied to indicate those that were mentioned (unaided) by the mayors during the interviews. Figure 5.1 indicates no relative importance but does indicate relative frequency. Some are seen as problems or challenges whereas others represent potential solutions to or support of future growth, and most are best viewed as a mixture of the two. In short, it is merely an indication of what is on the minds of today's micropolitan leadership.

Chapter 6

Seventy of America's Micropolitan Communities Examined

Seventy interviews with mayors of micropolitan cities were conducted. This was the yield from the initial research that selected more than 120 cities to be on the "short list." These communities represented the three types of micropolitan areas in all parts of the continental United States. Ultimately, 70 mayors consented to interviews, the summaries of which appear below. This represented an acceptance rate of nearly 60%, surprisingly high for this type of outreach.

Nearly all of these mayors are part-time—at least that is how their positions are described—and very few are paid. At the height of the national recession during which the invitations were extended, many had to be mayor and executive assistant all at once because budgetary resources could be saved by keeping positions vacant in city halls across America.

Some were difficult to reach; others declined. There was a clear suspicion on the part of many that they would end up being misquoted, cited in a negative way, or were ultimately going to be asked to buy something. It is unfortunate that our society has reached that level of mistrust although, in fairness, I can certainly understand their misgivings. What follows, then, is the summary of all the micropolitan cities from the initial list and the interview summaries from the 70 mayors who agreed to participate. These are some of America's first citizens and finest salesmen and women.

It should be kept in mind, as one reads the summaries of these interviews with America's micropolitan city mayors, that the interviews were conducted at the height of the nation's, the world's, worst economic environment since the Great Depression of the 1930s. I rather suspect that had a similar set of interviews been conducted in that decade, the outcomes and lessons would have been substantially different.

Several distinctions exist between the Great Depression and the so-called Great Recession. The lengths and depths of the disasters of the 1930s were clearly greater. Still, there seemed in these interviews to have been virtually none of the absence of hope that characterized the accounts of the Great Depression. Why? Why are individuals and cities and their leadership calmer, even more hopeful, now than before?

Although not all, most of the micropolitan city mayors interviewed in this research noted that they were either experiencing the beginning phases of recovery in their cities or expected to receive positive renewal in the near future. What came through clearly in those cases was the strength of conviction that they and their constituents would find a way to attract jobs, replace those that had been lost, and find the resources necessary to continue to provide strong public services. Many knew where the relief would come from whereas others had plans that included strategies they felt would help to drive a recovery.

Perhaps the difference today lies in a keener understanding of what can be done: the art of the possible. Many of the mayors discussed the potential for growing new companies or spinning off new technologies from a local university, or for working with a local hospital, military base, or other institution or facility to help generate job opportunities. They have involved other community stakeholders and have taken a long-term view of the types of economic growth and economic diversification that is sustainable in today's environment as well as that of tomorrow. So, the professionalism of both the elected and appointed officials in micropolitan cities may be substantially greater today; but that still begs the question: can micropolitan city economies survive and even thrive?

To answer that question, one must consider each of the three types of micropolitan cities individually. *Metropolitan* micropolitan cities are suburbs of larger conurbations and are therefore dependent upon the economic fortunes of their larger neighbors. When the core city is in growth mode, the suburbs grow to provide services and bedroom communities for the employees of the companies downtown. Even when the core city is in economic decline, there remains a degree of confidence that the city will not disappear and will, at some point, make a resurgence. Even in the most dire situations—Detroit, for example—the suburban micropolitan cities believed that they will survive and recover as the core city does so.

Hub micropolitan cities exist within a larger region and are the focus of a larger catchment area for retail, medical practices and various activities, and a host of other services. Within reasonable driving ranges (perhaps up to 50 or 60 miles) people will come to the city for that which they must purchase. If only for the purpose of providing absolute necessities, these hub micropolitans are more likely to survive regardless of what is happening in the macroeconomy.

An exception to this greater likelihood may be found within the larger regions that may be home to several hub micropolitan cities. As economic times become more dire, people will reduce spending on everything, even essential goods and services. When that happens, there potentially will be competition between the providers of those goods and services for a dwindling demand. When that occurs, the stronger of the service providers may survive and others may not. If this happens frequently enough, some hub micropolitan cities within close proximity to others may lose their tax base as their service providers lose their customer base to other hub micropolitan cities within a reasonable market area. This has the potential to jeopardize the existence of some hub micropolitan cities.

That potential exists within a larger region when people can access cheaper goods and services in exchange for a slightly longer drive. For isolated micropolitan cities, this is, by its very definition, not as likely. Isolated micropolitan cities stand alone within a larger geographic area. These cities typically need to be almost entirely self-sufficient in providing not just the essential goods and services required by families and businesses, but for the nonessentials and luxury items as well. Again, by definition, there are no alternatives; these cities will either continue to exist to provide those things to the residents and businesses in the region or may approach becoming ghost towns to an ever-diminishing population.

None of these conclusions are absolutes. Micropolitan cities can only survive, regardless of their geographic setting, if their states' tax policies support the types of economies that prevail or can be established in their communities. It will do these cities little or no good to serve as the regional source for the procurement of goods and services if they do not derive budget relief from the sales taxes generated thereby. If, for example, the city builds its general fund from real estate taxes, sales of goods and services are directly beneficial only to the extent that they generate enough demand for more goods and services to result in the construction of additional retail centers.

Absent such a direct correlation between the economic description of the city and the sources of the municipal budget, there must be a prevailing sentiment in that state to provide public support to these communities from tax revenues generated elsewhere. If that is not the case, these cities will wonder how they are to provide essential city services, and how they are to survive.

Some micropolitan cities in the United States, regardless of the degree of isolation, may be in slightly better circumstances as relates to the very survivability of the municipality if there is an anchor for the development of the city and its immediate surroundings. This may include a military base, or large medical facility, or the proximity of extractable natural resources. Even these assets, however, must be considered as potentially fleeting. Military bases can open, grow, contract, consolidate, or expand without much advance warning. More than one community has thought that they could rely on that source of revenue for stability in the local and regional economy only to be informed that the US government has decided to close them or move them or even expand them as a result of a process known as Base Realignment and Closure, or BRAC. The federal government and the Department of Defense must make these decisions in the name of national security as well as fiscal efficiency and responsibility. Still, communities can be hurt substantially by the resulting decisions and need to have alternative strategies for sustaining their local economies well into the future.

Hospital centers are strong drivers for some micropolitan economies. However, hospitals are a usually (although not always) responsive provider. The hospital is normally in place in response to existing demand. They are not generally built to attract residents but rather in response to the needs of a growing residential population. However, should primary jobs be lost in a community or region, one of the results will be the departure of those who have lost their jobs to find employment in other cities. When the demand for health services declines, so will the medical services being provided.

Natural resources are another strong asset around which micropolitan city economies have been built. Although these tend to have a longer-term, more dependable duration, they too can be diminished in value. Alternative fuel sources could hurt natural gas extracting communities, for example. Isolated and rural hubs can build long-term economies on these assets to a degree but are well advised by the mayors in this research to diversify their economic bases away from being overly dependent upon any single employer or single industry. Agricultural output or timber production are, for many of these communities, excellent means of providing that economic diversification and the stability that comes with it.

In addition, more than is the case with larger cities and metropolitan areas, micropolitan cities do not always have facilities or industrial or research parks ready to be occupied. This creates for many micropolitan cities a need to implement the now-timeworn catchphrase, "Build it and they will come." Larger cities generally have a more ready supply of office space or manufacturing or other facilities available to accommodate most prospective users. These facilities can usually be converted to new uses in relatively short periods and are therefore appealing to business prospects.

Micropolitan cities may have such facilities or office or industrial parks at the ready but that may seem much less likely than their larger counterparts, thus making the former less competitive. Many of the men and women interviewed made references either to the need for them or for plans in the works to develop them: build it and they will come. Of course, on the surface, this makes great sense. Once the bare bones are in place, an area can be more responsive to employers looking for sites. Hence, they can compete whereas other communities with raw land but no preparation may be out of the game if only due to the time that would be required to develop the infrastructure or to erect basic structures.

The course of action is certainly not as simple and clear as that. Those preparations are not cheap. It involves land purchase or purchases, investments in road and utility development or improvements, cable placement, facility construction, and possibly much more. Not only are those costs considerable, but they can be confronted at a time when other competing demands for those resources are keen. Finally, this approach is a gamble: many industrial and office parks exist around the

United States today, complete with invested dollars and debt service requirements, just waiting for the expected employers to arrive. Cities are faced with a difficult choice. To build and prepare these assets is expensive and distracts dollars from other needs; and the strategy may not pay off for a long time or at all. Yet, not to try will almost certainly put the city or the region out of competition for economic development prospects with those cities that are prepared.

Finally, just because a lot of public money has gone into the preparation of an industrial park doesn't mean that the costs are all in yet. Highly contested site location events will likely be between several locations, all of which could have the necessary facilities in place. The next step tends to be the competition for tax breaks, grants, and other incentives for a positive site location decision. These are calculations that small communities must make, in conjunction with return-on-investment forecasts, very carefully.

The distribution of the cities used in this research is depicted on the map.

The following provides a brief description of all of the cities on the original list as well as summaries of the 70 mayoral interviews conducted.

Aberdeen, South Dakota

The city of Aberdeen, South Dakota (Figure 6.1) remains the only municipality of any size within a radius of several hundred miles. Having initially grown as a regional hub where as many as eight railroad lines intersected, Aberdeen still enjoys a relatively vital economy and, as of June 2013, has an unemployment rate less than half of the national average: 3.4% versus 7.6%. Recent job growth (due to the recession)

Figure 6.1   Downtown Aberdeen, South Dakota. (Courtesy of City of Aberdeen)

is reported as slow but positive at 2.2%, again far better than the current national average of negative growth at −0.12% (http://www.bestplaces.net/economy).

However, as the economy has expanded, the population has not. The 2005 population of the city was 24,098, representing a decline of more than 1% from the 2000 level of 24,648, which in turn was 2.27% less than the 1995 figure of 24,927 (US Beacon, 2012).

The potential implication of a growing base of employment with a concurrent decline in population/workforce is that there may not be enough labor to satisfy the demands of employers. Northern Beef Packers concluded a deal that keeps the company in Aberdeen, a good thing as the company will pour more than $10 billion into the local economy over the ensuing five-year period, reaching as much as $2.5 billion by year five. This may not be pertinent, however, to the issue of available workforce because, presumably, "retained" jobs are already filled.

A more relevant issue for the mayor may be the dominance of agriculture in the region. Agricultural activities are reported to account for about 42% of all job growth in and around Aberdeen; and when the supply chain businesses are included, the proportion is more like 85%. But, the Beef Packers plant enables the further growth of other cluster businesses, including ranching, transportation, feed and other suppliers, and others. Will they be able to find the employees they need to grow in order to satisfy the demand (Natalie-Lees, 2011)?

The city's largest employers include a hospital that employs more than 1,500 people and the public school district employs more than 600 employees. These and other employers in the area (e.g., a 3M plant with 600 employees) may also have concerns about their ability to fill positions and keep them filled. In addition, the local media has written several stories in recent years regarding the shortage of housing. This may be a two-edged challenge in that workers cannot be attracted if there is not a range of housing available; yet, at the same time, there may not be enough construction workers to build the homes.

Interview with the Honorable Mike Levson, Mayor of Aberdeen, South Dakota

The population in Aberdeen, South Dakota has fluctuated over the past generation. Mayor Levson points out that the population gained about 10% between 2004 and the present but that had followed significant losses between 2000 and 2004. There are at least three probable causes for the recent resurgence of the population base in Aberdeen. First, farming and ranching have boomed during this period, largely based on the increasing prices for corn and soy beans. Federal crop insurance policies have been greatly improved in recent years also. Second, Northern Beef Packers has opened a new facility in the city. And, finally, the city did not have a significant run-up in property values in the preceding boom years and therefore had no subsequent bust as an offset to those values. The result has been that there has been no significant disruption in the local or in the regional economy.

Although it would appear that the relative dearth of housing when the new plant opened and the population base began to recover would result in higher housing prices, that did not happen. The city's growth in housing stock—in response to the increased demand, and despite the nation's financial woes—went from production levels of 30 new homes built per year to more than 100. Mayor Levson believes that this kind of responsiveness is often typical of smaller towns.

The city of Aberdeen is quite isolated from other population centers. To reach a city that is larger, one must travel 190 miles. Thus, Aberdeen provides most retail outlets and recreational opportunities, as well as the primary social services and health care for a larger region. As sales taxes represent about one-half of the city's budget (the other half coming from property taxes), these services are important to the city and its public service offerings. The same can be said of the farmers and ranchers in the city as they contribute to both the sales and property tax bases.

When it was suggested that retailers would thus seem to be strong economic development prospects, the mayor was quick to point out that a population base that spent sums of money is equally important as it generates sales taxes.

The region is home to a university and a college that generate the needed health care workers and other job classifications that are currently in demand locally, as well as providing the cultural and recreational outlets that enhance the community's quality of life. In micropolitan cities that are as isolated as Aberdeen, Mayor Levson avers, the boundary lines need to be ignored for purposes of economic development. He promotes the region constantly, "We're too close and too 'together' to be too competitive in this."

Lessons that he has learned include the need to unite the political and business leadership on both professional and personal levels. "There must be a meeting of the minds for a common purpose. After all," he notes, "those incomes earned in neighboring communities will be spent in Aberdeen." This is certainly true, given the economic and geographic isolation of his city, although such may not be the case for micropolitan cities in more densely populated regions.

Adrian, Michigan

As is the case with several communities in Michigan today, Adrian (Figure 6.2) is a micropolitan city with high unemployment and bleak prospects. Despite its proximity to the larger employment markets of Ann Arbor (30 miles) and Toledo (30 miles), the unemployment rate at the time of this writing is over 12% whereas the national average hovers around 9%. Recent job growth has compounded an existing problem: the negative level in Adrian exceeds the national (also negative) job growth numbers by a significant amount: −3.87% versus −0.12% (http://www.bestplaces.net/economy).

The city's population has remained relatively stable over time, declining by 2.4% between 1990 and 2000, from 22,097 to 21,574, then increasing very little through 2005 to 21,784 (US Beacon, 2012).

Industry classifications indicate that about one-third of the existing jobs in Adrian are in farming, construction, and production and shipping, which are not the highest paying positions in the panoply of salary ranges. There have been some recent announcements, however, that may help generate additional jobs with higher salaries and greater potential contributions to the state and local tax bases. In 2010,

Figure 6.2   Public art in Adrian, Michigan. (Courtesy of wePhoto Photography)

for example, the Wacker Chemical Corporation completed a $24 million expansion of its facility, resulting in the retention of nearly 160 higher-than-average-paying jobs in Adrian. The deal came at some cost, however, as the public sector had to agree to forgo $4.4 million in tax revenues. This included a 12-year, 5% tax abatement on future infrastructure development by the company.

This case raises the question of whether there are communities that are in such desperate need of jobs that the loss of tax base and the resultant impact on public services become increasingly acceptable. One must wonder, however, if such municipalities are mortgaging their future abilities to attract businesses and create the very public assets that will make them more attractive to businesses even in the absence of incentive payments or tax abatements. On the other hand, the city's industrial park was reported in prerecession 2009 to have gone five years without having attracted any new industries. The mayor may wish to comment on the value of such arrangements versus the need to enter into them regardless.

Interview with the Honorable Greg DuMars, Mayor of Adrian, Michigan

After eight years on the city commission and nine months as mayor, Greg DuMars describes the economic mood in Adrian, Michigan as "cautiously optimistic." This is seemingly a strong statement, given that the population of Adrian has declined by about 10,000 people in the last 10 years. Add to that the numerous plant closings in recent years, including a recent GM facility that once had 1,100 jobs in it and now is home to just 300 workers making convertible roofs for the Venture automobile. Another plant across the street from the city hall is being torn down. So, how can one claim any degree of optimism?

Mayor DuMars counts off nearly 20 oil wells being drilled outside of town. These represent a potential new source of revenue for the city. Another plant that makes fuel tanks and employs 350 people is expanding its workforce. And other manufacturing firms are interested in locations in Adrian, including one that could bring 300 to 400 new jobs the city's way. Furthermore, Adrian is home to three institutions of higher education, each of which is expanding. Adrian University has grown from 800 to 1,600 students in the past 10 years and both Siena Heights University and Jackson Community College are also growing. These institutions are critical if the Adrian workforce is to be rebuilt and offer a well-trained asset to potential new manufacturing-related employers.

Manufacturers are important to the city for another reason: the largest share of the city's revenue base for the provision of public services comes from the real estate tax base. In fact, more than 90% of the operating budget comes from the real estate tax base and state revenue-sharing resources. And those resources have declined so substantially in recent years that the number of city employees has been reduced from 165 to 128, largely in response to losses in the automotive manufacturing industries.

Finding replacement jobs and revenues is critical to Mayor DuMars. That is why one current potential economic development prospect has been offered a city incentive: 300 jobs are at stake. Incentive offers are vital, according to Mayor DuMars, because Adrian has "great difficulty in competing with Ohio and Indiana." In fact, when asked about asset gaps, Mayor DuMars noted that he would like to have greater capacity to grant tax credits to develop in the city or to redevelop some of the existing structures, 15 of which remain vacant in the city's downtown. He notes that "The downtown was once bustling. We probably have more downtown than we need right now."

As for lessons that could be instructive for other mayors of micropolitan cities, Mayor DuMars indicated that, as often as possible, debates and issues should be treated as nonpartisan. "We need to work together and get along, regardless of the political structure. A seven-to-nothing vote is the best outcome, but there will always be five-to-two votes. What I don't want is a four-to-three vote. And the minority votes should be different people all the time."

Albany, Oregon

Albany's position at the confluence of two rivers, the Willamette and the Calapooia, likely predetermined its exact location. During and following the Second World War, the city's and the region's economies grew as the result of the federal government's need for the local lumber and the establishment of a Bureau of Mines operation to develop new metallurgical processes. Today, a diverse economy benefits from inputs from a variety of sectors, including agriculture, lumber, health care, shipping, and several public entities.

Despite the evolution of an increasingly diverse economic base, today's unemployment rate in Albany (10.6%) exceeds the national average of 9.1%, and the recent job growth numbers (1.14%) lag behind the US average of −0.12%. More than one-third of jobs are in the following industries: agriculture, forestry, construction, and production and shipping (http://www.bestplaces.net). A variety of constraints to growth impede development; these include land zoned for commercial uses that sits on wetlands and flood plains. State of Oregon law requires municipalities to prepare land for development so this presents a conundrum to be addressed by the mayor.

As the job base and the city's limits have grown, the formal counts of population in Albany have changed dramatically. From 29,462 in 1990, the population base rose by more than 38% by 2000 and by almost another 10% to 44,797 in 2005 (http://www.usbeacon.com/oregon/albany.html).

Further expansion of commercial space is a challenge for Oregon's communities. On the one hand, economic development in Albany is constrained by wetlands and floodplain issues but state law requires cities in Oregon to prepare sites for immediate use by potential interested businesses. This is known as Statewide

Planning Goal 9. The 2011 to 2015 strategic plan for the city identifies this need as a specific goal.

Despite the apparent interest in business attraction, some industries are in decline. Even between the years of 2001 and 2005 (i.e., prerecession), manufacturing jobs declined by 10%, wholesale jobs fell off by 13%, and jobs in the information technology sector dropped by 16%. At the same time, employment in health and social assistance increased by 12%, in accommodations and food service by 13%, and in financial services by 22% against overall job growth in the same period of less than one-half of 1% (Sharp and Hansen, 2007). Within the category of manufacturing, the largest areas, as measured by employment, include primary metals, wood products and paper, and food processing.

The same report noted that the primary economic development projects in the years between 2000 and 2007 were in retail (four projects), industrial sites (eight), and a single project for production and distribution facilities (Sharp and Hansen, 2007). Given the nature of Albany's economic strengths, one point of discussion with the mayor should focus on the use of the 10 colleges and universities in the larger region as a means of producing new companies and supporting the growth of existing businesses in the city.

On the whole, the city is doing well. In 2011, the US Bureau of Economic Analysis ranked Albany 56th of 366 metro areas for the rate of growth (Albany's Economy Continues to Climb, 2011). The city refers to itself alternatively as the "Rare Metals Capital of the US" and the "Grass Seed Capital of the US." Are these emphases that will grow and sustain the economy in the future?

Albany, Oregon: Interview Declined

Ardmore, Oklahoma

The population of Ardmore, Oklahoma has reflected significant increases over the past two decades, growing from 23,079 in 1990 to 23,711 in 2000 and to 24,280 in 2005. This represents percentage increases between these years of 2.74 and 2.40, respectively (US Beacon, 2012).

With an economy that has always been dominated by oil, Ardmore suffers through the peaks and troughs in the demand for, and pricing of, oil worldwide. The bust of the 1980s encouraged the city's leadership to try to diversify the local base and they have done so to the extent that the city and the region are no longer solely dependent upon oil businesses for jobs and the tax base, but the significance of oil is still rather strong. Distribution centers and manufacturing complement the oil-based businesses and cluster support industries: oil-based jobs totaling about 800 and transportation-related industries amounting to about 5,000 (Talley, 2011). In addition, Ardmore is home to the Roberts Noble Foundation which conducts research and development in the use of various grasses for fuel production, which builds on an industry strength but in a way that has the potential to diversify the local economy even further.

Today, Ardmore is home to numerous and diverse businesses. These include Michelin North America, Mercy Memorial Health Center, several retail giants, Valero Energy, EJIW Foundry, and Flanders Filters. Each of those companies employs a minimum of 250 people in Ardmore. A focus on biotechnology development is reflected in the operations of the Noble Foundation (plant biology) as well as several local imaging and medical device companies. These businesses presumably exist in Ardmore due to the proximity to larger operations with similar interests in Dallas and Oklahoma City.

Ardmore's geographic position as a midway point between Dallas and Oklahoma City represents a significant potential economic development asset. It would be a point of discussion with the mayor to determine how that asset has been used to further the diversity of the economic base in Ardmore. Evident potential operations might include distribution and warehousing, mechanical and automotive servicing, and some manufacturing functions. Denton, Texas, which is the home of the University of North Texas, and Norman, Oklahoma, home to the University of Oklahoma, are a mere 40 and 75 miles distant. How have these assets been used by Ardmore to foster, enable, and encourage additional economic growth? The several local office parks with available space for businesses to locate, coupled with the low rate of unemployment, would suggest that the planners in Ardmore are using these assets in ways that may provide lessons for other micropolitan communities.

Ardmore, Oklahoma: Interview Declined

Athens, Ohio

Athens, Ohio is a city in decline. The population of the city held relatively stable in the decade of the 1990s, measuring 21,265 in 1990 and 21,342 in 2000; however, over the next five years (to 2005), the city's population declined by about 2% to 20,918 (http://www.beacon.com/ohio/athens.html). The unemployment rate in Athens presently sits at 8.9%, fractionally lower than the US average of 9.1%, a recent job growth posted in the negative (−3.54%) as opposed to the US average of −0.12%. Beyond the relative rates of unemployment, Athens demonstrates a significant gap (47.4%) in wages for the jobs that do exist in the city when compared to US averages: $12,819 per capita in Athens versus the current US average of $27,067 (http://www.bestplaces.net/economy/city/ohio/Athens).

Not surprisingly, poverty is an issue for Athens. When queried about possible federal relief, the two members of the House of Representatives from the region noted that it would be better to spend funds to create the necessary conditions for job growth and to eliminate burdensome taxes and regulations on business (DeWitt, 2011). Nonetheless, an economy that is lagging even a weak national picture translates into significant and severe problems of poverty and a host of related social issues for the city of Athens, Ohio.

Proximity to Ohio University is an economic development asset if used properly and to the mutual benefit of both the town and the institution. The University's Innovation Center and Biotechnology Institute and incubator are positive examples. The focus of these efforts appears to be not only on the generation of scientific research but also the manufacturing of medical devices, which could provide a strong stimulus for the economy of Athens and the region. A university report in 2010 indicated that 78 jobs had been created at the Innovation Center that year and that $3.8 million had been realized in new income. State and local tax coffers had benefited by a total of nearly $438,000 in incremental tax revenues for that single year of operation (Ohio University 2010 Economic Impact, 2011).

Dairy and food production also represent a significant opportunity for economic growth and the types of economic diversification that can help to sustain micropolitan economies through macroeconomic peaks and valleys.

Athens, Ohio: Interview Declined

Bangor, Maine

Bangor, Maine (Figure 6.3) offers several prominent strengths when seeking to attract or retain businesses. It also suffers in these efforts from several substantial detrimental traits. On the positive side, Bangor is within a densely populated region with about 400,000 residents. It is also within easy reach of many prominent

Figure 6.3 Bangor, Maine from the sky. (Courtesy of City of Bangor)

colleges and universities as well as other strong institutions of higher education. It has easy access to five airports, seaports, and the border with Canada.

Nonetheless, the unemployment rate, although not quite as high as the present US average of 9.1%, still sits right at 8%. And, recent job growth, although it is negative at −0.69% is not horrifically worse than the US average of −0.12% (http://www.bestplaces.net/economy/metro/maine/bangor).

The population of Bangor has declined steadily although not precipitously. Between 1990 and 2000, the decline from 33,181 to 31,473 represented a loss of a little over 5%. The decline through 2005 to 31,074 was roughly one and one-quarter percent, but still a loss (US Beacon, 2012).

Several primary employers give the local economy some stability. The fact that these employers are in diverse fields, including the public sector, adds to the economic stability over time. In this vein, Moody's Analytics (2012) cites the University of Maine and the University of Maine Medical Center as prime examples. Other considerations for businesses as well as residents considering relocation to or an expansion within the Bangor area include the relatively low cost of living and of doing business. Nonetheless, the local population is growing at a very slow rate and there is concern expressed in the press about the brain drain of students from excellent regional colleges and universities to other areas because of the lack of jobs, particularly in sectors other than the services sector.

Another concern for local officials is the great dependence on the public sector for the existing employment base. In Bangor, there are nearly 14,000 government jobs in a base of slightly over 65,000. This is more than 21% of the total jobs in the city. In fact, the same report lists employment growth in Bangor as ranking 236th of 392 US cities (http://www.city-data.com/us-cities/thenortheast/bangor-economy, 2012).

The presence of colleges and universities has meant that about 27% of adults have at least a bachelor's degree and about six of every seven has completed high school. And, one of the city's great advantages in terms of a stable economic outlook is that it is not overly dependent upon a single employer or a single industry. The city is home to seven employers with between 1,000 and 4,000 employees each, and eight with between 500 and 1,000 employees. And, today, trade leads all sectors in the city for economic impact. Various forms of trade contribute about $900 million to the local economic base, representing about 17% of the total. This is followed by education and health services at $880 million, and the financial activities category at about $663 million.

Interview with the Honorable Cary Weston, Mayor of Bangor, Maine

The economic mood in Bangor, Maine has shifted in the past 15 years. The region has passed through various iterations in the economy with logging, shoes, and a variety of other manufacturing activities as the focal points. In the 1950s, the closure of the local military base caused an "identity crisis" resulting in a new perspective on what the region can become, according to Mayor Weston. That self-perception is no longer one of blue-collar manufacturing alone but includes educational employers, medical services, and research and development functions built around Bangor University.

The outcome has been that Mayor Weston sees Bangor now as being "on the verge of an economic renaissance." Through a program called Mobilize Maine, a series of short- and long-term asset maps was prepared for Bangor. The short-term objectives of producing more STEM graduates and providing cultural attractions in the city will lead to the longer-term vision of becoming a center of innovation, creativity, and entrepreneurship. Additionally, the region will pursue more advanced manufacturing for that part of the labor force that possesses those skills. For example, an old mill that was closed has been converted to a facility for the construction of prebuilt prewired buildings that are being shipped to the Gulf of Mexico.

The asset mapping also revealed the assets that are needed to move the economy forward. Primary among them is the venture capital investment that could "create a burst of economic activity in the region." Along the city's waterfront, a conference center has been finished and has served as an attraction for additional investments in the corridor.

Mayor Weston's view of the economic future of micropolitan cities is that they will need to collaborate with one another to succeed. "No one in the room is smarter than all of us. City services and infrastructure cannot continue to be duplicated within the region; we simply can't afford it."

Baraboo, Wisconsin

Baraboo (Figure 6.4) has experienced steady, if not remarkable growth, since the early 1990s, beginning that time frame with a population of just over 9,200 and registering more than 12,000 in the census of 2010 (US Beacon, 2012). Unemployment has remained below the national average but the rate of recent job growth has been farther into the negative than national averages.

The area boasts access via several modes of transportation including rail and air service. The Wisconsin Department of Transportation issued a report indicating that, between the years 1997 and 2001, fully 85% of all expanded manufacturing businesses were located within 15 miles of an airport (Wisconsin Bureau of Aviation, 2008). Access by rail is also supportive of economic growth and expansion of the existing business based in Baraboo.

The city has placed great emphasis on the development of its waterfront. Situated between Wisconsin Dells and Madison along the Baraboo River, the city is poised for travel, tourism, and a variety of recreational pursuits. Economic

Figure 6.4 Downtown Baraboo, Wisconsin. (Courtesy of Morgan MacArthur)

development and land use planning goals seem to be focused on the development of high-end uses along the riverfront, including residential, entertainment, retail, hotels and dining, and hiking paths. As such, it would be important to query the mayor on the composition of the city's budget. The pursuit of high-end housing or upscale retail outlets may be indicators of a local budgetary dependence on property or sales taxes. A 2011 report on the retail market for the city of Baraboo (University of Wisconsin Extension, 2011) estimated that the city's population is but a small proportion (approximately 13%) of the total retail catchment area of about 93,000 residents.

The same report also notes that, although there are a significant number of retailers within the city limits, there are various types of retail uses that are not sufficiently provided to the residents of Baraboo. These include general merchandise stores, grocery stores, beauty parlors, hardware stores, women's clothing shops, and more. Another challenge for the city appears to be the lack of awareness beyond the city's limits as to what retail exists in the city as well as the lack of highway connections to access them. An asset that is contrary to the need for infrastructure is reported to be the Baraboo–Wisconsin Dells Airport, which serves the residential and business communities as well as creates jobs and revenues locally.

Not all signs are positive, however. When, in late December, 2011, Sears announced the closing of its Baraboo store, West Baraboo Village President Bruce Meyer responded, "This is going to have a big impact on the village tax base and the surrounding area. It's also going to cause a number of people to be unemployed, which always has an impact on the community" (Zagorski, 2011). Interestingly, the impact on the unemployment rate was a secondary consideration to the impact on the local tax base. In fact, Sears provided about 3% of the Village's tax receipts.

Interview with the Honorable Mike Palm, Mayor of Baraboo, Wisconsin

Mayor Palm and his city administrator, Ed Geick, characterized the economic mood in Baraboo, Wisconsin as having a "recent uptick." One office building is currently under construction and two companies (one of 30 employees and another of 5) have already signed leases to move in. A new stand-alone retail building is also under construction in the downtown. Like most of his counterparts, Mayor Palm focuses on the importance of having a vibrant downtown. Reflecting the pride evidenced by many of his peers, he calls downtown Baraboo "the most beautiful downtown in Wisconsin."

Retail outlets are important for jobs and the quality of life, however, they do not contribute to the city's ability to provide public services; there are no sales taxes. The city constitutes its budget on the back of property taxes (about 50% of general fund revenues) and a variety of usage fees. Baraboo has a number of economic development assets, perhaps the most significant of which is the extraordinary scenic beauty of the area in which it is located. Tourism is therefore very important to the city, and the mayor proudly discussed the means being implemented to increase visitation. As the origin of the Ringling family of Ringling Circus fame, Baraboo has created the Circus World Museum to attract visitors. This complements the use of the Baraboo River as a tourism attraction as well as the promotion of the city as the "Gateway to Devil's Lake State Park," which is Wisconsin's most oft-visited state park.

Another tourism opportunity the city is promoting relates to another favorite son, Aldo Leopold, the "Father of the Conservation Movement." The Aldo Leopold Foundation and the Legacy Center highlight his contributions to the conservation movement and is very much in keeping with the city's efforts to revitalize the river areas in town. The river falls 45 feet as it passes through Baraboo; it has been cleaned up, adjacent older structures have been razed, and the environmental impacts of the community on the river have been minimized. Sites have been prepared and are ready for development. This does not mean that manufacturing is not wanted in Baraboo. In fact, Teel manufactures plastic supplies for hospital uses and is planning to expand within the city limits, a welcome addition, according to Mayor Palm.

The University of Wisconsin campus in Baraboo is also seen as a significant economic development asset. The city, county, and the university have worked together on plans for the construction of a science building, which will be under way within two years.

One of the lessons Mayor Palm cites is that the city needs to do a better job of promoting itself. "We offer history, culture, recreation, and a Rockwellian downtown square." Like most of his peers in micropolitan cities, Mayor Palm is not only justifiably proud of his city, but he is a lifelong resident: "My children live here and my grandchildren live here." Professionally, he works with other communities to help them plan and implement municipal improvement programs, so he has a clear sense of what city leaders need to do. "We need to be ever optimistic. We must have a can-do attitude. There are always nay-sayers who oppose any kind of change. But, change can be good, too."

Bartlesville, Oklahoma

The discovery of the area's first productive oil well coincided with the incorporation of the city of Bartlesville in 1897, and the fortunes of the people of the region have been tied to oil ever since. From 1917 on, the area dug 80 consecutive productive wells. This led to the formation of the Phillips Petroleum Company that remains a primary employer today. The growth of the region's population to work in the oil fields led to growing demands for agricultural output and ranching, both of which also remain mainstays of the economy of Bartlesville today.

The population growth in Bartlesville continues apace, although it was relatively flat between 1990 and 2000 (from 34,256 to 34,748). Between 2000 and 2005, the residential population jumped by nearly 4.25% to 36,249, reflecting growing demands for domestic oil production (http://www.usbeacon.com/oklahoma/ brtlesville.html). The demand for workers is supported by a local cost of living that is 18.4% below the national average (http://www.bestplaces.net).

Some demographic analysis indicates possible concerns, however, not in the growth of the population but its composition. For example, the median age is 40 years old. This leads to questions about the aging of the workforce and the availability of replacement workers in skilled positions as the current generation retires, as the median age level of 40 is relatively high. Still, the unemployment rate in Bartlesville (4.3%) is much less than the current US average of 9.1%. And, recent job growth, although more negative than the national average (–1.53% versus –0.12%), does not seem to be of great concern to the leadership in Bartlesville.

The city's geographic position gives Bartlesville a range of options for attracting different industry segments. Bartlesville is situated 47 miles from Tulsa, Oklahoma and is part of the larger Tulsa Consolidated Statistical Area which, in 2009, approached one million residents.

A 2010 consultant's study prepared for the city identified potential targeted industries, including five in the category of technical and environmental services, four sectors in distribution and logistics, three in back-office services, four in instrumentation and control systems, and two in tourism development (Target Industries, 2010). These selections reflect the advantages Bartlesville has in terms of its location, relatively low land and labor costs, other business sectors already present in the region, highway and air access, and the prior work experience of the local labor pool. There is also a realization expressed on the part of the study that the local colleges and universities are providing classes that are compatible with the skillsets needed by those industry segments. The approach and the rationale employed in these decisions provide a good format for this type of selection process in other micropolitan communities (Target Industries, 2010).

Given its hub position as a micropolitan city, Bartlesville's largest employers, following Conoco Phillips, include primarily retail operations and distribution and hospital services.

Bartlesville, Oklahoma: Interview Declined

Beckley, West Virginia

The population of Beckley, West Virginia (Figure 6.5) had been in decline from 1990 (18,296) through 2005 (16,936), but rebounded in the following five years to a 2010 total of 17,614 (US Beacon, 2012). This may be the result, in part, of an unemployment rate that is somewhat lower than the national average, but there may be other factors involved as well. Job growth during that time frame was in a diverse array of industries including health care, mining, and manufacturing (West Virginia Economic Outlook, 2009).

The Bureau of Economic Analysis reported that the state of West Virginia enjoyed a 4.5% growth in its GDP (gross domestic product) from 2010 to 2011. This represented the third highest rate among the 50 states and was attributed to extraction industries (West Virginia Economy Among Fastest Growing Last Year, 2012). Although this is a positive sign, it is not the future of either the state's or Beckley's economy.

A 2012 report of the United States Energy Information Agency stated that coal production in the entire Appalachian region, which had reached 500 million tons in 1997, is forecast to decrease that amount to just 86 million tons by the year 2035 (Coal Decline, Economy is Shifting, 2012). Industries that have been noted

Figure 6.5 **Unique designs in Beckley, West Virginia. (Courtesy of City of Beckley)**

as having future potential for the city, the region, and the state in the press and on the city's economic development website include value-added wood products, tourism, teleservices, scientific services, and electronics assembly (Lifestyle of Southern West Virginia, 2012).

Interview with the Honorable Emmit Pugh, Mayor of Beckley, West Virginia

Mayor Pugh is like his peers in this study in that he is a native of the city of which he is now mayor and in that he has no further political aspirations. He is very different in one respect: he has served Beckley as an elected official for 33 years, nine as a member of the city council and 24 years as the mayor! Interestingly, his grandfather also served four terms as the city's mayor.

A business and occupation tax, which is based on a company's gross receipts, is the basis for nearly two-thirds of the revenues that support the city's $16 million general fund. About $2.5 million comes from the real estate base, and the remainder comes from a variety of user fees.

Economic development is now a regional effort for Beckley and the four surrounding counties formed a regional organization in 1989 to maximize the assets being offered and to minimize the local competition for private budget resources. Mayor Pugh believes that "a rising tide lifts all ships" and is not concerned about businesses locating outside the city limits. However, it should be noted that this works in this case only because Beckley represents the region's hub for retail, medical, and personal services, and because that in turn benefits the city's tax base. In fact, although the city of Beckley is micropolitan in population size, its retail catchment area is estimated by the mayor as between 260,000 and 280,000 residents. At one point, that base of residential buying power was redirected to malls outside the city but the mayor now feels that they are coming back to shop in the downtown area.

These developments are also welcome due to the loss of employment at local institutions of higher education now in a transitional phase as well as the general decline of the coal industry in the region. Other positive news includes a recent announcement by the Smithsonian Institution that includes Beckley as one of America's top 20 small cities for arts and culture.

One lesson offered by Mayor Pugh focuses on the need to tackle challenges in manageable amounts rather than trying to do too much at once. "Identify the goals, reach them, and then reset." The second lesson is that "You have to be careful with incentives. There is a cost–benefit ratio to consider."

Blackfoot, Idaho

Population gains in Blackfoot (Figure 6.6) in recent years have been substantial. From a 1990 total of 9,646 to a 2010 level of 11,899, the trend has been statistically

Figure 6.6 The Idaho Potato Museum, Blackfoot, Idaho. (Courtesy of City of Blackfoot)

significant as well as constant (US Beacon, 2012). Complemented by a level of unemployment at the time of this writing that was below the national average, Blackfoot appears to be in growth mode.

One example is the addition of 70 high-paying jobs to the city's employment base by Premier Technology. "The company regularly performs work for the Department of Energy and Department of Defense sites, as well as commercial customers … pharmaceutical, construction management, and commercial nuclear sectors" (Ellis, 2010). The mayor could help shed light on whether this is a one-time success or the first achievement in an element of economic development strategy for Blackfoot.

Interview with the Honorable Mike Virtue, Mayor of Blackfoot, Idaho

Mike Virtue firmly believes that his background in financial management and accounting has benefited him in his seven years as mayor of Blackfoot, Idaho. Furthermore, as with most of his colleague micropolitan mayors, he has no interest in further office. Mayor Virtue, who has spent his entire life in the region, maintains that elected officials in small towns should not seek further political careers. "It would make me subject to people's political whims and vote-counting. I can just do what's right."

Blackfoot is probably best classified as a metropolitan micropolitan city. It sits 25 miles from Idaho Falls and only 20 miles from Pocatello. To the south lies an American Indian reservation that means growth cannot proceed in that direction.

Blackfoot's economy is primarily based on agriculture, the presence of the Idaho National Laboratory (INL), and the proximity of three institutions of higher education. The remaining large sector of the economy is constituted by those businesses that exist to support those three sectors. The three higher education institutions—Idaho State, Eastern Idaho Technical College, and Brigham Young

University, Pocatello—serve to attract visitors to the city and the region as well as provide a workforce for, and support to, the INL.

The Idaho National Laboratory was the nation's first nuclear power generation facility. Initially created as a US Navy training facility, the INL is today home to more than 50 nuclear generating plants, has numerous contracts with the US Department of Energy, and employs in excess of 6,000 people. The grounds, which are highly secure, encompass nearly 900 square miles. Mayor Virtue notes that the relationship between the colleges and universities and the INL has resulted in the creation of new companies. Furthermore, although the city's $50 million budget is based largely on user fees for enterprise fund services, the property tax base is a significant share. This means that the region's localities benefit greatly and in various ways from the presence of the INL and, as a consequence, has not needed to raise the property tax rate in the past four years, right through the current recession.

Mayor Virtue offers a single emphatic lesson for growing and sustaining the economy of micropolitan cities. The several mayors in the region meet frequently to discuss common issues, concerns, and opportunities. Thus, economic development is conducted on a regional basis, thereby eliminating competition for business announcements.

Blytheville, Arkansas

The population base of Blytheville, Arkansas has been in constant decline since 1990 when it stood at nearly 23,000. Today, the total is 15,620 (US Beacon, 2012). A rate of unemployment at more than 12% when the national average is a fraction over 9% is the reason (http://www.bestplaces.net).

The city of Blytheville is located on the flat Mississippi Delta. Its farming (cotton) background helped the city thrive and the retailers and service providers in the city were the support industry for those who lived not only in the city itself but on the farms throughout the entire region.

A US Army airfield was opened during the Second World War and helped to drive additional economic growth and supported significant economic activity until it was finally closed in the early 1990s and was converted to civilian uses, but the current employment complement does not match the Army's figures of more than 7,000 military and civilian positions supported. Fortuitously, the steel industry emerged at about the same time that the base was shutting down its operations. Raw steel production still takes place in the region and supports approximately 15,000 jobs and higher levels of expenditure. Agriculture provides economic diversification for the region and the city of Blytheville. This includes the production of cotton, soy beans, and sorghum.

Arkansas Northeastern College is the result of a merger between the former Mississippi County Community College and the Cotton Boll Technical Institute, and now enrolls more than 1,800 students, provides jobs and tax revenues, and research in agricultural services and products that benefit the local farming com- munity. The college's role in the economic life of the community is a topic that should be explored in the interview with the mayor. This is a "good news and bad news" situation as the recent improvements in farming and the mechanization of farm operations has cost many jobs in the Blytheville area.

Blytheville, Arkansas: Interview Declined

Bowling Green, Ohio

Bowling Green, Ohio (Figure 6.7) is suffering from a relatively high unemployment rate (7.9%), however, it should be noted that it is well below the national average of 9.1%. And, although recent job growth across the United States is measured as a negative (at –0.12%), the rate of recent job growth for Bowling Green over the same period is reported as 1.25% (http://www.bestplaces.net/economy/city/ohio/bowling_green).

Bowling Green's population base has been growing for many years although the rates of growth have been very small. Between 1990 and 2000, the population of the city grew by 5.2%, from 28,176 to 29,636. Through 2005, the growth rate was about one-half of one percent, to 29,793 (US Beacon, 2012). Part of the attractiveness of Bowling Green, Ohio is reflected in a report by Moody's Analytics which list the costs of doing business in the city at less than 80% of the national average and the overall cost of living at about 86% of the national average (http://www.economy.com).

Figure 6.7 Bowling Green, Ohio from the air. (Courtesy of Debbie Walters Nabinger)

One of the assets that the city and the region have to market for business attraction and retention is Bowling Green State University, which engages in numerous partnerships with the city to help enhance the vitality of the local economy including the development and management of a business incubator. The university is not only an asset as a direct creator of jobs but as an economic engine in its own right. It supports over 9,000 jobs and contributes $700 million to the local economy on an annual basis. Visitors to its campus spend about $25 million in the community each year and contribute to the health of local small businesses. This is only one example of how colleges and universities, as well as hospital centers and other institutions, can contribute to communities' economic health. A 2006 report by the university estimated that, as a result of every state dollar spent on Bowling Green State University, eight dollars of economic activity was generated (Carroll, 2004).

Interview with the Honorable Richard Edwards, Mayor of Bowling Green, Ohio

Although not strictly a native of Bowling Green, Mayor Richard Edwards is a native of the area (having been born and raised within 60 miles of the city). He left the area several times over the course of his career as a public employee and administrator in a variety of higher education settings, and ultimately returned, initially to be the Executive Officer of Bowling Green State University and later to become the mayor.

Presently (at the time of this interview) in his first year as mayor, and without any prior experience as an elected official, Mayor Edwards notes the very important relationship between the city and Bowling Green State University. In a curious twist, the current and relatively new president of the university is a former colleague of the mayor's. This has enabled a strong relationship not only between these two key executives but also between their organizations as they move forward to build the local economic base. Together, they have called for and managed a strategic visioning process to examine the best means of identifying targets of opportunity for the city and the university. The mayor notes that "These town–gown relationships are very important but must be nurtured or they can become very fractious."

Specific economic development targets for the city rely on the close proximity to Interstate Highway 75 and the presence in the greater region of the automotive industry. But, the focus on businesses that are related to that industry is only part of the approach of Bowling Green's privately funded economic development program. Business retention is very important to Mayor Edwards, who recently joined the executive director of the economic development organization in paying calls on 30 or more CEOs and plant managers in the city. What they discovered was that many of them did not know everything that was happening in the local economy. As a result, many of the executives are now also holding conversations about possible collaborations with university departments and faculty. These visits also included many of the foreign-owned businesses that are located in the region. In brief, "There are many positive signs of turnaround in Bowling Green."

In terms of lessons offered to other micropolitan city mayors, he noted that

> A key component of a healthy small town is a flourishing downtown. Bowling Green still has room to build because we have three industrial parks with plenty of room and a lot of neighboring areas we could annex if we need them. But, the downtown is so important to us. Just because it is nice now doesn't mean that it will always be. Too many small towns have seen their downtowns go to seed. You have to make them attractive and keep working at it.

A second lesson offered is similar but in relation not to space but to people: "In small towns, you can't take relationships for granted. You have to work hard at them all the time too."

Bozeman, Montana

Bozeman, Montana (Figure 6.8) has witnessed a steady increase in population for more than 20 years (US Beacon, 2012). However, with the unemployment rate running at roughly two-thirds (6.7%) of the US national average of 9.1% (http://www.bestplaces.com), Bozeman seems to be faring reasonably well.

Prior to the recession, Bozeman's surrounding county, Gallatin County, averaged about 2,000 new residents a year; that has dropped to zero growth in the recession years of 2008 through 2010 (Lutey, 2011). At the same time, employment in the construction industry throughout the region declined by about 2,000 jobs.

Figure 6.8   Streetscape in Bozeman, Montana. (Courtesy of City of Bozeman)

Today, the largest employers in Bozeman are Montana State University with nearly 2,700 employees, Bozeman Deaconess Hospital with more than 1,200 employees, a variety of public agencies; Right Now Technologies with 400 workers, and a range of employers in the retail sector.

There are several bright spots in Bozeman. The high-tech and light manufacturing sectors are reportedly doing well and employ 3,200 people in the region (Lutey, 2011), and the Bozeman Airport has recently completed a $40 million expansion that enables it to accommodate direct flights to and from 10 major US destinations. The city sits on Interstate Highway 90, which runs all the way from Seattle to Boston. And, finally, Montana State University, particularly its laser program, has reportedly spun off a number of local businesses, including Bridger Photonics, which was recently included on the *Inc.* magazine Top 500 list. In addition, Policom research analyzed nearly 600 micropolitan cities in 2011 and ranked Bozeman seventh in the country for the quality of its economy (Ricker, 2011).

Local tourist attractions such as skiing at Big Sky and local trout fishing areas help to diversify Bozeman's local and regional economies even further. And tens of thousands of visitors pass through each year en route to Yellowstone National Park, 93 miles to the south. Economic diversification is critical to this isolated micropolitan city as it is to isolated micropolitan cities generally. Bozeman is more than 140 miles from Billings and about 200 miles from Missoula. Its economy needs to be self-sufficient. This would be a good topic for discussion with the mayor.

Another topic to review with Mayor Becker would be whether any lasting impacts exist from a 2003 city council decision to limit retail stores to no more than 75,000 square feet within a single structure. This was an effort to protect local retailers from overwhelming competition from the big-box retailers, but such measures in other states and cities have often resulted in net job losses.

Interview with the Honorable Sean Becker, Mayor of Bozeman, Montana

Relatively speaking, Sean Becker is unlike other mayors in the state of Montana. After his first year in office, he is still in his thirties and he is not from Bozeman. In fact, he is not from Montana. In fact, no one on the Bozeman City Council is from the state, which is highly unusual in Montana. Mayor Becker believes this to be an advantage because his city is not at all constrained by "how we have always done things." Rather, the council and the city are free to try new things and take risks.

In the 1990s, the city was overbuilt, both in terms of commercial and residential structures. When the 2008–2009 recession struck, roughly 5,000 people left town and the city was left with a lot of vacant properties. Over time, the vacancy rates declined but progress was halted by a downtown natural gas explosion that took out an entire city block.

Mayor Becker noted that Bozeman benefits from an interesting economic benefit. Because it is a relatively isolated university town, there seems always to be someone in town spending money in the shops. When the macro economy is strong, the companies and their employees increase in numbers. When it is weak, the population of the university increases. Today, there are about 15,000 students, up from about 12,000 before the recession, and another 3,000 faculty and staff.

When asked whether the city used the university well in its economic development efforts, Mayor Becker acknowledged that although that connection was better used now than it had been in the past, there is still much more that is possible. The university does, however, have faculty and staff who participate on city commissions and boards and also operates a technology park with a program called Techlink that helps facilitate small business growth. University labs and other facilities can also be rented by business people for private use.

Does the rate of spending affect the city's budget and its ability to provide public services? No, because Montana has no income tax; in fact, the state legislature in Montana annually tries to reduce or eliminate many taxes while capping the allowable growth on others. This means that municipalities such as Bozeman are constantly trying to catch up on the costs of public services, especially as the population grows. The city derives only about one-third of its $23 million general fund from real estate taxes and the rest from fees, grants, and other sources.

Certainly, a local income tax would be a boon for Bozeman as it sits in the middle of a region of more than 100,000 people. The nearest large communities are 8 miles and 140 miles away (Butte and Billings, respectively). The daytime population is roughly twice the nighttime population, but the absence of a state sales tax means that the city benefits only from the jobs and the real estate taxes and related usage fees. On the plus side, the city does not need to provide road maintenance as the main highways are state routes. This may be due to the fact that Bozeman is the "Gateway to Yellowstone."

When asked to recite lessons that could be beneficial to other micropolitan cities, Mayor Becker said that he had been successful in establishing a system that allows thoughtful processes infused with citizen input. He believes that the greater the citizen involvement in the process, the fewer the complaints about the outcomes.

Brigham City, Utah

The population gains registered by Brigham City (Figure 6.9) in the past 25 years have been impressive. From a 1990 level of 15,644, the numbers grew through the report of the census in 2010: (17,899; US Beacon, 2012). Coupled with relatively low unemployment rates, the city seems to have been enjoying significant economic growth. This seems to be consistent with and supported by the prevailing sentiments of the prominent force in the community represented by the Church of the Latter Day Saints. This would be an interesting area of inquiry for the interview with the mayor.

Vexxel Composites is a manufacturer of container products for the natural gas industry. With the aid of a state incentive, the company, in late 2012, added more

Figure 6.9 Welcome to Brigham City, Utah. (Courtesy of Paul Larsen, Brigham City)

than 100 new jobs to the local economy. Still, there are many articles in the local press regarding both the need to attract and create jobs and to increase business contributions to the city's tax base. Discussions that have taken place in the council's chambers about business incentives and tax and fee abatements that would support economic growth are also good fodder for conversations with the mayor.

Interview with the Honorable Dennis Fife, Mayor of Brigham City, Utah

As are many micropolitan city mayors, Dennis Fife of Brigham City, Utah, was very accomplished in numerous fields prior to entering public life. A chemist by training, Mayor Fife also served as an air force officer, served as the head of the chemistry department at the Air Force Academy, worked in the private sector, and earned a law degree. And as do many of the other mayors interviewed in this research, he credits those experiences with enhancing his performance as the mayor of Brigham City. "Cities get involved in everything, including chemistry and the law."

Brigham City has had some successes and some setbacks through the current recession. The unemployment rate remains relatively low but that is a function of significant job losses offset by smaller gains and the loss of many laid-off workers from the community. Mayor Fife notes that Procter & Gamble has begun hiring again, bringing in 250 new jobs, but that does not entirely offset the 2,500 positions the company eliminated a few years ago. One of the concerns Mayor Fife shared is that as jobs were lost without replacement opportunities for these high-end scientists, technicians, and engineers, they moved to other cities. This means that Brigham City no longer has one of its primary assets needed to attract new employers.

One of the largest employers in the region is Nucor, which not only hires local workers to produce steel but also thereby supports the employment of numerous residents in plants that fashion the steel into a wide range of products. After difficult times for Nucor, the company is hiring again. Through the course of the recession, Nucor did not lay anyone off, according to Mayor Fife; they simply reduced hours across the board. In addition, the company used the slower times to employ its workers in constructing various projects around the city.

The economy of Brigham City, which initially boomed in the 1960s and 1970s with the growth of the aerospace industry, was "devastated" by the loss of many of those jobs as the current (national) administration refocused its attention from that sector. Over the past two years, aerospace giant ATK "has had to lay off 2,500 people in a town of 18,000!" Mayor Fife noted that there is some good news to be told. The city will be the site of a new Temple of the Church of the Latter Day Saints, which the mayor believes will attract hundreds of people a day. They will patronize the city's hotels and restaurants and make purchases in the shops. This is vital to the city, which derives the bulk of its revenues from which public services are funded in the city from the sales taxes. That source has been stagnant for several years as people have often gone to Ogden or Salt Lake City for their retail needs.

One coming economic development announcement, although still in confidential discussions, has the potential for creating as many as 600 new jobs in the city in the initial phase and a like amount thereafter. A sports complex is in the planning stage and has the potential to attract numerous events that will generate sales tax revenues and help support city businesses. Proctor & Gamble is building its first US-based plant in 40 years in the area due to the availability of sufficient quantities of water. The plant, which will produce paper products, will be located on 750 acres of land, will have a value of $400 million, and will support 250 jobs and 50 contractors in the region. A Walmart distribution center is another large employer, and Storm Bowling manufactures more bowling balls than any other company in the world.

Still, the city needs both to diversify its local economic base further and to develop the support mechanisms for the clusters present in the area. Mayor Fife intends to develop a strategic plan for the economic development of the city, which will include a focus on cluster development. His advice to other micropolitan mayors is that "Economic development requires constant attention; nothing can be taken for granted. The only way to keep on top of things is to get out and meet the corporate CEOs and managers. Know what's on their minds."

Brookings, South Dakota

In the late 1870s, the area around current Brookings, South Dakota (please see Figure 6.10) was surveyed for railroad lines. Today, the city and the region are

Figure 6.10 Welcome to Brookings, South Dakota. (Courtesy of City of Brookings)

thriving centers of commerce with a relatively diverse set of industries and sectors represented. The rate of unemployment (4.0%) is not only less than half the national average of 9.1%, but it is well below any definition of what is "full" employment. Recent job growth also outpaces the national average, which is a negative growth figure (at −0.12%); in Brookings, recent job growth was measured at 1.7%, on the plus side of the ledger (http://www.bestplaces.net).

The city's population has grown substantially, from 16,270 in 1990 to 18,504 by 2000, an increase of nearly 14%, and again by 2005 to 18,715 (US Beacon, 2012). Between 2000 and 2011, the population base of Brookings rose by a total of 6.6%.

Brookings represents another community that has benefited in many ways from the presence of a university: South Dakota State University. However, such important institutions in communities can also be affected by downturns in the economy and in 2011 SDSU eliminated 90 jobs and reduced prior expenditure levels for faculty research grants (Fier, 2011). This will certainly have an impact on local businesses and the local economy as well as the city's tax base and public services.

Although the impact of university cuts will also affect local retailers and other small businesses in Brookings, the prerecession retail sales continued to rise annually and significantly, as is demonstrated in Table 6.1. A graphic representation of this trend highlights the impressive nature of the incline over this eight-year period in Brookings. It will also help the reader better understand some of the options that can be available to micropolitan cities if they are well situated and in states that permit their municipal governments to benefit from point-of-sales taxes when developing their local budgets.

Table 6.1   Retail Growth in Brookings, South Dakota, 2000 to 2007

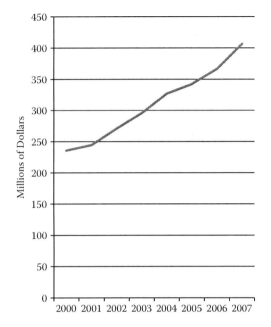

Source: Brookings Economic Development Corporation, 2011.

Other industries represented in the Brookings economic base include manufacturing, food production, and agricultural pursuits in general, and more. Daktronics is the largest employer in the city with 2,300 employees, followed by South Dakota State University with more than 2,100 employees, a 3M facility that supports nearly 800 jobs, and a Larson Manufacturing plant that employs in excess of 700 workers.

Also present in the city are a number of research and development entities, any of which could ultimately spin off commercial products or services. They include the Center for Infectious Disease and Vaccinology, the Drought Tolerance Biotechnology Research Center, the Center for Accelerated Applications at the Nano Scale, the Center for Research and Development of Light-Activated Materials, and the Center for Bioprocessing Research and Development.

Interview with the Honorable Tim Reed, Mayor of Brookings, South Dakota

There has been consistent growth since the late nineteenth century in the city, according to Brookings mayor, Tim Reed. The current iteration of growth has been fueled, at least in part, by the parallel growth of South Dakota State University. The university contributes specific areas of expertise to community discussions as well as the levels of spending that contribute directly to tourism and sales in and around the city. Mayor Reed also notes the joint partnership among the city, state, and SDSU to create a research park for start-ups as well as the commercialization of products resulting from the university's research programs.

The 138-acre research park includes a business incubator, a building for start-ups to occupy after leaving the incubator, and access to university and other support services to help the stabilization of the business side of these nascent companies. The mayor acknowledges that there were some issues to be resolved when the partnership was formed and the park conceived, but they were readily resolved and all partners have benefited since.

The city derives about two-thirds of its revenues from the sales taxes generated within its borders; the remaining portion comes largely from real estate taxes. This is an at-point system that enables the revenues generated to remain in the jurisdiction in which the sales were generated. Other micropolitan mayors have noted the inequities in states where the sales taxes generated go to a statewide pool and are subsequently redistributed by the state legislature. The effect is often to dampen the interest in expanding the local retail base.

However, in South Dakota, the sales taxes remain at the point of sale and thus encourage Brookings to seek to increase retail operations in the city. This is especially important as the city's residential population is still growing. Retailers provide goods for a growing community, create jobs, pay real estate taxes, and increase the critical sales tax base of the city.

The nearest city to Brookings is Sioux Falls, which is about 50 minutes away. This means that Brookings serves as the region's retail hub for many items although, in this way, Sioux Falls is a competitor for some services and for those who live within a similar proximity to both cities. And, of course, those revenues are important to both cities, thus increasing the sense of competition for the businesses and their customers.

Mayor Reed noted that the city has conducted "leakage studies" to assess the areas for which Brookings residents tend to do their shopping elsewhere. One such area is related to the home building and repair items that support a community with a growing population. As a result of one such study, and diligent city efforts, a Lowe's has been built in Brookings. As people began to patronize this business, other retailers built in proximity to the Lowe's, thus creating an opportunity for people to do all their shopping in one place and generating even greater revenues for the city.

Given its location, Brookings is also cognizant of the advantages it presents for the food processing industry. A partnership between the city and the state's economic development organization recently resulted in the establishment of a Bel Cheese facility in Brookings. An additional part of the attractiveness of the city to this company was the dairy sciences program at South Dakota State University, thereby demonstrating one significant advantage of a university for purposes of economic development outreach. Mayor Reed estimates that the plant will add about $160 million to the city's economy annually.

When asked about the future of micropolitan cities, Mayor Reed stated that they can be very successful in the future economy if they fully understand and capitalize on the assets they have in place. To the extent that smaller economies can be further diversified, that too will be important, as it will provide stability over time.

Burlington, Vermont

Over the past generation, Burlington, like many New England cities, has lost population, although the decline has not been precipitous. From a level of 39,127 in 1990, the slide was less than 1% through 2000 (38,889); but the decrease through 2005 to 38,531 was another nine-tenths of one percent (US Beacon, 2012). The unemployment rate at the time of this writing was 4.9%, slightly more than half of the national average of 9.1%, and recent job growth statistics also compared favorably to national averages at this time. In fact, Burlington had experienced a positive job growth at a rate of 1.3% whereas the national picture showed job losses at the rate of 0.12% (http://www.bestplaces.net).

Not surprisingly with those statistics as backdrop and, complemented by great scenic beauty around the region and the state, Burlington has been cited as one of the best cities (eighth in one such ranking) in which to live in the next decade (Rapacon, 2010). Supporting that appeal is a diversified economic base that includes a nascent green economy (wind farming), retail, transportation, utilities, professional and business services, and a range of public sector employment. The economic stability of this market, however, has not been sufficient to stave off losses in city tax revenues of nearly 14% from the beginning of the current recession (Kelley, 2011). One local economist attributes the loss in the tax base at the same time as job growth has occurred to the fact that the latter has largely occurred in two places. "Take away the university and the hospital, and the Burlington economy is generally shrinking" (Kelley, 2011).

One economic development strategy involves tourism attraction as it is estimated to account for about one-fourth of all retail revenues in the Burlington downtown area. An avenue to explore with the mayor would be the extent to which any reliance is being placed upon this strategy as a sales tax generator for the city: tourism is very highly sensitive to macroeconomic forces. The city has responded by investing millions in improvements at Burlington International Airport in the hopes that tourism traffic will be facilitated as the macroeconomy recovers.

Burlington, Vermont: Interview Declined

Carbondale, Illinois

The population base of Carbondale, Illinois demonstrates some rather unusual fluctuations. Between 1990 and 2000, the city's population declined by 23.5% from 27,033 to 20,681. Over the following five years, it increased by 20% to a level of

24,806 (US Beacon, 2012). This could be the result either of shifting economic fortunes or changes in the city's boundaries over time.

At the present time, the unemployment rate in Carbondale is at 7%, far below the national average of 9.1%; and the rate of recent job growth is essentially the same as the national average: –1.0% and –1.2%, respectively (http://www.bestplaces.net).

One of the city's primary assets for economic development and sustainability is the local campus of Southern Illinois University, which contributes nearly 2.3 billion to the local economy and supports about 24,000 jobs. Those jobs generate about $1.2 million in annual income, which generates additional spending in the region and throughout the state. Another 3,800 jobs are housed in the medical school.

A very important indicator of the health of the local economy, both at present as well as into the future, is the fact that about 50% (104,600) of all SIU graduates (210,000) are estimated still to be living in the state of Illinois. A question for the mayor, then, becomes the extent to which the future economic viability of the city is tied to the university and the continued retention of its alumni, and whether it is felt that the university is sufficiently tied into the economic development strategies of the city. Furthermore, for every state dollar given to Southern Illinois University Carbondale, an estimated $7.72 million of statewide economic activity is generated (Sharma, Diaby, and Harfst, 2011).

Specific components of SIUC, notably the School of Medicine, have the potential to create commercial activity in the city and the region and should be discussed with the mayor as well. A great deal of sponsored research is also taking place in SIUC's Colleges of Agricultural Sciences, Science, and Engineering. Some of this research relates to biotechnology, alternative energy sources, material sciences, biotechnology, and animal research that could produce new products or services that can be commercialized and translated into new companies, and even new industries, to support a sustainable economic base in Carbondale. It is reported that the university has, over the past 25 years, assisted more than 50 companies get started, thus creating more than 500 jobs in southern Illinois, obtaining 40 patents and nearly $4 million in royalties for SIUC (Sharma, Diaby, and Harfst, 2011).

Carbondale, Illinois: Interview Declined

Chambersburg, Pennsylvania

The population of Chambersburg, Pennsylvania (please see Figure 6.11) has been quite stable for the two decades from 16,647 (1990) and 20,268 (2010; US Beacon, 2012). Unemployment in the borough has run about three-fourths of the US national average, and recent job growth rates exceed 1% whereas the national average has been negative for the same period (http://www.bestplaces.net).

The recent development in the borough that has received some ballyhoo in the local press relates to one new hotel and several new restaurants. A local boiler manufacturer created 10 new jobs. Half of the landmass in surrounding Franklin

Figure 6.11   The heart of Chambersburg, Pennsylvania. (Pete Lagiovane, mayor of Chambersburg)

County is dedicated to agricultural uses, leaving Chambersburg to be a hub micropolitan city and the source of retail and health services for the greater region.

Nearby Letterkenny Army Depot also represents an economic development asset and net contributor to the Chambersburg and county employment pictures and tax revenue generation. The state and localities have added multimillion dollar improvements to the immediate area in order to convince the federal government not to close the installation in the recent round of BRAC (Base Realignment and Closure) decisions. In fact, 166 new positions were added to the depot. Perhaps the mayor can illuminate the economic returns expected for those investments as well as the various ways in which Letterkenny is involved either directly or indirectly in the present and future economic growth and stability of Chambersburg.

Interview with the Honorable Pete Lagiovane, Mayor of Chambersburg, Pennsylvania

Much of what occurs in terms of local economic growth and development throughout the small cities and towns of the Keystone State is the result of the controls imposed upon them by the state legislature, according to Mayor Lagiovane. The state is substantially overlegislated, having roughly one legislator for every 4,000 residents, as compared to one for about every 12,000 in nearby Maryland.

The borough constitutes its budget largely through property tax collections and has no ability to raise revenues through income taxes. As the formal economic development program is managed by the county, the city has little ability to generate the additional funds needed to build and maintain public works and public infrastructure, which is their primary responsibility. To do so more effectively is one of the means by which they can hope to increase the interest of businesses in Chambersburg. Relatively low prices for water, electricity, and gas are also attractive to employers.

Around the state, there are numerous small communities that are similarly unable to generate the revenues needed to provide good public services. Many must rely on volunteers, sometimes from other states, to provide services such as police and fire protection. Chambersburg has been forced to reduce its fire department by eight positions from a total of 21. This, Mayor Lagiovane believes, makes the community not only less protected but also less attractive to potential employers. "The future of micropolitan communities in Pennsylvania? I think we're in trouble. People are leaving and the demographics are changing." Forty percent of the $11 million budget goes to the police department.

The State of Pennsylvania has established a classification in state code known as Act 47, which is technically known as the Financially Distressed Municipalities Act and is a precursor to municipal bankruptcy. Eleven municipalities have been under it for more than 10 years and six others for more than 20. Compounding the problem for local governments is the state's policy of not taxing incomes derived from pensions. This yields new residents who draw significantly on the community's resources without having to contribute to their costs.

The intent of Act 47 was to forestall the state's communities finding themselves in federal court to access protection from creditors in exchange for various state-imposed sanctions and financial planning and processes requirements. In effect, the import of this provision of state code in Pennsylvania is to highlight the dire needs of the 19 communities that have sought protection under it.

Still, there are a number of assets in and around Chambersburg that are valuable for generating economic development. The interstate highway attracts travelers and has resulted in the growth of restaurants and retail outlets. A large hospital is the biggest employer, followed by a nearby Army depot. Affordable housing and good schools are also attractive assets to employers considering developing local facilities.

The lessons that were identified by Mayor Lagiovane do not include changing state policies. He has served as mayor in hopes of being able to coordinate the local communities, businesses, institutions, and volunteers to make a difference. His best advice is for smaller communities to use the good times to do that which does generate tax revenues. Home construction, for example, helped to create tax base enhancements. If more of that had been accomplished in the good years, the tough years could have been buoyed by those incremental revenues.

Chelsea, Massachusetts

Like much of New England, Chelsea, Massachusetts (please see Figure 6.12) is struggling to rebuild a viable economy. As it does so, the population demonstrates

Figure 6.12   Chelsea, Massachusetts and the Boston skyline. (Courtesy of Chelsea City Hall)

a more transient character than the region has typically known. Between 1990 and 2000, for example, Chelsea grew by more than 20%, from 28,710 to 35,080. But, between 2000 and 2005, it shrank by more than 7% to 32,518 (US Beacon, 2012). At the time of this research, recent job growth was about net zero whereas the national totals were somewhat into the negative. Unemployment levels slightly exceeded national averages: 10.3% to 9.1% (http://www.bestplaces.net).

The very nature of the city has changed substantially over this period as much of the population growth came from in-migration. Nearly 40% of that which occurred between 1980 and 2000 was Hispanic (http://www.bestplaces.net).

This micropolitan city within the greater Boston area dates back to the early 1600s as a place and to 1857 as an incorporated city. Initially having developed as a transportation hub, the city remains at the intersection of multimodal transportation connections that include roadways, waterways, and Logan International Airport. To further the economic growth of the city of Chelsea, some emphasis has been placed on the creation of Tax Increment Financing districts—or TIFs—that enable growth through a self-taxation that is guaranteed to return to that specific area in the form of support for infrastructure development and improvements. One avenue of inquiry for the mayor is the extent to which these have been successful in Chelsea and whether they will continue to use them as a facilitator for economic growth.

It would also be interesting to hear the mayor's perspective, in light of discussions regarding casinos and other industries to pursue, on the types of jobs being sought and what is being done to attract them and the assets those efforts require.

The city is now looking forward to the development of a 100-room hotel in the urban renewal area of Chelsea. The hotel will include a 200-seat function space.

At a time when recession has stalled improvements in other, competitive cities, Chelsea's bold move could prove to be a wise investment in future growth. It also gives the city a reputation for being prodevelopment and collaborative with the business community. This is an important consideration because it also requires boldness on the part of the private partners in the project. The immediate payoff will be 100 new jobs in a city that desperately needs the boost. In the long-term, it may be that the reputation as being business-friendly in a state that is not always, will be the biggest prize.

Interview with Jay Ash, City Manager of Chelsea, Massachusetts

Jay Ash serves as the city manager of Chelsea, Massachusetts. The city does not have a mayor, not even a member of the city council who holds the titular title of mayor. Full executive authority lies in the hands of the city manager.

Chelsea has the unfortunate distinction of being the first city in the United States since the Great Depression to enter into receivership, which it did in 1991. This occurred as the result of years of mismanagement (each of the last four mayors was indicted for criminal activities). The receivers brought together about 20 communitywide stakeholders and concluded that the city would no longer have a mayor, but rather a professional, appointed by the council: a city manager. Mr. Ash, a native of Chelsea, now serves in that capacity.

He describes the city's mood in economic terms as "surprisingly positive." The city has most recently seen the beginning of the development of a Marriott Hotel and the comeback of a major retail center. Hotels have a special place for Ash and for a variety of reasons. They generate jobs and income as well as property taxes and hotel taxes (the room excise tax) that help support city services. Hotels also bring in revenues from outside the community and enable the provision of services to those visiting Boston, to which Chelsea is a bedroom community. Finally, hotels can be built vertically rather than horizontally, an important consideration for a highly densely populated city of less than two square miles in area.

But, even with growth, Chelsea will never be able to exist solely on the basis of the taxes they can generate from within. Chelsea is, in fact, one of the poorest cities in the state, so it is not surprising that 90% of the city's school budget comes from state tax sources and 20% of the city's nonschool budget comes from the tax coffers of the state of Massachusetts.

Initially a manufacturing center, Chelsea has, over the past 20 years, tried to shed that image and has begun to pursue a number of selected categories of commerce: airport-related activities due to their proximity to Logan International Airport, support services for those businesses in downtown Boston, back-office functions and hotels, traditional health care and biotechnology, food industries, and the growth of the residential communities.

The substantial diversity of Chelsea's residential base is regarded as a generally positive trend, however, it does also result in attendant costs for the city. Many of today's Latino immigrants do not possess marketable skills outside agriculture. It is for this reason that food industries are one of the targeted commercial segments noted above. Once language training has been provided, such jobs will be more appropriate for these new immigrants.

Mr. Ash believes that micropolitan communities can survive because there are many supports and lessons to enable them. However, he expresses concerns that have been echoed in other of these interviews that the federal government no longer appears to be a partner in growth for the nation's smaller cities. In fact, the federal supports go to the larger cities, meaning that Chelsea must often compete for federal support with the city of Boston. He feels good about Chelsea's future because of its proximity to Boston, however, he expresses grave concerns about other micropolitan communities throughout the state due to the changed federal focus.

Mr. Ash lists several lessons for other micropolitan cities:

- Ensure that the entire city is on the same page when it comes to economic development, including elected officials, appointed officials, planning staff, and others.
- Don't chase what everyone else is chasing. Know your city's strengths and build on them. For example, Chelsea does not chase high-tech companies because they will prefer to locate in nearby Boston and Cambridge.
- Relationships are critical. Leadership must convince businesses that they really do have their best interests at heart and mean to be helpful.

In terms of concerns for future growth, the list includes the ever-crumbling infrastructure, the low education and skill levels, especially of the immigrant population, and the loss of federal partnership with smaller cities.

Chillicothe, Ohio

The population base of Chillicothe, Ohio has remained remarkably stable over the past 20 years. With some minor fluctuations registered between, the 1990 base was 21,923 and the 2010 mark was 21,901 (US Beacon, 2012). With an unemployment rate that mirrored the national average (high 8% range) at the time of this writing, Chillicothe represents a picture similar to many of the micropolitan rust belt cities.

Recent developments have been mixed. Pent-up demand for trucks caused the local Kenworth Truck plant to expand their workforce by 1,000 jobs as has a paper plant. Health care positions have been cut because births are down 30% in the recession, which has further reduced the demand for health care services in Chillicothe (Peralta, 2011).

Chillicothe, Ohio: Interview Declined

Clarksburg, West Virginia

The micropolitan city of Clarksburg, West Virginia has seen its population base decline over the past two decades. From the 1990 census level of slightly more than 18,000, the city declined through 2005 to 16,500 but saw a slight reversal of that trend in the 2010 census, registering 16,578 residents (US Beacon, 2012).

Unemployment hovers just below the national average (8.1% versus 9.1%), however, that must be considered in light of the population losses. The number of jobs has likely declined significantly but has been offset by the movement of families out of town. This would be an area of inquiry to be explored with the mayor.

The city has some natural economic advantages, not the least of which are the numerous US interstate highways in close proximity, and Pittsburgh lies only about 100 miles away. The recent relocation of the FBI's Criminal Justice Information Services Division has begun to revive both the local job base and the residential levels of the city and the region as well.

Clarksburg, West Virginia: Interview Declined

Clinton, Iowa

Clinton, Iowa, as do many American cities large and small, owes its existence to the navigable waterway it enjoys, in this case the Mississippi River. Commerce settles in proximity to routes that enable the smooth flow of products and people to and from primary and secondary markets. Clinton enjoys a 12-mile stretch of waterfront and that has shaped its local economy.

The city's population, however, reflects a significant decline in recent years. The 1990 level of 29,201 dropped off by nearly 2.5% by 2000 (27,720), and again by almost 5% more by 2005 (27,086; US Beacon, 2012). Its unemployment rate, at a time when the US average was 9.1%, was only slightly lower at 8%. And its recent job growth was at a positive 0.7% when the US average remained in the net loss column at −0.12% (http://www.bestplaces.net).

In the Clinton catchment area for workforce, the total in 2006 was given as more than 223,000, about 22% of whom were engaged in some form of manufacturing occupation (Gilliam, 2009).

Much of the development news out of Clinton relates to the best uses for development along the Mississippi River. Tourism dominates the outreach, complemented by news of the development of a marina, a minor league baseball stadium, a theater, parks, a walking trail, and a skateboard park. Although these are attractive and pleasant additions to the quality of life in a city, one must question whether they will generate employment opportunities or tax revenues. If, of course, the intent is beautification and a general enhancement of the overall quality of life, these projects make sense. If there is an expectation of job creation or the generation of tax revenues, one must ask whether these were the best uses for the funding thus allocated. These would be good avenues of inquiry for the mayor of Clinton.

The recent groundbreaking for a rail line of the Union Pacific Railroad to the city's industrial park signals a significant growth opportunity for the park and for the city. In addition to the $30 million investment, the park will soon be connected to the rest of the nation. The office of the governor estimated as many as 3,000 to 4,000 jobs as the other benefit of the line. It is an example of cities making economic development investments for the future when the economy is at a low point.

Clinton, Iowa: Interview Declined

Clovis, New Mexico

Clovis, New Mexico originally developed as a center for people involved in farming and ranching concerns, and was formally incorporated as a city in 1909. One of the early commercial assets was the railroad, which continues to be important to doing business in Clovis today.

The city's population has increased marginally in recent years, growing by more than 5.5% between 1990 (30,954) and 2000 (32,667), and again by over 2% more by 2005 (33,357; US Beacon, 2012). At the time of this writing, its level of unemployment was 4.7%, nearly half of the 9.1% US average, although its recent job growth paralleled that national average at −0.14 and −0.12, respectively; http://www.bestplaces.net).

The population statistics for the city belie the strength of the region around it. There are about 10,000 more people who live within 10 miles of Clovis and more than another 85,000 within a 60-mile radius of the city (City of Clovis Website, Statistical Data and Links, 2012).

One of the drivers of the economy of Clovis today is Cannon Air Force Base. Its 2010 report states that it is the home to an employee payroll that exceeds $224 million and an annual expenditure rate of over $200 million more. This may make the city and the region (and perhaps even the state) overly dependent upon this single employer and one must consider the potential impacts of a cutback at the base, or even a closure of the base.

Food processing plants also can be found in and around Clovis due to the dairy farming in the region. These include Gold Star Dairy, Clovis Grain Processing, and the FrozFruit Company, a plant capable of producing more than 300,000 fruit bars per day (Pressley, 1993).

Other major employers include Eastern New Mexico University, the public school system, Plains Regional Medical Center, Walmart, the Burlington Northern Santa Fe Railroad, and Clovis Community College. Much of this employment is dependent upon the continued existence of Cannon Air Force Base in the area. Small manufacturers do help to bolster the economic diversity of the city and the region but the question of greater economic diversity is one that would be addressed with the mayor. On a related matter, a severe drought and subsequent wildfire in 2011 cost more than 160,000 acres, one impact of which was the loss of hay production that supported the farms in the region. Again, economic diversification may be an important consideration.

Clovis, New Mexico: Interview Declined

Coeur d'Alene, Idaho

One comparative report for Coeur d'Alene (please see Figure 6.13) shows that its cost of doing business ranks fourth in US standings whereas its overall cost of living ranks 149th (*Forbes*, 2011). There is a variety of possible explanations for this disparity, however, it is important to understand whether this is an indication that taxes are overly favorable for businesses, leaving the residential community to carry the burden of public service expenditures. The same report indicates that the adult population is well educated, with over 92% possessing high school diplomas and 23% a college degree.

Prior to the recession, in 2007, one reporter indicated that with an unemployment rate of just 3.5%, if there was a problem in the economy looking forward, it would be the inability to fill positions. By 2009, the Milliken Institute was reporting that Coeur d'Alene was the fourth best performing city in America, up from the number six spot two years earlier (Allbusiness, 2011). As this book is being written (2012), Coeur d'Alene may be facing another potential issue regarding its future economic vitality: the state of Idaho ranks thirtieth among US states

Figure 6.13 From shore to mountains in Coeur d'Alene, Idaho. (Aerial photo courtesy of Big Country Helicopters, Coeur d'Alene, Idaho)

for economic rates of growth. And, the city's unemployment rate stood at 12.3%, compared to the national average of 9.1%. On the bright side, however, recent job growth was recorded at 2.9% against a national average of –0.12% (US Beacon, 2012). Another factor that is casting a potential pall over the area's economy is the demand for, and therefore the price of, silver as a result of global economic problems. As a consequence, financial activities are now the leading sector, representing about 22% of the economic output of Coeur d'Alene (EconPost, 2011).

An interesting avenue of inquiry would be to determine whether, as a result of the extended national and global recession, the 2007 sentiments of the city's leadership remain intact. At that time, the use of economic incentives to attract and retain businesses was disallowed. The economy was rather diverse and relied not just on mining, but also on agriculture, technology, business and personal services, and tourism (particularly skiing and whitewater rafting; Gauchon, 2007).

Interview with the Honorable Sandi Bloem, Mayor of Coeur d'Alene, Idaho

The Honorable Sandi Bloem is the mayor of Coeur d'Alene, Idaho. Mayor Bloem refers to the local mood in regard to the current state of the economy with caution, yet she remains hopeful and believes that the community does as well. The reason for the rosy outlook is that she feels that, when the nation and the world emerge finally from recession, Coeur d'Alene is "prepared to recover" and that, as a result, it will likely emerge from the recession more quickly than other cities of its size.

That preparation comes in the form of infrastructure and appearances. The infrastructure that companies seek is already in place in the city; businesses will neither have to develop it themselves nor will they have to wait as the public sector approves plans, solicits builders, and then conducts the processes necessary to prepare sites. In the parlance used earlier in this book, the city has prepared an environment that is conducive to economic growth and vitality. As such, Coeur d'Alene does not use cash incentives or tax abatements to support business attraction or retention efforts. Mayor Bloem feels that the environment is attractive enough and the city is maintained well enough that employers are attracted without the use of incentives, and that today's technology enables working from micropolitan cities for employers that are located elsewhere.

In terms of appearances, Mayor Bloem places a great deal of importance on the preparation and maintenance of public spaces, believing that if people see a pleasant and vital community, they will want to be part of it and to invest private dollars to complement the public investments. And, by state law in Idaho, the city is permitted to use urban renewal funds to support infrastructure development and maintenance as well as the maintenance of public spaces.

Another reason for a positive outlook is that the city's budget has not been decimated in the current recession to the same extent that they have been in other cities of a like size. The revenue sources are quite diverse, including a range of taxes and user fees. This supports her belief that growth should pay for itself. That breadth of diversity also extends to the industries in the community, which also gives the mayor a cause for hope: "There is a great advantage in such diversity because it provides stability."

Although modestly not given to advising others, Mayor Bloem, when asked for the lessons of Coeur d'Alene from which others could benefit, noted that "The decisions you make today will decide your city's future. If you build a quality place, quality people will want to locate there."

Concord, New Hampshire

The population base of the city of Concord, New Hampshire is toward the higher end of the definitional range for micropolitan cities and it is still growing. In 1990, the US census reports set the level at just over 36,000. By 2005, the level was up well over 42,000 (US Beacon, 2012). And that trend continued through the 2010 census, which reported 42,695 residents of Concord, an increase in five years of 359. As of this writing, the level of unemployment among the residents of Concord is almost precisely half the national average of 9.1%. Only about 4.6% of Concord's workforce is unemployed, well below what is generally considered to be "full employment."

A 2008 city planning exercise Crossroads focused on potential enhancements of the city's "creative" sectors, which support nearly 4,500 jobs and generate more than $150 million in annual payrolls in the city. Priorities highlighted in the plan include tourism marketing, loan funds, arts incubators and artist housing projects, expansion of relevant courses at the local community college, creation of a signature arts event, and more. As this plan was released just as the recession was beginning, it would be important to discuss with the mayor the extent to which these strategies have been implemented and what the immediate effects have been.

Beyond the arts and cultural scene, Concord has several other significant employers. Concord Hospital employs 3,200 people and Steeplegate Mall another 1,200 plus. Others include Genesis Healthcare, with 1,200 employees, Lincoln Financial Group with 600, and more.

Concord, New Hampshire: Interview Declined

Cookeville, Tennessee

Cookeville is, if not the fastest growing (in terms of population) micropolitan city in the country, certainly one of the fastest growing. From 1990 to 2000, the city's population base grew by 10%, from 21,744 to 23,923. Over the ensuing five years (to 2005) it grew by an additional 16.8% to 27,743 (US Beacon, 2012). Its mid-2011 unemployment level of 8.8% sat near the national average of 9.1% and its recent job growth was a positive 1.2% as compared to the national average of a negative −.012% (http://www.bestplaces.net). The community is certainly not without assets for business attraction and growth. It is home to Tennessee Tech and its 8,500 students, which is ranked highly by US periodicals as one of the best public institutions in the southeast. And it has been named one of the nation's best options for retirement.

Yet, there are also some concerns that are identified in the literature by and about this micropolitan city in Tennessee. The high levels of unemployment have given way to a concern about the attitudes of the residents regarding their ability to recover lost economic ground. This is not uncommon and is not restricted to cities of this (micropolitan) size. Prior studies have indicated that large metropolitan communities have experienced similar crises of the collective psyche (see Gordon, 2010). In the case of Cookeville, the issue is given its best airing by a local article: "Though the numbers tell part of the story, the real question for area employees is creating readiness for change and the new jobs that may be emerging in the area ... those who live in the Upper Cumberland and want to stay seem confident that they will find a way to remain in place and find their opportunity for advancement, building skills in readiness ..." (Local Area Unemployment Rates Stay High, 2011).

Another concern in the local press is worthy of inquiry with the mayor. There is a concern expressed that the state economic development efforts are overly focused on large-scale economic development projects because they capture press attention and make political hay. Although large businesses are good for cities and do a great deal to generate business for a city's small and midsized companies, the concern in Cookeville is that the support being given the larger employers is coming at the expense of other businesses. This may be especially disconcerting at this time of relatively higher unemployment levels, when manufacturing jobs have been lost and replaced only by lower-paying jobs in the retail and service economies.

Poverty is substantial in Cookeville. Nearly one in five people is enrolled in a food stamp program (September 2011), equating to 13,385 people in Putnam County (Swallows, 2011). The region is relying on Cookeville to recover. Some 25,000 people commute into the city for work each day. Diversification of the local economy has begun and includes retail, health and medical services, hotels, and restaurants. These are positive signs but the salaries in these occupations tend to be lower than the manufacturing jobs held by the previous generations of Cookeville's workforce.

Cookeville, Tennessee: Interview Declined

Covina, California

Covina is a suburb of the sprawling Los Angeles metropolis. Following the Second World War, Covina began to grow its economy on the basis of citrus farming and juice production, but an agricultural virus was devastating, and made clear the need to diversify the local economy. Over time, the population grew, in part due to the growth of Los Angeles and California generally. From 1990 to 2000 the base grew by nearly 8.5% from 43,207 to 46,837; and again from 2000 to 2005 by 2.2% to a total of 47,850 (US Beacon, 2012).

Recent job growth in Covina has underperformed against national averages, losing at the rate of –0.53%, compared to the US average of –.012%. At the time of this writing, the unemployment rate is higher than the national rate of 9.1% sitting at 10.7%.

Covina, California: Interview Declined

Culver City, California

Culver City is an example of a micropolitan city in which the economic viability is wholly dependent upon its proximity to a larger industrial base with a primary industry. In the case of Culver City, the proximity to the entertainment industry in southern California drives a lot of the employment opportunities.

Industrial segments present in Culver City include several functions supporting the production of motion pictures as well as other entertainment sectors. In addition, information and telecommunications businesses are present in the city as well as a wide range of health care positions (more than 9,000). A full 6% of the jobs in the city are in finance and real estate (http://www.americity.org, 2011).

Thus, Culver City is the beneficiary of the motion picture industry but has also significantly diversified its economic base. And that has led to stability in the local population base. From 1990 to 2000, the level grew by 0.6% from 38,793 to 38,816, and from that time to 2005 by another 2% to 39,813 (US Beacon, 2012).

Given the proximity not only to the motion picture industry but also to the beaches and scenic beauty of the state of California, Culver City's economy also benefits from a thriving trade in tourism, hospitality, restaurants, and retail. In mid-2011, the city elevated its Transient Occupancy Tax rate to 14% in order to capture additional revenues from tourists who take back very little in public services. In effect, a strong tourism economy helps the city provide public services to the residents who *do* benefit from them while minimizing, to the extent possible, the cost to local constituents. One area to explore with the mayor would be whether the 14% rate is too high. At some point, the deterrence of a higher tax may cost the city's hospitality industry more in visitors than it gains from the marginal revenues from the increase. Has Culver City reached that point yet?

Culver City, California: Interview Declined

Danville, Virginia

As has been the case in much of the southern part of the Commonwealth of Virginia, Danville (please see Figure 6.14) has been hurt in the current extended recessionary period, although its economic problems had begun much earlier.

Figure 6.14 Downtown Danville, Virginia. (Courtesy of Mackenzie Osadchuk, City of Danville)

Many of those challenges began with the loss of jobs in traditional areas of strength including lumber, textiles, and tobacco.

As one would expect in such a situation, the population base declined precipitously. From a 1990 level of 53,056, the city had declined by the census of 2000 to 48,411, and again by 2005 to 46,143, and finally to 43,055 in the census reports of 2010 (US Beacon, 2012). This represents a 20-year population decline of nearly 19%.

The state of Virginia has placed significant emphasis on assisting Danville and other similarly affected areas in the redevelopment of their local economies. It and the city have created numerous incentive programs for business attraction and support as well as allowances and fee reimbursement opportunities for power, water, and other services.

Master planning for the redevelopment of Danville's downtown area has proceeded apace and the city has become a true partner with the employers who have selected the city as a location. And although challenges abound, there have been some encouraging signs. The Regional Medical Center supports more than 2,000 jobs throughout the region and serves a wide geographic area. This represents about one-fourth of the jobs in the region it serves. A number of community colleges, technical schools, and universities within easy access also represent economic development assets. Stated needs include more restaurants in the downtown as well as other retail uses to reverse an estimated $45 million annually in leakage to other cities' retail centers (Greenberg Development Services, 2008). A good conversation with the mayor would address how a micropolitan community can seek to overcome such dramatic economic downturns and begin to grow again in a way that is sustainable over time.

But, it will need to do so with an eye toward land use planning. A 2008 report of the city's potential markets and market area (Greenberg Development Services, 2008) stated that "The city ... will need to monitor the location of proposed projects to ensure that they are compatible with one another and meet the city's objectives for the area. Projects also will need to be monitored to be sure that they enhance other investments rather than function as 'stand-alone' projects." This, too, would be a good topic of discussion for the interview with Mayor Saunders.

Interview with the Honorable Sherman Saunders, Mayor of Danville, Virginia

Mayor Saunders and one of the professional staff from the city of Danville (Jeremy Stratton) described Danville's economy in substantially more positive terms than the press. The city, which is located near the Virginia border with North Carolina, is about a one-hour drive from the Raleigh–Durham area. Its geographic position enables it to serve as a hub for retail and other business and personal services throughout a greater region.

The total loss of jobs equated to about 12,000, according to the mayor. Mayor Saunders described the comeback from the loss of those textile and lumber and tobacco jobs as being well under way. The mood: "Great!" The sights for future economic growth are now set on manufacturing and technology broadly. The city feels it is able to provide high-speed data connections and a strong workforce for data centers and other applications. Mayor Saunders feels businesses that wish to take advantage of the Danville location will also benefit from reasonable highway access and strong rail connections with the Norfolk Southern Railroad.

However, the mayor is also a realist. He spoke of the need to improve educational levels in his community, especially to those at greatest risk. He believes this to be critical if Danville is to become a serious economic development location. Toward that end, he proudly speaks of the local community college and the fact that the percentage of the workforce with two-year degrees has grown from between 10 and 11% to between 14 and 15%.

Still, even with these improvements, Danville needs state support to attract businesses. Virginia has used its tobacco settlement money to assist areas of high unemployment and great need such as Danville in attracting companies by providing cash incentives to locate operations there. Mayor Saunders indicated that every business which has done so recently has received this type of support. Without that help, Danville's travails would have been much greater.

One of the advantages Mayor Saunders sees in a micropolitan-sized community is the volunteerism that takes place. Today, many local residents are teaching others to read and increase the literacy rate. Residents help each other because, in a small community, people learn to rely on one another, "We're all in this together."

When asked about what he has learned that might prove to be instructive to other cities of like size facing similar issues, Mayor Saunders replied that regions also need to work together. Danville's partnership with surrounding Pittsylvania County has proven to be productive. Together, the city and the county have purchased land for an industrial park, both entities contributing about $6.5 million. For Danville, and many other micropolitan cities, this is vital because the cities have finite land resources available, so much of the land that is or can be zoned for commercial uses lies outside the city's borders.

Another lesson the mayor notes is to revitalize the downtown, which he equates to one's living room. "It's what makes people think well of your home and it's what makes people think well of your city." And once a success is achieved, emphasize it. "People want to know that there is not just talk but that things are really happening. You can't just rest on your laurels. We have to fight every day to make Danville a better place."

Denison, Texas

Denison has been steadily growing in population for the past 20 years. Between 1990 and 2000, the city's population base increased by nearly 6% from 21,505 to 22,773. Over the next five years, it realized another 3.8% increase to 23,648 (US Beacon, 2012). The city is situated about 75 miles from Dallas so its housing values during the recession declined by a relatively small 5% as the region lost about 2.5% of its employment base (United States Department of Housing and Urban Development, 2010). There are not just a few industry segments from which those jobs were lost; rather, they came from many industries. At the same time, education, health services, and the hospitality trade all held their own in terms of the numbers of people employed in and around Denison. For example, the Texoma Medical Center employs between 4,000 and 5,000 people at the present time.

In this part of the country, Denison promotes its abundant supplies of water and electrical power as strong assets. In addition, a new 17,500-square-foot meeting facility is expected to attract conferences and the resulting revenues. This facility was built at the cost, in part, of $2.7 million of publicly granted incentives. The city's economic development website announces that Denison is "aggressive in incentive payments." This would be a topic to explore with the mayor: do incentives yield a positive return on investment? And what other demands had to be ignored to provide the incentives?

In addition to using incentives to spur economic growth, the city has begun to beautify its downtown as a means of creating an environment that is conducive to business growth. These types of projects have been successful in some micropolitan cities in attracting buyers back to the retail opportunities that exist. As important, such programs need not always be costly: façade improvements and basic cleanup efforts can make substantial improvements, enhance residents' pride in the city, and bring in shoppers and revenues as well.

Major employers in Denison include Tyson's Fresh Meats, the Texoma Health Care System, Jones Hospital, the public schools, CIGNA, Texas Instruments, Ruiz Foods, and Trailblazer Health Enterprises. This list represents significant employers in a well-diversified economic base. Multiple incentive programs are designed to enhance that diversity in the local economy, indicating an appreciation of the value that both growth and diversity bring to micropolitan cities and regions.

Denison, Texas: Interview Declined

Dodge City, Kansas

Dodge City has witnessed strong residential growth over the past 20 years, growing from 21,129 in 1990 to 27,340 by the 2010 census report (US Beacon, 2012). At the time of this writing, the city's unemployment rate of 3.4% was substantially below the national average of 8.6% (http://www.bestplaces.net).

Two business parks across 525 acres in Dodge City provide abundant shovel-ready development sites for companies to locate. Numerous media references have been found that refer to the need to revitalize and beautify the downtown area. This would be a good point of discussion with the mayor.

Another avenue of inquiry would be the success in moving toward the city's stated objective of becoming the entertainment capital of western Kansas. And if that has been successful as a strategy, how has it generated revenues that support the municipal budget and enable the city to provide public services? Much of the employment base is tied to agriculture and farming production. The two largest employers are listed as beef processing businesses that, together, employ nearly 5,400 residents. Higher education, retail establishments, and the public sector appear next on the list of primary employers. Does the mayor feel a need to diversify the local economy further?

Dodge City, Kansas: Interview Declined

Doral, Florida

Doral, Florida, as an incorporated city, is relatively new, having been formally established as a city in 2003 (please see Figure 6.15). Its proximity to Miami means that Doral is attractive to both businesses and residents because the area is generally sunny and warm and enjoys beautiful ocean views. Doral also benefits from being near Miami International Airport, but its geographic location can also be detrimental because it means that there are significant traffic issues.

Although the economy of Doral and the surrounding area has a history of dynamism, it has struggled in recent years due to job losses and the resultant high rate of residential mortgage foreclosures. Today, the state of Florida ranks only behind the state of Nevada in terms of the number of foreclosures. Job growth has continued

Figure 6.15   City building in Doral, Florida. (Courtesy of City of Doral)

to be negative in the present economic downturn at –2.76% (www.bestplaces.net/economy/city/florida/doral) whereas the US average was at –0.12%.

As a result of job losses, the residential population of Doral has also declined. The "nighttime population" of the city went from 22,102 in 2000 to 21,895 in 2005 (US Beacon, 2012). The 2000 census also reported that the city's population was overwhelmingly Hispanic (nearly two of every three residents). But it is the shifts in population from the daytime (workers) to the nighttime (residents) population that must be a key consideration for the leadership of Doral. The National League of Cities reported that Doral ranks third in the entire nation among cities with populations between 15,000 and 25,000 people in terms of that shift. In the daytime, Doral hosts 63,802 workers whereas it has a residential population of only 20,438.

For the leadership of communities with such dramatic swings in daytime and nighttime populations, a vital consideration must be how they generate the tax base from which they provide public services. If the predominant source of general fund revenues is the real estate tax base, the administrators in Doral would be delighted because they would be reaping great real estate tax revenues from the private sector and can use that to provide quality public services (including public education, public safety, public works, and more) without expecting residents (who vote) to bear the full burden of those expenses. They receive positive effects to the real estate tax base and someone else has to educate the children of those workers.

On the other hand, if a substantial percentage of the local tax base is generated by income taxes, then Doral's leadership would have the opposite problem: they are required to pay for infrastructure development and improvement at the same time the wages earned in Doral are being taxed by their neighboring jurisdictions.

Interview with the Honorable J. C. Bermudez, Mayor of Doral, Florida

Mayor Bermudez acknowledges that the economy of Doral has been affected in the same way that many other cities in Florida and around the United States have experienced. Yet he remains optimistic for his city because there are many assets and recent developments that have helped Doral grow. He is very proud of the recent construction of significant Class A office space that has enabled the attraction of some major employers to the west side of Miami, where Doral is the largest city. The most recent of these economic development wins involved the attraction of the headquarters offices and plant of the *Miami Herald*, which moved in 2013. Another headquarters in Doral is the Carnival Cruise Line.

Still, Mayor Bermudez wants more. Why? The city's budget is based in large part on the real estate tax base: more buildings yield the greater taxes Doral needs to provide high-quality, low-cost public services. Of course, a major complementary asset for the tax base is the world-renowned Doral Golf and Country Club, site of numerous PGA (Professional Golfers Association) tournaments over the years. But that is not the only game in town. Doral is now home to more than 40 banks, the Latin American Division of Harley Davidson, and air service that both provides jobs (logistics is a prime example) and enables economic development targeting in Latin America and Asia.

In terms of gaps in the asset base, the mayor notes that the city needs to attract more restaurants, retail, and residential units in the downtown to complement its growing business base.

Mayor Bermudez considers the future of micropolitan cities like Doral as "Great." By way of explanation, he cites the fact that Doral has been built without raising taxes. "There is definitely a place for these cities and communities that were once traditional suburban neighborhoods and have now been urbanized. We have a nice downtown, jobs, housing, and wonderful people you get to know."

When asked if there were lessons from the Doral experience that he thought could be useful to other micropolitan cities, Mayor Bermudez said that they need a "proactive mentality" as well as the foresight to understand that economic development is not an afterthought; it needs to be a constant objective. Furthermore, these communities must attract jobs because employers help to provide quality of life and keep the taxes lower for residents. "Government should be run like a business."

Douglas, Georgia

Douglas, Georgia, named for the presidential competitor to Abraham Lincoln, Stephen A. Douglas, was chartered in 1899. Its location was largely determined by its proximity to the nearby railroad line and is positioned about 120 miles north of Jacksonville, Florida and about a three-hour drive from Atlanta. One avenue of discussion for the mayor would need to be the dramatic fluctuations in the city's population over the past generation. In 1990, the population base of Douglas was 22,099. By 2000 it had declined by 52% to 10,639. Then, over the next five-year period, the city's population reflected an increase of 3.2% to 10,978 (US Beacon, 2012).

The city's unemployment rate (10.8%) at the time of this writing exceeded the national level of 9.1%; and Douglas' recent job growth of −0.76% compared unfavorably to the US average of −0.12% (http://www.bestplaces.net). The city's poverty level in 2000 was reported as a very high 24%.

A small industry cluster exists in the poultry business. This includes about 2,000 jobs and a $75 million contribution to the local economy as well as sup-port positions in trucking, feed sales, and more. This is complemented by the 1,200 jobs in warehousing and distribution and the 600 positions at the Coffee Regional Medical Center. South Georgia College, a two-year institution, supports 1,865 students. This would be an area for discussion with the mayor: in addition to the contributions it makes to the economic viability of Douglas, how is SGC involved in supporting economic development in and around Douglas?

Local media coverage indicates that great emphasis is being placed by local elected and economic development officials on support for the growth of exist-ing small businesses and the start-up of new small businesses. This also provides fertile ground for discussion with the mayor. Is this the future of Douglas? Is that adequate? Is this the future of all micropolitan cities?

Douglas, Georgia: Interview Declined

Durango, Colorado

The population of Durango (please see Figure 6.16) has grown steadily from 1990 on, moving over that period from 12,430 to nearly 17,000 today. Unemployment in the city is below the national average at this time and recent job growth has been in the positive 2 to 3% range whereas national performance has been negative. Surprisingly, it is very difficult to find any coverage in an Internet search of any business or economic activity in Durango. This may simply mean that there is either no local press or that the coverage relates to other matters.

Interview with the Honorable Doug Lyon, Mayor of Durango, Colorado

Durango, Colorado is an example of an isolated micropolitan city. The city provides a wide array of services and needs for the approximately 50,000 residents of the area that stretches for a considerable distance in all directions from Durango. The fact that the sales levels are up by more than 6% over the previous year is testimony to the significance and extent of that isolation. The mayor cited this as a great positive because the city derives nearly two-thirds of its general fund revenues from sales taxes.

Figure 6.16   The mountainous setting of Durango, Colorado. (Courtesy of Durango Area Tourism Office)

The summer preceding the date of the interview was a very successful one for the city's retailers. The city also serves as the region's center for cultural experiences, fine dining, and the thriving arts scene. Another attraction for visitors, as well as an asset for economic development, is Fort Lewis College, which acts in partnership with the city on a number of fronts. To further the mutual benefits of the "town–gown" relationship, the city created a dedicated sales tax, the revenue from which may only be used for parks, trails, and open spaces. Sixteen acres of those open spaces are on the college's campus in Durango. In this partnership, the city provided the infrastructure development and the university provides the ongoing maintenance. The two bodies also cohosted a bicycle race, as well as other activities designed to bring the students and the residents of Durango together.

Although retailers are important to Durango's economic growth, there are several primary economy companies in town as well. The Mercury Company manufactures credit card processors and, while it is finishing its headquarters building, employs 300 people and plans to add as many as an additional 350 over time. Others include Chinook, Allied Pipe, and a regional medical center that employs nearly 1,000 people in Durango. The largest employer in the region is the Southern Ute Indian Tribe, which extracts natural gas reserves and manages development projects nationwide.

Mayor Lyon, who has served on the City Council for eight years is, as are most of the mayors interviewed for this book, a native of his city and graduated from Fort

Lewis College. Another similarity with his peers in micropolitan cities is that he has no interest in pursuing statewide elective office. Partnerships are the means to what he attributes his success in Durango. "We work together well here. We must all feel that we are part of the team. It is simply the culture of this community."

Elk Grove, Illinois

Elk Grove is a micropolitan community in the suburban Chicago region (please see Figure 6.17). Its location only 20 miles southwest of the city shapes its internal economic stability. Moreover, its one-mile distance from the approach to O'Hare Airport means that its economy is largely responsive to, and does not shape, the external forces that support its economic viability. Not surprisingly, the Elk Grove cost of living is significantly higher (by nearly 23%) than the US average. The population base grew slightly between 1990 and 2000 from 33,429 to 34,727, or by nearly 4%. However, the decline in the city's population by nearly 6.5% between 2000 and 2011 (to 32,473) paralleled a loss in recent job growth that was further into the negative than was the national average: –1.4% versus –0.12% (http://www.bestplaces.net).

The Second World War stimulated the Elk Grove economy, which did not even have paved roads until that time. The manufacture of the Douglas Aircraft C-54 transport in Elk Grove began its aviation economy, one high point of which was the location of the United Airlines headquarters in Elk Grove until 2006.

As aviation manufacturing has long dominated the economic scene, the leadership in Elk Grove developed a business park in which there are presently 3,600 businesses and more than 100,000 jobs. This helps to make Elk Grove home to the second highest number of manufacturing jobs in Illinois, more than 21,000. One avenue to explore with the mayor would be whether there is a sense that the economy is sufficiently diversified to ensure future stability. There are indeed secondary businesses. The presence of the airport, for example, has meant that Elk Grove has become home to 30 shopping centers, however, these tend to support primarily low-skill, low-wage employment.

Figure 6.17   A park in Elk Grove, Illinois. (Courtesy of Village of Elk Grove)

Interview with the Honorable Craig Johnson, Mayor of Elk Grove, Illinois

Elk Grove, Illinois is a suburb of the city of Chicago and sits adjacent to O'Hare Airport. Mayor Johnson says that this makes this metropolitan micropolitan city unusual. "It has a small town feel and also has 100,000 jobs. I can walk down the street and talk to old friends or *Fortune* 500 CEOs."

The mayor is also unique because he has served as mayor for 16 years. Although this is unlike the other mayors in this study, Mayor Johnson maintains that it is not at all unusual in his part of the country. Elk Grove was established in the 1950s and his family was the fiftieth to arrive. The mayor maintains that Elk Grove is a great place to do business despite the fact that its home state of Illinois is regularly ranked at the bottom of every index of business-friendly states. He calls the economic mood of Elk Grove today "phenomenal." The city is home to Illinois' second largest base of manufacturing jobs. And, although the city had a vacancy rate in commercial buildings that rose to 14% during the recession, it had, at the time of this writing, declined to less than 5%.

Despite the impacts of business activity on the tax generation of the city, the mayor and city council were able to "right-size" the city's staff complement and reduce 45 jobs without either layoffs or loss of service levels. This also saved the city $450,000 per year in expenses. Forty percent of the city's budget comes from the sales tax base and another 30% from real estate taxes. Thus, companies that manufacture products, many of which are sold from the point of manufacture, generate tax revenues on those sales.

As for lessons learned that he would impart to other micropolitan city mayors, Mayor Johnson notes that government should have a "business-oriented mindset. Departments must be seen as responsive and business-friendly. The last thing a business wants is to be sent to see 'someone else' all the time."

Another thought he offered was that businesses need good roads and infrastructure. "If trucks are sitting in traffic that costs the business money." But, his favorite lesson? "A politician does what is popular; a statesman does what is right!" The primary asset gap Mayor Johnson can identify is a business-friendly state. "We see that as an obstacle that we just have to work around: we'll just be the most business-friendly city. Businesses want to feel welcome and appreciated."

Elko, Nevada

Between 1990 and 2010, the residential population of Elko, Nevada (please see Figure 6.18) grew by nearly one-fourth, from 14,736 to 18,297 (US Beacon, 2012). With an unemployment rate below the national average, Elko appears to be in a relatively strong economic position.

Figure 6.18 Open landscapes of Elko, Nevada. (Courtesy of Shannell Owen, City of Elko)

One of the city's and the region's strongest sectors has been, and continues to be, cattle ranching and farming. As a consequence, much can be found in the local process regarding public land use decisions that have an impact on those business sectors. The local economy clearly benefits from what are significantly high-value exports. As such, an interesting line of inquiry for the interview with Elko's mayor would be what the city is doing to create a comprehensive business cluster around cattle ranching and farming sectors.

Still, there are an estimated 142 different economic clusters that are active in what is described in the current literature as an extremely diverse economic base in Elko; and cattle ranching produces only an estimated 3% of the total value of output in Elko County (Harris, 2004). Still, taxable sales in the county around the city of Elko declined by nearly 14% in February of 2012 over the previous February. An important topic of conversation for the mayor would be the extent to which that has had an impact on the local tax revenues that comprise the city's budget. At a time when construction and manufacturing totals also declined, there may be an issue in terms of the city's ability to provide the full range and level of quality of public services.

Although the city uses its relative isolation and "wide open spaces" to promote itself for both residential and business relocations as well as tourism, the city sits in a region that is a long way from larger agglomerations. Reno is 286 miles away, and Salt Lake City 230 miles distant. This means that Elko is likely the hub for the entire region's retail sales and medical services, which would provide a strong source of economic continuity and growth. The city's website may provide the explanation: "Elko has steadily plodded forward. We're not flashy. We're slower to change with fads or economic whims." This approach, coupled with six casinos and some of the world's most active mining operations (especially for gold), seems to have sustained the local economy through the recent national recession (Nevada Regional History, 2012).

Interview with the Honorable Chris Johnson, Mayor of Elko, Nevada

Through the late 1980s, Elko, Nevada was a significantly smaller community than it is today. The basis for the economy at that time was largely ranching. In the late 1980s, the local mining interests became more productive and the city population swelled, and that of the larger region did so even more dramatically. Today, with nearly 20,000 residents, Elko serves as the regional hub for retail, cultural opportunities, health care, and more. The catchment area for Elko for these kinds of services is roughly 200 miles in all directions.

The retail component of the economy is an important one as the city of Elko constitutes its local budget largely from its sales tax base; this represents between 60 and 70% of the general fund expenditures annually. However, the sales tax revenues from retail outlets are not the primary driver of the sales tax base. That distinction belongs to the construction industry, which represents about 70% of the local economy generally. In boom times, people come to work in the mining industry and they need to purchase homes. The sales tax on those purchases help to sustain the budget.

The fact that the construction industry can rise and fall quickly led Mayor Johnson to answer the inquiry about lessons learned by preaching conservatism in spending. He believes that micropolitan cities need to invest in infrastructure in the good times but to ensure that they are still putting something away for bad times. "Downturns occur and we need to be ready for them. There was a time when Elko was overbuilt and the sales taxes were down. We've turned that corner now—and see a big push at present for apartments—but it's important to not be overconfident with the booms, and prepare for those downturns."

Other areas of the local economy help Elko sustain its constituents and its quality of life, including revenues from the state. Nevada is not a state in which the city of origin for revenues is permitted to retain such revenues. Indeed, to the contrary, Mayor Johnson maintains that Las Vegas exports revenues to all the cities of Nevada and that Elko fares very well in that regard. The local economy also benefits from farming and tourism. The future of the economy in Elko appears stable as reports indicate that the mining industry should remain strong well into the future. Indeed, a local operation was recently purchased for multimillions of dollars, a strong indication of that company's level of comfort in the potential yields of Elko's mines.

Mayor Johnson is different from most of the mayors interviewed as part of this research, who have professed no interest in higher elective office. Mayor Johnson has enjoyed his time in office and repeatedly noted what an honor it is to hold the office and "to serve such good people." The mayor, who owns a plumbing and heating construction business, was Nevada-born and moved to Elko at the age of six. He may have a possible interest in public service at a higher level.

When asked for additional lessons that could be instructive to other mayors of other micropolitan cities across the country, Mayor Johnson notes that it is vital to understand the budget in and out and always to prepare for the downturns and never bank on the good times continuing forever. Furthermore, he adds that "There are a lot of good people out there. Many of them, you don't hear from. They are the silent majority, but they're there when you need them. Mayors don't have a lot of direct power but, with good people around them, they can get a lot of things done."

Elmira, New York

Upper New York state has had many economic reversals in the recent past, many of which mirror losses throughout the American rust belt. Population losses in Elmira are, against that background, not too surprising, although they have been quite substantial. In the final decade of the 1990s, Elmira's population declined by nearly 19%, from 38,083 to 30,940. In the next five years, the decline registered an additional 3.3% to 29,928 (US Beacon, 2012). Please see Figure 6.19.

Elmira's unemployment rate at this writing (9.4%) exceeded even a relatively high US average of 9.1%; and its recent job growth was even further into the negative: −1.29% versus −0.12% (http://www.bestplaces.net). Furthermore, Moody's Analytics ranks Elmira as 162nd out of 392 US cities for employment growth, yielding a cost of

Figure 6.19 The Chemung River entering Elmira, New York. (Courtesy of Doug Kerr)

doing business that is 90% of the national average and an overall cost of living that is 82% of the national average (http://www.moodoysanalytics.com).

The economy still retains significant components of manufacturing as well as elements of other business sectors, including food services and hospitality. For example, the demand for electrical equipment assemblers exceeds the national average by more than 15% and machine tool operators by 10%. However, a look at the list of Elmira's largest employers reads as follows: the public school system, a hospital, another public school system, a prison, and another hospital. Most of these are not primary employers and are both responsive to demand and highly dependent upon local tax revenues and very sensitive to fluctuations in the local population. This indicates a strong avenue of discussion for the interview with Elmira's mayor.

Assets that can be used for business attraction include a relatively low cost of housing that has resulted from the loss of population over the years, and low income requirements of the population who possess a relatively low level of education. That can also be a significant deterrent to business attraction as well as to the retention of the existing business community. The mayor should also be asked about the preparedness of the labor force for new employers.

Interview with the Honorable Sue Skidmore, Mayor of Elmira, New York

Mayor Skidmore conducted a very candid interview, not trying to hide the challenges her town is facing. Elmira, New York sits about midway along the New York border with the state of Pennsylvania. An old industrial city, Elmira has now lost most of the manufacturing plants that were the hallmark of its economy before much of the production went overseas and before two floods (the latest in 1972) created such havoc that the city and its people have never quite recovered. An aged community, Elmira is left with relatively high levels of unemployment and poverty.

Although not a native of the city, Mayor Skidmore has lived in Elmira for 20 years, served on the city council for six years, and has been mayor for six months. One key question had to be why she would want to be mayor in such a situation. Like so many of her colleagues included in this research, Mayor Skidmore saw a need: nothing was happening; someone needed to try to do something positive. Many of her constituents had lost hope and spoke loudly of "the good old days," which she translates to mean "before the '72 flood."

Against such a description of despair, what can possibly be done to advance the collective well-being? The list is both extensive and expensive. The downtown has vacancies and vacant lots. Although the mayor is addressing this, the city's finances are struggling. The mayor has managed to get the municipal bond ratings back to an A– rating. The city has no professional planner so there is no strategy for economic development and there are no recent updates to the master plan. The mayor has made arrangements to "share" the relevant employees of the surrounding county's government to help out.

The city sits on a major interstate highway, three hours from Albany, three hours from New York City, and three hours from Canada. Tourism is difficult to sell, however, because Elmira only has one hotel. The mayor is now working to attract the attention of other hospitality companies.

Not only does the laundry list of accomplishments to date sound quite remarkable against the backdrop of the economic situation in Elmira, but the mayor's determination comes through loud and clear. She notes the economic stability provided by several institutions in the community including a maximum security prison, a college, and a community college. On the downside, these are public institutions and add to a tax base problem caused by the city being home to 125 churches. More than 40% of the city's land base is tax exempt!

This leaves the city overly dependent for the revenues from which to provide public services on state aid and formulaic disbursements, which are, of course, always declining. This leaves Mayor Skidmore with one primary lesson: as a person whose background was in business, not politics, she has come to learn that moving the process forward in the public sector requires much more time than in the private sector. She firmly believes that good things will happen, but equally that one must be patient.

Enid, Oklahoma

The city of Enid (please see Figure 6.20) was built around the 1890s site of a railroad station. It later became a hub for the railroad lines that spread throughout the state. Although the state of Oklahoma has built and sustained its statewide economy on oil production, the city of Enid is very highly dependent upon the presence of Vance Air Force Base. Vance, with a primary mission to train more than 400 pilots each year for all the American armed forces, is the city's largest employer and accounts for about $220 million of the local gross regional product. The base also employs more than 2,600 military and civilian personnel who reside in and around Enid. In total, and including the contractors that are located in Enid specifically because of the air force base, there are about an even number of military personnel (1,347) and civilian personnel (1,354) who are thus employed as well as the military dependents.

This has sustained the economy in the city and in the region, however, one significant reduction in base mission or billets could spell disaster for the Enid economic base. This would need to be explored with the mayor in terms of plans and efforts to diversify the economy of the city.

Population fluctuations may be the result of changes either in demand for employment at the air force base or in the oil industry over time. The city's population levels

Figure 6.20 Beautiful buildings of Enid, Oklahoma. (Courtesy of Mike Klemme)

increased in the decade of the 1990s by nearly 4%, from 45,309 to 47,045, but then had declined by 2005 by −1.34% to 46,416 (US Beacon, 2012).

Nonetheless, the unemployment rate stood at only 3.7% whereas the national average exceeded 9%. This may be a reflection of the loss of jobs. Enid is somewhat isolated within its larger region; the city is situated about 90 miles north of Oklahoma City. This means that individuals who lose their jobs have few alternatives and would likely have to leave the area for further employment. Indeed, recent job growth was reported as −0.6% when the national average was at −0.12% (http://www.bestplaces.net).

The economy of the city of Enid, like that of the state of Oklahoma, rose and fell for many years on the basis of the oil sales generated by local extraction companies. From the 1960s through the early part of the 1980s, the oil boom helped the area grow. But the bust in oil prices of the 1980s spelled difficulties for the city. Farmland prices declined and credit weakened for farmers throughout the area as a result.

The city, as the hub of sales and services for a larger region, has since diversified its economy to some extent. Major local employers today include Advance Pierre Food Company, Computer Science Corporation, the public school system, and two medical centers. The need for further diversification of the city's business base would be a matter of discussion with the mayor. In the meantime, concerns continue about the future of the oil industry, the future of Vance Air Force Base, and the potential for economic decline in future Enid, Oklahoma. Recent business relocations and expansions give the city hope for a sustainable, diverse economic base in Enid. New areas of research, including wind farming and research into other alternative energy sources, also give hope to new and diverse business opportunities for Enid.

Interview with Eric Benson, City Manager of Enid, Oklahoma

Enid, Oklahoma has a weak mayor form of government so the city manager is the executive officer and the individual primarily responsible for creating a vision and driving toward it for the city. Eric Benson, a former military brat and military officer, offers that his experience as an officer in the US Navy provided him with the necessary skillsets to lead the city of Enid. "Management is the same: you have issues to solve, resources to use, and a lot of people to direct."

In Oklahoma, cities cannot access property taxes for the provision of public services. They must be used for infrastructure development or the budgets of the local school systems. This means that sales taxes are vital to the growth of Enid's budget. Mr. Benson points with pride to the fact that their sales tax revenues have increased by double digits month over month for the past two years. The reason for this growth is the presence of the oil fields in and around the city. One of every three dollars in Enid's sales tax base is associated with the oil industry.

Enid is geographically isolated, a fact that, when combined with the importance of sales taxes for the city, draws retail development into the economic development target for the city. Although health services is the city's largest employment sector, it is essentially built out, whereas the expansion of the retail base is not only valuable but needed by the residents of Enid and the region.

Another generator of sales tax revenues for the city is tourism, much of which is centered around the presence of Vance Air Force Base. Today, hotels in the region enjoy a 95% occupancy rate, yielding a demand for additional hotel development, which the city is also pursuing.

Budgetary pressures can come from many directions in an isolated micropolitan city. Enid also has an unusual situation with various of the city's faith-based organizations not only serving homeless people but attracting them from out of town to provide them with food and shelter. Although a worthwhile objective in general, it creates tremendous pressures on the local budget for the provision of public services to a group of individuals who do not make any contributions. As the city's homeless population has increased fourfold in the past four years, one can easily imagine the budgetary strains that has caused.

The low rate of unemployment in Enid (less than 3% according to Mr. Benson) means that jobs can be, at times, difficult to fill. But that has not yet been a drag on either business attraction or business retention. Mr. Benson explains: "We are a town that failed to believe in itself for 25 years after the last oil bust." Has that changed? "No; I spend a lot of time pumping up my elected officials to withstand the objections of the public to various decisions."

One such decision drew a lot of fire from citizens who defeated a bond issue to improve the downtown, only to have the city council allocate $25 million for the same purposes. Mr. Benson said that the objections, "began to die down after the steel began to come out of the ground and people could begin to see what they would be getting for the money."

Still, the residents continue to voice some displeasure over the changes being wrought in the city. The complaints are constant and pervasive enough that developers often ask the city manager, "Why am I so positive on your town when your residents are not? Why are they discouraging us from coming here?" Mr. Benson says that one has to do what is best for the city and its people even if they don't agree. Still, he cautions that "In a small town, you have to go to church with these people; you have to see them on the streets." His conclusion then is that city officials have to be prepared to have one-term tenures. Change is hard and is sometimes resented.

Eureka, California

Eureka (please see Figure 6.21) was incorporated as a city in the state of California in 1874. It is a port city located on Humboldt Bay some 270 miles north of San Francisco. As with many isolated micropolitan communities, the population base of Eureka declined between 1990 and 2000 and again between 2000 and 2005. In the first instance the decline from 27,025 to 26,128 represented about 3.3%, and in the latter period the decline to 25,579 represented another 2.1% (US Beacon, 2012).

Much of the recent economic history of the city relates to the natural resources of the area: fishing and lumber. Today, those businesses are joined by others in health care and education, all of which are complemented by the tourism trade. The major employers are indeed in health care and higher education and include the local government, the College of the Redwoods, and St. Joseph's Hospital.

Figure 6.21 Downtown Eureka, California. (Courtesy of City of Eureka)

In the current recession, Eureka has experienced a continued decline in the population base with a continuously rising unemployment rate, which reached 12.8% at a time when the national average was 9.1%. At the same time, the national average for recent job growth remained negative at −0.12%. In Eureka, it was still lower at −1.8% (http://www.bestplaces.net). Despite the declining population base, Eureka has been experiencing significant in-migration, which has clearly been more than offset by departures. Natural population growth is a far smaller factor in the stabilization of the population base for Eureka than is the level of in-migration.

Discussions with cruise lines that could increase tourism to the city are now underway and would be a topic of discussion with the mayor. Additionally, food products preparation, packaging, and distribution, based on the region's agricultural output, seem to buttress the local economy and provide future opportunities for growth. Manufacturers of boating and water-related sporting equipment also provide possible growth opportunities for Eureka. And many of the skills required imply progressively higher-paying jobs. One such example is the computer-aided design work being done by boat manufacturers. This also means opportunities for training and retraining in those skills areas at nearby Humbolt State University and the College of the Redwoods. The mayor should be asked to shine a light on plans to enhance the growth of these industry segments by creating the assets the various clusters will need to be as successful as possible in Eureka.

Interview with the Honorable Frank Jager, Mayor of Eureka, California

Eureka, California is situated 300 miles north of San Francisco, adjacent to Humbolt Bay, the largest port between San Francisco and Portland, Oregon. Although a micropolitan city, it is the largest community for significant distances in every direction: 150 miles to the east is Redding and even further southward is Santa Rosa.

The city's budget growth is controlled by external forces, according to Mayor Jager. The state's Proposition 13 limits the allowable amount of increases in property taxes, leaving the sales tax base as the primary generator of revenues to support city services. This means that, in recessionary times, revenues can decline dramatically. Compounded by declining prices affecting the local timber and fishing industries, the city has struggled in recent years and currently has a double-digit unemployment rate. Environmental considerations about people overfishing certain types of fish as well as environmental degradation forced the state-imposed restrictions nearly a decade ago.

A complicating factor for Eureka's future economic development relates to access. Rail service has declined over the years and the area is served by only one airline. Everything needs to be trucked in and out of the city. These impacts are also felt in the tourism area, resulting in still lower sales tax revenues. Furthermore, although the deepwater port is a potential asset for the city, it remains underutilized because cargo can only be brought in by truck and the rail access is minimal. Some recent hope has come in the form of increased demand for timber production from Asia, although concern is expressed about the impacts of various environmental restrictions on the logging industry. Finally, an extremely powerful California Coastal Commission has imposed very restrictive policies regarding development along the coast.

The mayor's lesson learned from this set of confining circumstances is that the primary asset, Humbolt Bay, should have been improved more significantly during the good economic times. That would have helped sustain operations and even growth during the recent recession. Tourism remains a primary economic driver for this coastal community. The city is safe and enjoys a high quality of life. Humbolt State University is an economic driver as well as a source of new residents, those who come to study and then remain in the area. This, according to Mayor Jager, makes the situation difficult but the outlook optimistic.

Farmers Branch, Texas

Farmers Branch, Texas (please see Figure 6.22) has seen some fluctuations in its residential base, at first increasing by more than 13% between 1990 and 2000, from 24,250 to 27,508. However, that trend was reversed between 2001 and 2005, as the population totals declined by nearly 4% back to 26,487. Then, by 2010, it had grown again to 28,616 (US Beacon, 2012). Yet the level of unemployment at the time of this writing was 7.6%, significantly below the national average of 9.1%. This explains the recent job growth figure of +1.27% whereas that of the nation was still in the negative at −0.12% (http://www.bestplaces.net). The causes of the return to a growing economy and a growing community would be the focus for the discussion with Farmers Branch's mayor.

Figure 6.22 Redevelopment in Farmers Branch, Texas. (Courtesy of Derrick Birdsall, Amy Cooper, and Tom Bryson, City of Farmers Branch)

As a suburb of the city of Dallas, Farmers Branch is home to a diverse and relatively large employment base. Major employers in the city in 2009 included IBM with 4,200 employees, JP Morgan Chase Investment Services with nearly 2,400 employees, the Federal Internal Revenue Service with 1,200 jobs, Televista with 1,500 workers, and GEICO with nearly 1,200 more. An important policy matter to discuss with the mayor would be any lingering effects of the city council's 2007 decision (the first in the nation) to prohibit landlords from renting to most illegal immigrants. This is the kind of policy that can leave a bad taste in the mouths of prospective employers for a long time.

Interview with the Honorable Bill Glancy, Mayor of Farmers Branch, Texas

Farmers Branch is a "first-ring" city in suburban Dallas, Texas. One of its challenges is to provide services not just for a full-time population of less than 30,000 residents, but also to the 65,000 to 75,000 individuals who come to their jobs in the city every workday. Serving as a suburban job center is a positive for the city, which derives about one-third of its budget resources from *ad valorem* taxes. The other two-thirds are derived relatively evenly from sales taxes and a variety of fees.

As the city emerged from being a blue-collar job center to a professional marketplace playing off its proximity to Dallas, the leadership realized that the infrastructure needed to be upgraded. They regarded those costs as investments because it was clear that residential growth resulted in a negative for the city's budget, and businesses took back far less in public services than they contributed in the way of taxes.

An interesting aspect of micropolitan city mayors is that they tend not to be professional politicians, but businessmen and women who understand the value of promoting their cities as being business-friendly and responsive to its "customers." Mayor Glancy is a clear example of these concepts. One lesson he offered was that the city cannot "keep changing its positions. Make a decision and stick to it. Businesses want to see consistency and reliability."

Another lesson offered to other micropolitan cities by Mayor Glancy was that "We are living in fast-changing times. Cities that aren't always thinking about what is coming next will go backward. And there is no standing still. You're either moving forward or backward." Farmers Branch is moving forward and wants to do so by being a community for everyone. The mayor's vision is of a city in which young people can buy their first home and stay in it until they are ready to move up to a still bigger home in Farmers Branch.

Findlay, Ohio

The population of Findlay, Ohio (please see Figure 6.23) has grown steadily through the recession, increasing from the 1990 level of 35,703 to 38,967 in 2000, and

Figure 6.23 Finding the way in downtown Findlay, Ohio. (Image courtesy of Elizabeth Weddington)

41,202 in the census reports of 2010. This represents an increase of more than 15% over that 20-year period (US Beacon, 2012). An unemployment rate of 6.5% at the time of this writing (http://www.bestplaces.net) is somewhat unusual for this part of the United States and for Ohio in general. An interesting topic for the mayor would be to understand why Findlay is not suffering more with the rest of the state and the region. An aside to this conversation would need to address what constitutes acceptable jobs for those in Findlay. There is press coverage expressing concerns about the pay rates of the jobs being created (Wilin, 2011). This was also referenced in recent news coverage of the opening of a Hamlet plant that will produce soy-based proteins for animal feeds. The gist of the stories relates to the $22-an-hour wages and the associated benefits (Findlay Hancock Economic Development Org., 2012).

Interview with the Honorable Lydia Mihalik, Mayor of Findlay, Ohio

Lydia Mihalik is the mayor of a micropolitan city but she is unlike most of the mayors in this study. First, she is relatively young, only 32, and she is not a native of the city she leads. She came to Findlay from Indiana to attend the local university. And, although she has no immediate higher political ambitions, her intention, unlike most of the others interviewed, is not to serve a term or two as mayor and move on. Mayor Mihalik likes the job and looks forward to a long run as mayor of Findlay. Still in her first year as mayor, Ms. Mihalik was a professional in the area of community and economic development for 10 years and possesses a better knowledge of the issues than most mayors in their initial terms.

Findlay, too, has had a different experience than that of the other micropolitan communities studied during the current recession. Things are not too bad in Findlay; the mood is "pretty positive" and the city has seen an influx of investments in recent years, including two foreign owned businesses—one German and one Danish—that work in the areas of automotive parts and livestock feed production, respectively. This diversifies the economies in two ways: diverse industries and diverse origins. The latter helps smooth out the peaks and valleys of purely national or regional economic forces. Together, these two companies alone represent about 250 new jobs in Findlay.

Recent economic development activity in Findlay has included everything from strong growth of small businesses to the establishment of the Marathon Petroleum Corporation's Downstream Marketing Division. Because the latter has located its operations right on Main Street in the downtown, attention to Main Street and downtown beautification programs is less urgent; it is taking place organically.

And, that isn't even the biggest name in town. That distinction goes to Cooper Tire and Rubber, which is also located in Findlay, and although not on the *Fortune 500* list, it does rank at number 707 and is located within the Findlay city limits. The city has also seen a recent "uptick" in other automotive manufacturing operations, notably the creation of 300 new jobs at the Mission Brake Corporation. And all of Whirlpool's dishwashers are manufactured in Findlay, Ohio. Additional land for development still exists within Findlay's city limits.

Other regional activity includes a new Honda Acura plant in the community of Marysville, just south of Findlay. This raised the issue of how the city of Findlay derives the general fund revenues from which the city provides public services. With all of the development discussed, a real estate tax base would be productive; however, that source represents only about 10% of all general fund revenues. Findlay builds its budget primarily on the basis of a 1.25% income tax. From this, one might assume that the target for economic development programs would be higher-paying jobs; however, Mayor Mihalik notes that the jobs being attracted need to be compatible with the workforce available. The city is working with the state of Ohio on a variety of workforce programs to prepare residents for the newer and coming technologies. This includes a model program borrowed from a community in Indiana that begins such training in the fourth grade and works up.

There are several lessons from Findlay that may be instructive to other communities and other mayors. First, the development of the economy cannot be seen as being solely a public responsibility. The relationship between the public sector and its private sector partners must be strong and must be constantly nurtured. One cannot presume that it will continue over time. Second, Findlay has been attentive to the maintenance and development of its infrastructure in good times. As a result, it has sites and facilities to show companies that may consider Findlay as a future location.

Curiously, one lesson offered by Mayor Mihalik is that the continued diversification of the economy must be enhanced. Despite the presence of the diverse array of business sectors cited, the loss of one of these primary employers would leave a lot of residents out of work and would have effects on other businesses and support services throughout the community and the region. Perhaps that constant attention to economic diversification in the future is an indicator of why it remains relatively strong today.

Frankfurt, Kentucky

Frankfurt, Kentucky has experienced very difficult economic times in recent years. Part of this can be attributed to its existence in the state of Kentucky, which has consistently been in the bottom levels of most rankings reflecting education levels, job creation, and income levels. It has not, however, halted recent population growth in the city of Frankfurt.

Between 1990 and 2000, the city's population increased by nearly 7%, from 25,968 to 27,741; and over the next five years it declined, but only by less than 2% to 27,210 (US Beacon, 2012). Frankfurt's recent job growth has registered net growth at 1.3% against national averages in the negative at −0.12%; and the current level of unemployment is reported at 8.9%, slightly lower than the national average of 9.1% (http://www.bestplaces.net).

After many years of what could be termed an over-reliance on manufacturing as the core of the economic base in Frankfurt, a discussion with the mayor about targeted industries should prove very interesting. What types of jobs are being sought? Are the appropriate assets present for those jobs in Frankfurt, and is the labor force prepared for them? And how do, and how can, local institutions of higher education support those objectives?

Frankfurt, Kentucky: Interview Declined

Fremont, Nebraska

The micropolitan city of Fremont, Nebraska (please see Figure 6.24) has a fairly diverse economy that has held the city and the region relatively unharmed during the current recession. At the time of this writing, the national unemployment rate tops 9% whereas it is at 4.7% in Fremont. Recent job growth is positive at nearly .50% whereas the US average is negative at −0.12% (http://www.bestplaces.net). Population in the city has increased over the past generation, rising between 1990 and 2000 by 6.3% from 23,680 to 25,174, then again by .56% between 2000 and 2005, to 25,314 (US Beacon, 2012).

The economic base includes strengths in agriculture, metal processing, and electronics manufacturing. Fremont serves as a regional employment hub attracting many workers from Elkhorn and even Omaha and Lincoln. This raises a question for the mayor concerning how the city's budget is constituted; for example, what is

Figure 6.24   Fremont, Nebraska from the sky. (Courtesy of Rader's Photography)

the relative importance of income taxes? Furthermore, as there is an effort to attract tourists to the city's opera house, museum, and other attractions, the mayor may wish to comment on the relative importance of transient occupancy taxes to the city's budget.

In an effort to diversify the city's economic base, Christensen Business Park has been developed and has begun to be occupied. By adopting a "build it and they will come" approach, Fremont has been able to attract to the park Southwark Metal Manufacturing Company, Charleston Inc., and Natural Pet Products over the past decade.

Midland University is also located in the city but there is no evidence either on the college's website or in the local press about how the institution might contribute to the economic growth of Fremont. This would also be a discussion topic for the interview with the mayor.

Interview with the Honorable Scott Getzschman, Mayor of Fremont, Nebraska

The mayor of Fremont, Nebraska is a business owner (Getzschman Heating) who is currently serving his first year as mayor after six years on the city council. Fremont is just far enough from two major cities, Omaha and Lincoln, that it serves as a regional hub for some services, such as health services. But, it is close enough that the mayor can promote his micropolitan city as a nice quiet community with safe neighborhoods and a progressive school system that is less than an hour from the amenities of two larger cities.

The economy continues to grow in the area although the population growth remains slow. The city is surrounded for miles in any direction by agriculture: the farming of corn and soy, and the raising of cattle. These businesses are complemented by cluster support businesses such as feed producers, heavy equipment dealers, a high-end dog food manufacturer (Matura), a Hormel (pork) plant, and a sheet metal plant. All of this gives the base economy stability over time and is enabled by the two major highways that intersect in Fremont.

The city's budget is based on several primary sources, including real estate taxes, sales taxes, and a hotel and lodging tax. About 50% of the latter is used to promote the area's tourism attractions, including hunting, fishing, boating, and a major festival.

When asked about the economic lessons learned by Fremont that might be useful to other, similarly located micropolitan cities, Mayor Getzschman's advice is to maintain an open government, be more progressive rather than reactive, and to focus on the positive attributes of each individual in the community.

Galesburg, Illinois

Galesburg's (please see Figure 6.25) economy is, in one sense, a reflection of the national economy. They have similar levels of unemployment at present: 8.9% in Galesburg, and 9.1% nationally. And both have experienced negative recent job growth at −0.17% in Galesburg and −0.12% for the nation (http://www.bestplaces.net). The city's population has fluctuated: increasing by .50% between 1990 and 2000 (from 33,530 to 33,706), and then declining by 5% between 2000 and 2005, to 32,017 (US Beacon, 2012).

Figure 6.25   A downtown street in Galesburg, Illinois. (Courtesy of City of Galesburg)

To help attract jobs to the city, an incubator facility has been developed totaling 120,000 square feet. It would be an avenue of interest to pursue with the mayor: Was this a "build it and they will come" strategy, and how has that worked out? Tourism also appears to be a potential growth industry for Galesburg, which was the site of a Lincoln–Douglas presidential debate as well as one of the stops on the underground railroad. Its geographic position relatively proximate to Indianapolis, St. Louis, Des Moines, and Milwaukee also gives credence to a tourism attraction strategy in the city's economic development plan.

Galesburg has a poverty issue to deal with, also a good topic for discussion with the mayor. Although the per capita income in the United States was $26,505, and $27,027 throughout Illinois, it was only $20,657 in Galesburg. Similarly, the poverty rate in the city at that time was 14.7%, much higher than the statewide average of 8.5% or the national average of 12.3% (AreaVibes, 2011). What jobs do exist in Galesburg are low-paying. What is being done to attract higher-paying jobs to Galesburg? The downtown needs to be made more attractive in order to bring businesses and residents back to the city. What cleanup programs are in operation and how effective are they? Has there been a brain drain from Galesburg? What can be done to reverse that trend?

Interview with the Honorable Sal Garza, Mayor of Galesburg, Illinois

Mayor Garza came to his position with a background in the State of Illinois Department of Commerce, in which he had worked on projects related to economic development and regionalism. This clearly shaped his thinking as he took the reins of leadership for the city three years prior to this interview. Still, although he acknowledges that Galesburg has some serious issues to resolve, he senses a shift from hopelessness to a more positive outlook among the citizenry. "Galesburg," he says, "was in recession long before the rest of the nation."

As was the case in many micropolitan cities in this part of the United States, manufacturers had departed for cheaper climes: Mayor Garza estimated that 4,000 or 5,000 jobs were lost in the manufacturing sector and the relevant secondary jobs (i.e., those that were supported by the existence of the jobs in the primary sector, such as retail).

This was a wake-up call for the people of Galesburg who passed through a series of stages not unlike those people experience upon the loss of a loved one, including disbelief, anger, and a loss of hope for the future. When asked how the city moved away from this sense of hopelessness to what the mayor characterized as "hope and a sense of competitiveness," he stated that there had been no specific precipitating event. It was a slow and arduous movement during which the city leadership had first to create hope and then manage the resulting expectations.

In part, this was the result of initial efforts to cooperate regionally for economic development rather than "going it alone" and competing intraregionally. This necessity is in part geographical in nature: Galesburg sits about 45 minutes from the Quad Cities and from Peoria. The region was fortunate that two primary employers, Caterpillar and John Deere, did not leave the area. But others did, and both the unemployment and the poverty levels climbed. As they did, the region was more inclined to pull together for economic development purposes. To some extent, it was a forced collaboration, but one that made sense.

Of course, the initial focus had to be to stop the "hemorrhaging of jobs." The second effort was to try to make investments that would be attractive to employers even though the return on those investments might be years away. The city thus invested about $20 million in a water treatment facility that will make the region an attractive location to those businesses presently located in regions of the country where there is or may be in the future an inadequate water supply. Mayor Garza noted that down economies are good times to conduct planning for economic growth as well.

Two local colleges, Knox College and Carl Sandburg Community College, help to further economic growth in Galesburg as does a local penitentiary that is not only a generator of jobs and contracting for goods and services, but also a "good and quiet neighbor." The colleges are producing graduates in the relatively few areas that are still in demand throughout the region, such as nursing and other health care professions. They have also been partners in the recent establishment of a "green tech" incubator. With all of these assets and the newly found sense of hope, Mayor Garza states, "We can actually come out of this stronger than before." As with other mayors of micropolitan cities that are trying to recover from economic decline, Mayor Garza has defined what appears to be a brand of municipal leadership that is different for these situations than for other municipal functions and issues. It appears to need to be more daring and more encouraging.

In terms of lessons learned in Galesburg, Mayor Garza suggests early planning of strategies that revolve around layoff aversion. In other words, what can the city do to help keep companies from leaving or downsizing? Another note of caution is that, when approaching companies, do so from a business perspective: don't address that which is in the best interest of the community but what is in the best interest of the businesses. How will these actions contribute to the bottom line of the company and how can we help enhance those impacts? At a minimum, if someone is considering leaving Galesburg, "We want to be part of the discussion."

Gallup, New Mexico

Despite the relatively diverse nature of the economic base in and around Gallup, the city's population has fluctuated in recent decades. Between 1990 and 2000, the level rose from 19,154 to 20,209, or by 5.5%; however, over the next five years, it declined by more than 4% to 19,378 (US Beacon, 2012). Although there is the kind of diversity (government employment, mining, and refining industries to name a few) that might lead one to expect greater stability in the employment base, the unemployment rate at the time of this writing (8.7%) rivals the US average of 9.1%. And, recent job growth is further into the negative in Gallup than it is across the rest of the country (−0.38% to −0.12%; http://www.bestplaces.net).

A look at the primary types of industry in the region may help to explain the reason for the fluctuations. Mining is a traditional source of employment in the region and although it is complemented by native American crafts (75% of the population of Gallup is native American), personal services, retail, and tourism, it is extremely susceptible to price variations.

As unemployment levels climb, retail, tourism, and personal services all suffer. One question for the mayor would be whether the local tax base is overly dependent upon the sales taxes from those types of businesses and how that has affected the city's ability to provide public services. One of the consequences of these trends is that Gallup historically has one of the lowest per capita income levels in the state of New Mexico.

Gallup, New Mexico: Interview Declined

Gillette, Wyoming

At least one ranking (http://www.policom.com) has placed the Gillette (please see Figure 6.26) economy in the top ten (eighth) among 574 micropolitan communities in the United States. The city's population has increased steadily over the recent past, climbing between 1990 and 2000 by 11.4% (from 17,635 to 19,646) and again by 15.5% between 2000 and 2005, when it reached a high of 22,685 (US Beacon, 2012). At the same time, the unemployment rate remained fairly stable and is, at the time of this writing, far below the 9.1% national average, sitting comfortably at 5.0%. However, recent job growth at −2.42% has been further into the negative than the national average of −0.12% (http://www.bestplaces.net).

When one looks behind the population numbers, one finds that the growth is related to changes in the city's boundaries, which have increased between 2000 and 2010 by 43% through 50 separate annexations.

In order to encourage growth, Gillette developed its infrastructure, including building a new library, three new schools, a recreation center, a fire department, and a hospital, as well as facilities to provide additional water and power capacity, all at the cost of about $3.2 billion. The result: more than 50 new commercial buildings were constructed between 2000 and 2009 and more than 620 permits were issued in the same period for alterations and upgrades to existing commercial structures (Surface and Allen, 2010). This has yielded an increasingly diverse economic base in Gillette. The largest employers are an energy company, the public schools, another energy company, a hospital, and a coal extraction concern.

Figure 6.26   A parade for the community in Gillette, Wyoming. (Courtesy of City of Gillette)

One missing asset for growth is sufficient housing to accommodate the employers already in the city, plus the demand that would be created by newly arriving companies. The mayor would need to explain what is being done to address this shortage and the implications for economic development.

Interview with the Honorable Tom Murphy, Mayor of Gillette, Wyoming

A fourth-generation resident of Gillette, Mayor Murphy has served eight years on the city council, the past two as mayor. His forebears were homesteaders who immigrated to Wyoming because the federal government was offering 160 acres of farmland to those who would help populate the territory. Unlike most of his peers in the other cities in this study, Mayor Murphy "may" indeed have an interest in further office because, as he stated it, "I like building coalitions and getting things done."

Today, Mayor Murphy is "cautiously optimistic" about the economic future of his city. Fifty percent of the country's electric power is generated by burning coal, and about half of that comes from his community and the region. Every day, about 200 miles of train cars (if they were placed end to end) take coal out of this region in Wyoming. But the mayor believes that not everyone knows all of the facts about coal mining; too many people envision the mountain top removals of other states. Mayor Murphy maintains that the mining and its aftermath can be managed responsibly. Furthermore, he believes that Gillette is the model for that type of responsible extraction. "You can't even tell where the coal areas are."

Regardless, the city's economy is very dependent upon its mining and minerals treatment businesses. Fortunately, there is forecast at least 200 years of coal to be mined in the area, in addition to natural gas, methane gas, oil, and uranium. The diversification of Gillette's economy does not, however, stop with the variations in the minerals industry. Wind farming is being developed in the region as well as a thriving tourism industry built around national parks and mountain ranges. Further diversification in the future may involve the value-added manufacturing processes that would take place after the extraction and before it is transported from Gillette.

The city builds its budget, in large part, on the basis of sales tax; the state rate is 4% and the city gets back one-third of that total.

In terms of missing parts of the economic future of Gillette, Mayor Murphy bemoans the absence of a real US energy policy that would include an emphasis on the mining of coal. More and more coal is in demand in the developing world, including two particular great areas of demand: China and India. Still, the lesson that Mayor Murphy offers to other mayors of micropolitan-sized cities is to develop the area's natural strengths.

Grand Junction, Colorado

Moody's Analytics cites the strengths of Grand Junction, Colorado for job growth as a relatively low cost of doing business and the abundance of natural resources, including oil, coal, natural gas, and uranium. On the negative side, the city has insufficient diversity in its economic base and relatively low levels of education among the population.

When compared to national averages, Grand Junction ranked near the bottom in terms of employment growth between 2009 and 2011, placing 323rd of 362. And, despite the lack of great economic opportunity in the city, the cost of living remains at 94% of the US average and the cost of doing business at 85% of the national average (http://www.bestplaces.net). With that background, one has to wonder why there has been such dramatic growth in the population base: from 29,034 in 1990 to 41,986 in 2000 (+44.6%), and to 45,299 by 2005 (+7.9%; US Beacon, 2012).

Economic output over that period of 15 years has risen and declined due to changes in the costs of natural resources, primarily natural gas, leaving the host county to Grand Junction—Mesa County—one of the most economically depressed counties in the United States. At the time of this writing, the unemployment rate in Grand Junction far exceeded the national rate of 9.1%, standing at 11.2%. And, the recent job growth was further into the negative at −2.32% than the national figure of −0.12% (http://www.bestplaces.net).

There are a few significant employers in the city, including St. Mary's Hospital (with 2,235 employees), Halliburton Energy (977 employees in 2008), Walmart (860), and the City Market (650). Still, in that timeframe, the mining of natural resources accounted for more than 12.6% of the local economic output ($657 million; US Department of Housing and Urban Development Comprehensive Housing Market Analysis, 2005).

As is the case with many of the other micropolitan cities examined in this research, Grand Junction serves as the hub for activities within a fairly wide region that includes not only western Colorado but some of eastern Utah as well. This explains the presence of the relatively large employers in retail, which accounts for about 14% of the jobs in the city, and health care, which accounts for another 12%. Against such a background, it is not surprising that the media consistently cite Grand Junction as "the only city in Colorado still in recession" (Kennedy, 2010).

Grand Junction, Colorado: Interview Declined

Greenwood, South Carolina

Greenwood, South Carolina registered a population base of 23,222 in the 2010 census (US Beacon, 2012) and a double-digit unemployment rate (10.3%) at the time of this writing (http://www.bestplaces.net). Although it will not produce a great number of jobs, the city will benefit in tax revenues from the development of a $6.5 million genetic research center that Clemson University announced in April of 2012 it will add to their existing Greenwood Research Center (Greenwood Partnership Alliance, 2008). Discussion with the mayor could indicate the economic impacts of that investment as well as the means by which the city and the region will seek to enhance a related cluster of businesses, organizations, and jobs.

A detailed strategic plan for economic development was produced in late 2008 (Greenwood Partnership Alliance, 2008). The mayor should be able to elaborate as to how much of this prerecession plan has been implemented and the extent to which those plans were interrupted by the larger economic downturn. Despite the downturn, surveys performed as part of the planning exercise indicated that residents would not leave Greenwood for better employment opportunities. Thus, the SWOT Analysis (strengths, weaknesses, opportunities, and threats) properly identify the city's quality of life as a strength. Other strengths included highway and rail access, an available though not necessarily well-prepared workforce, an "exceptional health care system," solid infrastructure, and low tax rates.

Community weaknesses cited in the 2008 strategic plan include lack of easily accessible air service, the skills and education levels of the workforce, amenities for younger people, affordable housing, public transportation, and investments for the growth of biotech companies. Plans were developed at the time around the development of a business park and various public facilities as well as the improved preparation of the local workforce. Other areas of concern expressed related to the image of Greenwood as a good place to do business and the need for additional (city) budgetary resources. Yet, in the face of the need for greater tax base generation, the Greenwood Partnership Alliance lists several pages of incentives for businesses including grants and tax abatements in exchange for positive relocation or expansion decisions. These would all be fertile topical areas for an interview with the mayor.

The surrounding county to Greenwood is also called Greenwood. Its poverty level more than doubled (to nearly one in four residents) between 2007 and 2010. This was the largest percentage increase during that period for any county in the United States (Tavernise, 2011).

Greenwood, South Carolina: Interview Declined

Hannibal, Missouri

Hannibal's population has remained remarkably constant over the past 20 years, declining from the 1990 level of 18,004 to 17,916 in the 2010 census (US Beacon, 2012) and has a relatively low unemployment level (6.1% versus the current national average of 8.6%; http://www.bestplaces.net). However, the recent news has not been very positive. General Mills cut more than 850 jobs in May, 2012 although the impacts on the plant located in Hannibal were not clear in the press coverage. This is a question for the interview with the mayor.

Of course, as the boyhood home of Mark Twain (Samuel Clemens) and the site of many of his tales, Hannibal does enjoy a fairly steady and strong tourism trade. Tourism spending represents one of the largest sources of revenues for the area, behind health care, manufacturing, and farming. Health care and manufacturing alone accounted in 2009 for 34.4% of all jobs in the city (Northeast Missouri Hotspot–Hannibal, n.d.). This implies a need for greater diversification in the Hannibal economy.

Hannibal, Missouri: Interview Declined

Hays, Kansas

The population base of Hays, Kansas declined precipitously between 1990 and 2000 (from 26,131 to 20,013) but has held steady since and registered a total of 20,510 in the 2010 census (US Beacon, 2012). The causes for the reversal of the trend after 2000 should be discussed with the mayor. The current level of unemployment of 3.1% compares extremely favorably with the US average of 8.6% (http://www.bestplaces.net). Hays is located about midway between Denver and Kansas City. In the surrounding Ellis County, the largest employers include Hays Medical Center and other health services, Fort Hays State University (with an enrollment of about 12,000 students), various public sector agencies, a call center, and several small manufacturers. Ellis County is also home to nearly 750 farms, giving the area some economic diversity in its base.

Hays, Kansas: Interview Declined

Helena, Montana

There is an interesting shift in the population reporting for Helena, Montana that bears discussion with the mayor. In the 1990 US decennial census, the city is shown as having more than 40,000 residents; however, by 2005, reports set the level at just over 27,000 (US Beacon, 2012). Whether this is the result of out-migration stimulated by some economic or natural event, or whether certain parts of the city were ceded away is a topic that bears explanation. The city has made a bit of a comeback in this regard in recent years, growing to 28,190 by 2010, as reported in the census of that year.

Nonetheless, the economy appears very stable with an unemployment rate at the time of this writing of 5.2%, far less than the national average, which exceeds 9% (http://www.bestplaces.net). Part of this is due to the fact that Helena is home to many public employees. It not only hosts 7,000 state employees as the capital of Montana, but it also serves as the county seat of Lewis and Clark County. This helps to prevent dramatic shifts as the macroeconomy fluctuates.

Helena, Montana: Interview Declined

Hobbs, New Mexico

The population of Hobbs, New Mexico (please see Figure 6.27) held fairly constant between 1990 and 2005, declining only slightly from 29,115 to 29,006. However, over the next five-year period, the population grew to 34,122, representing nearly a 17% growth in just five years. The causes of this would be an important topic for discussion with the mayor. Equally important would be how the city has accommodated such rapid growth and whether the tax base and infrastructural impacts have been, and are expected to be, positive or negative.

As currently being reported, the 4.0% unemployment rate is less than half of the US average (8.6%; http://www.bestplaces.net). Prerecession plans available online indicated a need to develop additional housing to support business and community growth. Another area identified for change at that time related to the need to diversify the local economy away from an overdependence on oil and natural gas extraction. A third area that was cited related to the need to improve and revitalize the downtown sections of Hobbs. Whether these have been addressed and the extent to which successes have been realized are fodder for the interview with Hobbs' mayor.

Diversification of the city's economy was bolstered by the 2008 construction of a medium-security prison. Reports attribute a $125 million infusion to the economy to the facility as well as 800 jobs for the initial construction as well as another 1,200 that were supported thereby in the secondary and tertiary economies. The 800 prison workers account for an annual payroll of about $16 million, yielding a demand for more than 300 homes and generating a property tax base addition of more than $260,000 annually (Chiri, 1996).

The construction of a "ghost town" in Hobbs, where testing and research can be commissioned with all the structures of a city but none of the residents, will also reportedly add revenues to the community. The estimated cost for the development of the test city is about $1 million (Crum, 2012). New hotel and highway

Figure 6.27 Welcoming sights in Hobbs, New Mexico. (Courtesy of EDC of Lea County)

construction has reportedly already begun to house those who will contract to conduct research in the ghost town.

In the city's actual downtown, Hobbs faces a challenge born of widely varying income levels. One study tallies the downtown population as being less than 2% of the city's total but heavily Hispanic and not as well educated or skilled and less affluent. The question of haves and have-nots in Hobbs would be a point of discussion with Mayor Cobb.

Interview with the Honorable Sam Cobb, Mayor of Hobbs, New Mexico

Mayor Cobb noted the peaks and valleys associated with oil and gas extraction of previous decades: "The eighties were really tough." New technologies, however, have enabled the reopening of wells and fields long dormant, thus permitting an economic resurgence in Hobbs and the surrounding counties. Hobbs had to reinvent itself and diversify the economic base or it would continue to suffer whenever the extractions were less productive or world prices dropped. Solar and biofuel production were initiated and a uranium enrichment facility was opened.

Subsequent growth faced the challenge of where to house the workers who a rapid increase in employment demand brought to town. With a current unemployment rate in the mid-2% range, the challenge has not yet been conquered but is being addressed. To complement the diversification process, Hobbs was pleased to become the site selected for the establishment of a modern "ghost town." This is a typical town in terms of structures and infrastructure; all that is missing are the people.

The objective of the ghost town is to permit the testing of products and materials that can later be used in real cities across America. The construction phase alone will provide a substantial capital injection into Hobbs. In the operations phase, more than 350 jobs will be created, plus the capital injections created by the companies and researchers testing projects under contract with the "town."

The ghost town will not generate significant tax revenues for the community, which derives three-fourths of its general fund from the extraction businesses; the remainder comes from homeowners. State law requires cities in New Mexico to retain a minimum of 8% of its tax revenues per year for reserves. In Hobbs, that number is well over 30%. This enables the mayor and council to operate construction on a pay-as-you-go basis.

Further diversification of the local economy is derived from the geographic position of the city. The mayor estimated that Hobbs' retail trade area includes between 135,000 and 140,000 people. The city benefits from a local 6.875% sales tax. Despite press reports, Mayor Cobb maintains that the downtown is very attractive. This is due, in part, to a partnership with the local Maddox Foundation, the result of which has been several extensive beautification projects in the shopping district.

Mayor Cobb is a businessman (third-generation sole manufacturer of Oscar Mayer products with 200 employees). He approaches city issues in this way and speaks broadly of returns on investments and pay as you go. His challenge is workforce housing and he has approached the need as a businessman, providing incentives for developers. His only regret is that the process was not engaged three years earlier to accommodate today's growth.

Holyoke, Massachusetts

As have many of New England's cities (of all sizes), the economic base of Holyoke (please see Figure 6.28) has fluctuated in the past 20 years. Population counts for 1990 and 2000 show nearly a 9% loss from 43,704 to 38,838. The rebound through 2005 to 39,958 is encouraging, although marginal at about three-tenths of one percent (US Beacon, 2012). Recent job growth has been reported at a positive

Figure 6.28 Holyoke, Massachusetts at night. (Courtesy of Rob Deza. www .Robdezaphoto.com)

four-tenths of one percent, fractionally higher than the US average of –0.12%, but the rate of unemployment at the time of this writing stood at 11.3%, somewhat higher than the national level of 9.1% (http://www.bestplaces.net).

The city has demonstrated an interest in using technology to provide public services while reducing those costs and has partnered with Cisco to do so. This would clearly be a necessary avenue of inquiry in the interview with the mayor. Another area to discuss would be the extent to which Holyoke's relatively low levels of educational attainment make economic development a difficult task. Thirty percent of adults are reported to have less than a high school education and another 30% to have just a high school diploma. Another 16% have some college, leaving only one in four adults in the workforce who possess college degrees. Holyoke continues to be one of the state's poorest cities. One in five public school students is either homeless, residing in a shelter, or is in foster care or some other form of transitional living (Badkhen, 2008).

Interview with the Honorable Alex Morse, Mayor of Holyoke, Massachusetts

Alex Morse began his run for the position of mayor of Holyoke, Massachusetts while still a student at Brown University and unseated the incumbent mayor as well as besting two other candidates. All three were over 60 years of age and Morse assembled a coalition of voters who wanted change and some youthful enthusiasm in the office. He took the oath of office at the age of 22 and began to work on the emphases of his campaign: the arts, technology, and innovation.

Holyoke was, at the time of his election, characterized by the new mayor (still in his first year in office at the time of this interview) as having "high unemployment and a dead downtown." One of his early actions was to create a new position in the city for a creative economy industry officer whose role it is to help bring people back to town and to revitalize the downtown area. The mayor firmly believes that by bringing the arts to the downtown area, the people will follow and that there will be built up a demand for new restaurants and other retail opportunities. Toward that end, the city has built trails along the canal that have begun to spur interest in restaurants and other forms of growth.

The city has also created a tax incentive to induce the construction of arts spaces and has now made its first award under that program. These spaces include live–work areas as well as performance spaces. This is quite a change in tone for a city that was America's very first planned industrial city and remains the home of several paper mills.

The focus on technology and innovation led to a consortium of five Boston-based universities (Harvard, MIT, Boston University, Northeastern University, and Boston College) to use a single data center, located in Holyoke, about one hour away. The driver for the universities was that the energy costs are remarkably lower in Holyoke, which generates 100% of the electric power used by the facility from hydroelectric generators in the city's canal. For the city, another result was a signifi-cant boost in the business community's awareness of Holyoke and an enhancement of its overall image.

As for lessons the mayor has learned and that may be instructive to other micro-politan mayors, it may yet be "early days." Nonetheless, Mayor Morse does offer that "Cities need to market themselves. Let people know that the future will be different and that's OK. To get there, we need to stick to the three Rs: retain our businesses, recruit new businesses, and reform the processes of the city."

Hutchinson, Kansas

The economic base of Hutchinson, Kansas has grown increasingly diverse in recent years while still relying to a large extent on its traditional strength in dairy produc-tion and agriculture. To this, the city has added strengths in visitor services and tourism as well as health care professions. In 2009, Siemens Energy began work on wind projects in the area and now employs more than 400 people and contributes more than $35 million annually to the local economy.

Some of the growth has been encouraged by the use of incentive programs that sacrifice as much as 100% of the taxes if 10 or more jobs are created and more than one-quarter of one million dollars is invested. An area of inquiry with the mayor will be whether the expected return on investment has been measured and is positive.

The city's population has grown as a result, jumping by 3.76% from 1990 to 2000 (39,308 to 40,787), and again by 0.43% to 40,961 in 2005 (US Beacon, 2012). And the unemployment rate, although high at 7.7%, is lower than the US average of 9.1%. However, recent job growth has been further in the negative (–0.7%) than the national average of –0.12% (http://www.bestplaces.net).

Hutchinson, Kansas: Interview Declined

Jamestown, New York

Jamestown (please see Figure 6.29) is an older community in upstate New York. Nearly two-thirds of the current housing stock is of pre-World War II vintage. As with many of the communities in the region, the population base of Jamestown is in decline, dropping by a full 15% between 1990 and 2000 from 37,314 to 31,730, and again by 4.25% by 2005 (30,381) (US Beacon, 2012).

The observed decline in population probably stemmed from a similar decline in the furniture production industry generally. This would certainly need to be an avenue of inquiry with the city's mayor: what were the full causes of this decline and what have been the results? Also, what can be done to reverse that trend, especially with a cost of living that exceeds the national average by more than 10%? Although there is some evidence in the local news coverage of economic diversification in the region, the city's unemployment at the time of this writing (8.6%) is nearly as high as the national average of 9.1%. And the city's recent job growth has been a whopping negative −4.53%, compared to the national average of −0.12% (http://www.bestplaces.net).

Interview with the Honorable Sam Teresi, Mayor of Jamestown, New York

Jamestown, New York is somewhat, although not completely, isolated from other cities in its region, according to Mayor Sam Teresi. It is generally considered to be

Figure 6.29   Street festival in Jamestown, New York. (Courtesy of Downtown Jamestown Development Corporation, Jamestown, New York)

situated in the "Buffalo orbit," although not a bedroom community to that city because the distance is too great to commute (one and one-half hours). In fact, Erie, Pennsylvania is closer: a 45-minute drive.

Still, Jamestown does serve as the retail center of the region, which means that sales taxes are very important to the city's budget. The state of New York levies a 4% sales tax of which the county receives three percentile points. That figure can be shared with the local governments on the basis of negotiated agreements. Jamestown thus receives half of that which goes to the county.

In addition to trying to attract additional retail outlets, the city's economic development strategy also focuses on preventing the leakage of retail sales to Erie. Indeed, that becomes increasingly important when one considers that Jamestown is only nine square miles in area and thus much of the growth occurs outside its borders. Mayor Teresi also expressed concerns with the population counts provided by the United States Bureau of the Census. Jamestown is home to many "snowbirds" who leave the region for warmer climes in the cold months. Because the official date of the decennial census counts are in April, many of those people are away and are not included. When one then considers that college students who have left the city for school have not yet returned in April are also undercounted, the matter becomes worse. Finally, a large itinerant Hispanic population that does not always respond to census outreach provides still more undercounting. For a micropoliltan community, small percentage changes can have dramatic consequences in both the counts and the resultant payments from the state and federal governments that are formulaic and needs-based.

One lesson that Mayor Teresi passes on from his experience in Jamestown is to learn from one's colleagues. At the time of the interview, he had recently concluded his service as the chair of the New York Association of Cities and Villages and reported that his greatest learning had come from those of his peers who had lived through similar experiences. This is related to another element of his background that has contributed to his actions as mayor of Jamestown. Prior to his election 12 years earlier, Mayor Teresi had served as the city's director of planning, a post in which he learned that economic growth is not just the city's responsibility. Rather, the private sector has a role to play as well. "The city controls the environment so public investment must precede private investment, but the city cannot go it alone." Over the last 12 years, the private sector has gotten involved in economic development, especially in the city's downtown development programs. "This has been indispensable," said the mayor. "You have to figure out how to get everyone to the table. That's when we began to make real progress. Business decision makers want to see a place that looks good and that works well together."

A second lesson offered is to be mindful of the community's weaknesses and attempt to do what can be done to alleviate the effects of those weaknesses, and to place the bulk of the focus on taking maximum advantage of the community's strengths and positive assets.

An additional lesson relates to the kind of economic diversity that keeps the economy going on an even keel in spite of the changes in the economic fortunes of one or another industry segment. One major employer left Jamestown recently and the loss equated to between 400 to 500 jobs in the city. "It was tough, but not devastating," said Mayor Teresi. An engine manufacturer soon brought several hundred jobs to the city and is expected to bring another hundred or more. The hospital accounts for 1,200 to 1,300 positions. Small businesses are growing; and manufacturing, in which about 20% of the workforce is still employed, remains strong. Tourism is the source of both jobs and tax revenues for Jamestown, and makes a statement to residents about the beauty of their community and their region. "Diversification has made it steady as you go."

Jasper, Indiana

Jasper, Indiana (please see Figure 6.30) is located in Bainbridge Township and is the county seat of Dubois County. It sits within a larger region that places it about 120 miles from Indianapolis, 55 miles from Evansville, Illinois, and about 80 miles from Louisville, Kentucky. The city has seen an increase of about 50% in its residential base in just the past 20 years, growing from just over 10,000 in 1990 to just over 15,000 by 2010 (US Beacon, 2012). With the city's unemployment rate hovering just over 5% at the time of this writing, compared to the national average of 8.6%, Jasper seems to be bucking the trends seen elsewhere in the state of Indiana (http://www.bestplaces.net). The city has the economic advantage of serving as the hub for retail and other services. Close proximity to Interstate Highway 64 gives

Figure 6.30 **The City Mill and the Patoka River, Jasper, Indiana. (Courtesy of Sam Voelkel)**

the city good access to other destinations. The city has enjoyed some economic development success as the recession begins to abate. Power equipment parts manufacturer Stens announced in late 2011 that it would expand local operations, adding nearly 100 new jobs to the plant. The $2.3 million investment by the company will be used to upgrade an existing facility in town for its new operations.

To seal the deal, the city agreed to three-quarters of a million dollars in tax credits. Perhaps the mayor would clarify the potential for a positive return on investment for the city from this incentive. Agriculture, manufacturing, and service industries presently dominate the area's economic landscape. It would be interesting to ask the mayor how incentives will be applied to each of those sectors.

Interview with the Honorable Terry Seitz, Mayor of Jasper, Indiana

Terry Seitz' first year in office as the mayor of Jasper, Indiana represents his first foray into public service. He feels that the city had become complacent and "did not want to play the economic development game." The result, as characterized by Mayor Seitz, is that Jasper has "unclaimed potential."

With a background in media marketing, the mayor set out first to develop a brand that can be promoted. His first step in that direction, however, has been what he terms the "internal marketing" that needs to be done to prepare the city for economic development targeting of specific companies or industries. The mayor also makes clear the need for the branding and promotions to address not just the attraction of employers, but also the workforce that once called Jasper home. "Many of our kids go to Nashville, Indianapolis, or Louisville. When they reach their 30s, and begin to raise families, they come back and we need them to come back."

Jasper has traditionally been an economy based on manufacturing. The mayor quickly points out that the city does not have easy access to an interstate highway but still has a large logistics center, including warehousing, in and around the city. "Drivers can reach 40 US states overnight from Jasper." Mayor Seitz maintains that this is a good start but, in terms of lessons for other cities and other mayors, he asserts that one must constantly look for ways to do things better.

In terms of the city's budget, the state of Indiana exerts considerable control over growth of the tax base. In the current fiscal year, local governments in the Hoosier State can only increase the property tax rate by a maximum of 2.83%. Jasper, however, budgets very conservatively; the council plans to spend only 90% of its projected revenues, and then only actually spends up to the 85% mark.

Mayor Seitz concurs with many of his colleague micropolitan mayors in terms of his personal role: "Remember why you became mayor and what your core values are. Always be opportunistic. Don't do things one way just because that's how they have always been done. Always listen to others and look for new ideas."

Jesup, Georgia

Jesup, Georgia represents one of the smallest micropolitan cities included in this study. In fact, it was not until the 2010 census report that Jesup even qualified as a micropolitan city, with 10,214 residents (US Beacon, 2012). At a time when the national rate of unemployment stood at 8.6%, Jesup's rate was reported to be 11.6% (http://www.bestplaces.net).

The city had originally been founded at the intersection of railroad lines and the primary components of local economic growth were initially (and, to some extent, remain) agriculture and timber, although the latter is not as strong an industry today as it once had been. The largest employer is the Rayonier Corporation, which reportedly has more than 900 employees in and around Jesup. The company provides paper, timber, and wood fiber products.

Jesup, Georgia: Interview Declined

Kearney, Nebraska

Kearney, Nebraska has seen steady, although not substantial, growth in its population over time. From the 1990 level of 24,396, the city grew by 2005 to 28,643 (US Beacon, 2012). Unemployment is extremely low at this time, registering only 3.4% whereas the national average is 9.1% (http://www.bestplaces.net). As with many micropolitan cities that are either somewhat or very isolated, Kearney serves as the county seat of Buffalo County.

But there are other major employers in Kearney as well. These include a branch of the University of Montana (1,700 employees) as well as Central Community College, two major hospitals (Good Samaritan Health Systems has 1,600 employees), shopping and personal services for a very large region, and a substantial primary business sector (including Baldwin Filters with 900 employees, Eaton Corporation with 620 employees, and Cabela's with 400 employees). The county has a total population of about 41,000 in addition to those who live within the city limits of Kearney.

In addition to the more than 1,100 farms in the region, manufacturing operations employ more than 3,500 people, trade and retail more than 5,600, services nearly 4,800, and government an additional 3,600. The most recently completed and approved Comprehensive Development Plan for the city of Kearney indicates that the vision is to transform the city from its agricultural and college foundation to a regional service center with an urbanizing core. To achieve this transformation, the city needs to focus on numerous key issues, including the transportation infrastructure, affordable and other housing inventories, improved regional air transportation, some crime issues, and the assurance of adequate public facilities to support the subsequent growth. And all of this must be accomplished while maintaining the type and quality of lifestyle which the residents prize.

Kearney, Nebraska: Interview Declined

Kerrville, Texas

Much of the current economic literature for this part of the state of Texas characterizes Kerrville only as a component part of a larger region that includes Ingram and Kerr County. Does this reflect an inability of the city to stand alone economically or does it reflect a positive effort to collaborate within the region, thus taking advantage of the collective assets for economic development marketing and promotion? The city's population has grown substantially over the recent past. Between 1990 and 2000, the level rose from 17,384 to 20,425, or 17.5%. Through the next five years, the population base of Kerrville grew again to 22,010, or by an additional 7.8% (US Beacon, 2012). Still, the unemployment rate is just 6.3%, far below the national average at the same time of 9.1%. And the recent job growth was measured at a positive 0.02%, compared to the national average of a negative –0.12% (http://www.bestplaces.net).

A 2008 policy document found online includes literally several pages of incentive programs that can be used to entice companies to locate in Kerrville. One has to question not only whether the return on investment has been a positive one but also what had to be postponed or unfunded in order to sacrifice the potential revenues that were abated or returned to the companies.

Kerrville, Texas: Interview Declined

Kinston, North Carolina

The city of Kinston, North Carolina (please see Figure 6.31) was founded in 1784 due to its position near the coast and the relative ease of access to its port from Great Britain. Indeed, its settlers simply dropped the "g" when naming the area for the king, George III. Its economic history has largely been one of agricultural production, however, the late twentieth century saw two serious floods within a period of less than five years that caused the city's leadership to begin looking toward a more diverse economy.

The hardships caused by these events resulted in a loss of population from the city; between 1990 and 2000 the base decreased by 6.35% from 25,295 to 23,688, and again by 3.53% between 2000 and 2005, to 22,851 (US Beacon, 2012). Unemployment at the time of this writing stood at 11.1%, higher than the national average of 9.1%, but recent job growth was a positive 0.44% whereas the nation had lost jobs at –0.12% (http://www.bestplaces.net).

There are some assets that will be attractive in support of the city's economic development outreach efforts. The North Carolina Global Transpark covers 2,400 acres of ready land with strong rail, road, and air access. In effect, companies can bypass much of the development and permit scheduling. The Lenoir Community

Figure 6.31   Kinston, North Carolina from the air. (Courtesy of City of Kinston)

College has an attractive campus and can provide training to supply employers with a skilled workforce as well as upgrading the skills of their existing workers. It would be an area of discussion with the mayor to see if these assets are being effectively used.

Another clear area for discussion with the mayor would be incentives to attract businesses to, or retain them in, the region. North Carolina has been alternatively more and less aggressive about the use of cash incentives, tax abatements, and more for these purposes. Over time, some criticisms have been leveled at the state for applying these programs only to the more visible deals with larger companies, to the exclusion of small businesses. One group wrote that "Economic development policy, as it has developed, has become simply a term used for state management of entrepreneurial activity and an excuse for funneling favors to privileged businesses and industries" (John Locke Foundation, 2008).

Whether this represents fact or overstatement, the important question is really whether such programs have been effective in helping cities like Kinston to increase their economic well-being and the residents' overall quality of life. One must wonder at this when reading such statements as Kinston has "fallen into economic and physical distress in recent years, as the immediate area has experienced steep increases in the volume of condemned housing, crime, and unemployment" (Monaco, 2011).

Interview with the Honorable B. J. Murphy, Mayor of Kinston, North Carolina

The city of Kinston and Lenoir County, of which Kinston is the county seat, are located in the middle of the North Carolina coastline. This location is very attractive to residents, companies, and visitors, but it also explains the two hurricanes that produced a "100-year flood" more than a decade ago. The flood left many properties in the city that had to be purchased by the federal government and on which no further building may take place. Combined with the national loss of jobs in the textile industry and the decline in the United States of tobacco farming, Kinston's economy has suffered repeatedly in recent years.

Mayor Murphy notes that the population had declined dramatically as a result of the clear overdependence on tobacco and textiles. As those employers left the area, many positions in the secondary economy also departed. Today, the economy has evolved. The nearby Global Transpark was created by the state of North Carolina in hopes of being an attraction for businesses over time but was not effective in doing so for about 20 years. This made the vision appear for many to be a waste of resources. However, a recent decision by aircraft manufacturer Spirit Aero to manufacture parts for the Airbus at Global Transpark has brought new hope. This announcement will mean 300 new jobs in the near future and perhaps as many as 1,100 in the next five to ten years. These are relatively high-paying positions, averaging $48,000 per year.

Mayor Murphy relates the frustration of the interim period as people looked for the Global Transpark to help alleviate some of their economic woes. He noted that the leadership of that day needed to manage expectations more effectively as local hopes began to diminish. Other recent announcements have also helped to bring positive results. Large local employers also include Sanderson Farms, a poultry producer with about 1,000 employees (albeit in lower wage positions), Smithfield Hams, and Lennox China.

The economic development assets of Kinston that are identified as strengths by Mayor Murphy include a very high quality of life, international ports within an hour and a half of the city workforce, a workforce that has manufacturing experience, five military bases within 50 miles, and a community college system that is nimble and adept at training for the specific needs of local employers. When asked what is missing, the mayor cites two needs. First, the access to an interstate highway needs to be improved; and second, better use can be made of the city's waterfront area.

When asked about lessons learned in Kinston that could be useful to other micropolitan cities, Mayor Murphy noted that the earlier overdependence on textiles and tobacco led to a steady decline in the local economic base. Today, the city is much more diligent about surveying both the micro- and macroeconomic changes that could have local implications. In this way, the mayor expects to be able to anticipate future threats sooner and to take better advantage of the resulting opportunities.

Kokomo, Indiana

The population of Kokomo, Indiana (please see Figure 6.32) has generally been increasing at a time when that of many micropolitan communities has been

Figure 6.32   A streetscape in Kokomo, Indiana. (Courtesy of City Kokomo)

contracting. The 2005 population of 46,178 reflected an increase of .14% over the 2000 base of 46,113 which had, in turn, reflected an increase of nearly 2.6% over the 1990 level of 44,962 (US Beacon, 2012). The city appears to have been thriving during that time period despite the loss of a significant number of jobs in the manufacturing sector. This may be due to the attraction or creation of replacement jobs, an effort that has aided the area's overall cost of living, which is more than 13% below the national average (http://www.bestplaces.net).

This is part of the explanation of how Kokomo began to attract automobile manufacturers back to the city. More than $89 million federal dollars were used to prepare the facilities that helped to attract a hybrid vehicle components manufacturing plant. A local transmission plant has been retooled by Chrysler, helping to retain more than 1,000 employees in the region, according to the US Department of Commerce. Many more jobs are supported among the many suppliers throughout the region to these types of primary employers. And, of course, additional employment is supported in the tertiary or service economies as well.

Despite the cited successes, at least one economist feels that it will be another decade before Kokomo regains its prerecession employment levels: "It looks quite alarming to see that Kokomo won't return to previous … levels until after 2021, but it is important to keep in mind how far it fell in the recession. We will see job growth in the next couple years. It just has a lot of ground to cover" (Human, 2011). Of course, many of the former manufacturing jobs went overseas and will probably not be coming back. Federal largesse enables the city to offset some of the marginal costs for manufacturing onshore, but only in the short term. The challenge for

Kokomo, and cities like it, will be to capture the more advanced manufacturing functions and to train their respective labor forces to give them the necessary skill-sets and to set them apart from workers outside the United States.

For smaller cities such as Kokomo, however, this creates a "chicken and egg" challenge. One must train the workforce for jobs that do not yet exist in the region. This requires a willingness to make investments in the future that will often either come at, or will seem to come at, the expense of other more immediate employment and budgetary needs.

Interview with the Honorable Gregory Goodnight, Mayor of Kokomo, Indiana

Unlike many of the mayors of micropolitan communities who were interviewed for this research, Gregory Goodnight, mayor of Kokomo, Indiana, is not a part-time mayor. His is a full-time position. A second distinction Kokomo has from the other areas referenced in this book is that the city has grown beyond the definition of micropolitan, and now has nearly 57,000 residents. This has been accomplished neither through natural increase nor through in-migration, but from the annexation of surrounding areas. These newly annexed areas were included in the Kokomo boundaries for two reasons: first, the new areas somewhat "squared off the map" and had geographic reasons for inclusion; and, second, about 70% of the annexed areas were contracting for various city services anyway.

Nearly two-thirds of Kokomo's tax revenues are generated from real estate tax levies, not income or sales taxes. As such, a growing economy in Kokomo is one that enjoys new commercial construction. One challenge to this is that the city has lost a significant number of manufacturing jobs in recent years and retains much of the facilities in the city. Still, Mayor Goodnight uses the same phrase that many of his colleague mayors used to describe the local outlook: "Cautiously optimistic." Despite this, the mayor noted that, among micropolitan cities, the future will see some winners and some losers. No one, he stated, will be immune from the economic pressures he is seeing in Kokomo, but some will grow stronger and survive and others will not be able to survive. He is emphatic about one thing in this regard: cities will grow or they will decline; "You can't stand still."

Kokomo's economy is traditionally based on manufacturing, including large employers such as General Motors, who, over the years, have grown in workforce, shrunk, and either regrown or closed and moved away. The future of Kokomo's economy, although entirely based on a strong manufacturing base, will not be as dependent upon it for its long-term stability. Mayor Goodnight feels the city is ready for a range of economic uses. The existing facilities and the labor force skill-sets are appropriate for manufacturing, but they should be complemented by technology companies and other industries. Some of that has already begun, as a few small start-ups have sprung up in the city.

The mayor believes that micropolitan communities are appealing to many people who long for a smaller environment in which to live and raise a family. Thus, the competition for economic development prospects tends to be other similarly sized cities within the state of Indiana. People who will look at a community the size of Kokomo are probably not going to be interested in a larger city such as Indianapolis as well. Cities of this size afford people nearly all of the same opportunities as those of larger cities, as well as the ability to know everyone a little better and to be as involved as one wishes in the activities around town.

Kokomo possesses safe neighborhoods (54th safest in the United States), higher education, hospitals and health care, and a good school system. As such, the appeal is to people and companies for whom these assets are most important. Local incentives are largely used to train employees and to make loans for a variety of purposes. They are available only for business attraction, not for the retention or expansion of existing businesses.

Mayor Goodnight, upon being asked about lessons from the Kokomo experience that could be instructive for other micropolitan communities, notes that he continually looks at what others are doing. In this way, he can learn new ways of doing things that can benefit his city. "You can always learn something that could help."

LaGrange, Georgia

The micropolitan city of LaGrange, Georgia (please see Figure 6.33) is located approximately 60 miles southwest of Atlanta. Thirty-six percent of all its in-city jobs are in the production and transportation sectors, which provide relatively

Figure 6.33 Open spaces in LaGrange, Georgia. (Courtesy of Keith McDow, City of LaGrange)

low-paying occupations. The current rate of unemployment is 11.5%, compared to the national average of 9.1%. Recent job growth has been strong at 2.38%, compared to the national average of –0.12% (http://www.bestplaces.net). The population grew from 2000 to 2005 by more than 5%, growing from 25,998 to 27,362 (US Beacon, 2012). Not surprisingly, given the predominance of low-wage industries, the poverty rate in the city tends to be high and is mirrored by a reportedly high rate of health issues including teen pregnancy. On the other hand, LaGrange High School was designated by *USA Today* as the top high school in the state of Georgia, based largely on its advanced placement courses.

It is not clear from the initial research whether the city serves the region as a hub for services. The immediate county, Troup County, has a population approaching 70,000 and the surrounding seven-county region totals nearly 320,000 residents. The mayor should be asked to shed a light on this potential for economic growth within the city.

In December 2011, good news on the economic front was received when Daewon announced its new manufacturing facility that will serve as a supplier to the nearby Kia plant. The company will invest about $14 million and create nearly 100 jobs in a three-year period. This plant will add to the existing 3,500 jobs in local employers that provide services to the Kia plant. According to the local press coverage, much hope is being pinned on the "Kia effect," meaning that smaller suppliers will colocate as well as help generate new businesses in the secondary economy (serving Kia and the related suppliers) as well as in the tertiary economy (jobs not directly related to Kia or its suppliers but that are supported by that general growth). Will the city and the region take specific actions that will accelerate that secondary and tertiary growth?

Another question for the mayor would be the extent to which there exists an overdependence on this one economic sector. Also, it would be of interest to discuss with the mayor the extent to which the above-cited problems are being addressed and whether they influence business site-location decisions, either in terms of business attraction or retention. Finally, as the city's economy does become increasingly more diversified, how will the public schools and the local higher education institutions (West Georgia Technical College and LaGrange College) become involved? A similar query will relate to how regionally based are such appeals to the business community. Does LaGrange coordinate those efforts with neighboring communities or does it collaborate on land use and infrastructure issues as they relate to economic growth?

In terms of regionwide opportunities, LaGrange benefits from its relative proximity to Fort Benning, which in the recent round of BRAC (Base Realignment and Closure) decisions, acquired 28,000 soldiers from Fort Knox. One reaction was the construction of a new tower at the regional West Georgia Medical Center. Are there plans for additional growth in infrastructure to support that movement?

Interview with the Honorable Jeff Lukken, Mayor of LaGrange, Georgia

Jeff Lukken has been the mayor of LaGrange, Georgia for 14 years but that is not the beginning of his exposure to the city's public leadership. When his father moved to Georgia from Chicago 40 years ago, he became involved with other leaders in the community and concluded that something needed to be done to protect the local workforce from being overly dependent upon a single industry: textiles. The group coordinated the purchase of a tract of property for the purpose of creating a research park and brought infrastructure and utilities to the area. The lesson to be drawn from that experience, according to Mayor Lukken, is to prepare for business growth when the times are good. Of course, many communities are not able, or at least not willing, to lay out the expenses for such developments now in the expectation of later returns. This chicken-and-egg argument must be considered within the context of political and budgetary decisions: can we afford to invest now, and not do other things that are needed more immediately, and wait to reap the benefits later?

Mayor Lukken asserts that these decisions and actions were critical because the textile industry did ultimately collapse in the region. Three mills have been lost from the area in the last five years, however, the unemployment rate has remained fairly constant because the economy has become larger and diversified enough to offset the losses. Recently, a Kia automotive plant opened near the city and announced plans not only for 3,200 direct hires, but an estimated 10,000 other jobs in the supplier and secondary and tertiary economies. In fact, a Georgia Tech study has placed the number at a much higher level, $23,000, and growing.

LaGrange is in a somewhat rural area but lies only 55 minutes from Atlanta. This makes it a retail and services center for a small region, and that also helps to drive economic growth.

LaGrange has also been successful in taking some advantage from the presence of four colleges and universities in the area, however, more could be done to collaborate with them to drive further economic development in the future. The four institutions, LaGrange College, Columbus State, Western Georgia Technology College, and Point College, provide leadership, cultural opportunities, research support, and notoriety as a "college town." The mayor thinks more can be gained by cooperating to commercialize research and create employment opportunities in the resultant businesses.

When asked how the city constitutes its budget, the mayor proudly points out that they curtailed the assessment of property taxes when he became mayor. The city owns or co-owns coal and natural gas production plants, water and sewer treatment facilities, broadband lines, and more. The user fees assessed for these items cover the costs of city services. When businesses ask how much of the local property taxes the city is willing to abate as an incentive, the mayor proudly states that they are already 100% abated for everyone.

Mayor Lukken feels that micropolitan cities will come under great stresses in the future. There are great benefits to living in towns that are large enough to offer services and a high-quality lifestyle but small enough to be safe. If cities like this can understand what their strengths are and promote them, they can thrive, but no one wants to compromise their quality of life.

The mayor offered two lessons for micropolitan city economic development. "Engage the community; volunteers are our best assets." And second, prepare and train the workforce, including basic workforce skills, so they become an asset when marketing to companies.

Laramie, Wyoming

Laramie has enjoyed a relatively stable economy and a relatively constant level of population in recent decades. From 1990 to 2000, the population base grew from 26,687 to 27,204 (+1.94%). Over the following five years, it declined by 4.24%, to a total of 26,050 (US Beacon, 2012).

The unemployment rate at the time of this research was less than half of the national average of 9.1%, and stood at 4.2% in Laramie. Recent job growth was down by −0.46%, somewhat more than the national average of −0.12% (http://www.bestplaces.net).

An important topic of discussion with the mayor would be how the city constitutes its budget. With more than one-third of all jobs in the government sector, real property taxes, if a primary source of budget revenues, could be lost. With the city's high rate of tourism attraction, however, a positive feature of budget development could be a high transient occupancy, or hotel, tax. A related topic would be what the city is doing to enhance the gross of those industries, thereby generating additional revenues for the provision of municipal public services.

Additional economic stability comes to Laramie from the University of Wyoming. When the agricultural and ranching sectors are down, the university provides a steady stream of spending and visitors to city hotels and restaurants. A variety of small businesses have been spun off from university research and a business incubator on campus helps small businesses get started.

Laramie, Wyoming: Interview Declined

Lewiston, Maine

Lewiston, Maine (please see Figure 6.34) is located in Adroscoggin County and has a 2010 population count of 36,592. This, however, represents growth from the 36,050 of 2005 but a loss of more than 10% from the 1990 apex of 39,757 (US Beacon, 2012). The current rate of unemployment is shy of the national rate of 9.1%, at 8.7%, although the current job growth is further into the negative than

Figure 6.34 Water sports on the Androscoggin River in Lewiston, Maine. (Courtesy of Lisa Dixon's Shoot for Maine Photography)

the national level of −0.12%, standing now at −1.33% (http://www.bestplaces.net). Furthermore, in mid-2012, Moody's Analytics listed Lewiston among the 76 metropolitan areas in the United States still "at risk" (Dedman, 2012).

Interview with the Honorable Robert MacDonald, Mayor of Lewiston, Maine

Mayor MacDonald has a background that is dissimilar from most of the mayors interviewed as part of this research. He was formerly a police detective and an employee of the local public schools prior to running for mayor. He never served on the city council (although he did once chair the state's Republican Party) and has no interest in either a second term or higher office in the future. However, much like his counterpart mayors who have had careers in business or other non-political pursuits, Mayor MacDonald also believes that his career experiences help him be successful in public life. As the police department's hostage negotiator, he learned how to talk to people and that is an asset he believes he brings to his job as mayor.

The city of Lewiston, Maine is, according to its mayor, an isolated micropolitan city that provides retail and other services to the residents of a wide region. The mayor points out that the city's isolation is due to the fact that it is proximate to a turnpike on which the only two tolls are immediately south and immediately north of his city. "People just take the other roads to save on the tolls and drive right around us. That is why we are so isolated."

Lewiston also suffers from a serious image problem. The city itself has several older and poverty-ridden neighborhoods, which have become what most people know about Lewiston. "Outside of the city, the neighborhoods are much more prosperous but people still know us by the downtown. And, it has even become the butt of jokes around the state." The mayor has been trying to improve both the downtown area and the city's image.

Unfortunately, the downtown is challenged not only by its income levels and appearance but also by the absence of jobs. Given that the city builds its local budget largely on the real estate tax base, there is the double-edged sword of minimal revenues coupled with greater-than-average demands for public services and transfer payments.

There are some positive signs for the downtown, however. One restaurateur in the city has now built three restaurants, one of which is somewhat more expensive than most local residents can afford. Still, its patronage is 55% from outside the area and, "You absolutely must have a reservation to get in." Another advance for the downtown area has been the development of apartments (also more upscale and expensive than the rest of the stock of multifamily units in the city) over retail establishments. "The city is coming along."

In terms of lessons learned, Mayor MacDonald notes that elected officials should "always be out there talking to people, especially the young people," whom he defines as late 20s and early 30s. Find out what they want. "They told us they wanted bike trails so we put in some bike trails."

Another lesson learned in Lewiston has related to the greater inclusion of local Bates College in civic activities. The new president has "worked more closely with the city and spends time in town. And she advises the students to do likewise. Mayor MacDonald notes that "If we didn't have Bates College here, we would be in a real bind." So, he concludes, "We have a great staff and the best city manager in the state. The college has a new, wonderful president, and the city is definitely coming back. In 15 years, you won't even know the place!"

Littleton, Colorado

Littleton's population boom of the 1990s has leveled off in the first decade of the new millennium. Please see Figure 6.35. The 1990 level of 33,685 was increased by nearly 20%, to 40,340, by 2000; however, by 2005, the growth had flattened (40,396). The jump over the next five years, to 41,737 (US Beacon, 2012), coupled with an unemployment rate of 8.0% whereas the national average stood at 9.1%, seems to be inconsistent with the current rate of job growth (−0.57%), which is further into the negative than the national average of −0.12% (http://www.bestplaces). This would be a topic to broach with Mayor Brinkman. Another topic for the discussion with the mayor would be the frequently expressed (in the media) practice of not offering financial incentives.

Figure 6.35 At the foot of mountains in Littleton, Colorado. (Courtesy of Cathy Weaver, City of Littleton)

Interview with the Honorable Debbie Brinkman, Mayor of Littleton, Colorado

When Debbie Brinkman, the mayor of Littleton, Colorado, was asked about the economic mood of her residents and businesspeople, she reported that they are "OK about the locality, concerned about the state, and nervous beyond that." Unemployment locally is down to under 7%, which, Mayor Brinkman believes, is due to the fact that the economy of Littleton is not based on a few large firms but rather a great many smaller companies.

As a result of the conclusion reached by the city that its base is primarily smaller businesses, the city developed the concept of "economic gardening," which uses collective public resources to provide the otherwise expensive (for the small businesses) market data, analysis, and coaching to small companies. This enables small businesses to refine their marketing and outreach to richer targets. Mayor Brinkman, a part-time mayor, also has a one-woman interior design business. By using the resources made available through the economic gardening program (which costs about $500,000 per year and is open to all Littleton residents), she was able to identify families with certain income levels and specified numbers of children in specified areas of town, and then focused her marketing efforts to those addresses. As a result, sales tax revenues are up in 2011 by 3.6% over 2010.

Growing businesses organically is critically important for Littleton because the city is essentially built out. With a total area of 13.52 square miles, only about 200 acres are available for development. Economic growth is not going to result from the attraction of major new employers to the city. Mayor Brinkman is satisfied with that; she reports that many small start-up businesses are in technology areas and, after they get established, obtain contracts or grants and begin hiring more people into positions with relatively higher salaries. This provides stability to the local economic base as well as creating the demand for new business and personal services companies. That latter growth is important to the city because of the relative importance of sales tax revenues in the city's general fund. Mayor Brinkman expressed pleasure that there are not too many large chain retail employers in the city because that enables the local retailers to thrive and because no single shutdown will greatly affect city revenues. Furthermore, with much of the local retail scene being the property of residents, the revenues stay in Littleton rather than being shipped back to the headquarters in other cities and states. This, too, may be a reason that micropolitan communities will continue to enhance their own local economies.

Finally, Mayor Brinkman notes with not a little pride that Colorado has a long history of intercommunity collaboration. She feels that "Cities will be broke if they do not learn to collaborate with each other as well as with their respective private sectors." By way of example, she cites the use of public and private funding to leverage a state grant (from the lottery fund) that was used to buy properties along the river and develop a 150-mile trail. "It's the only way we'll survive."

Lompoc, California

Lompoc, California has derived great economic stability over time from its proximity to Vandenberg Air Force Base. That may explain the 1990 to 2000 increase of 9.2% (as the base grew) in population from 37,649 to 41,103. A question arises, however, as to the decline of 2.72% to 39,985 by 2005 (US Beacon, 2012), neither does the presence of Vandenburg Air Force Base explain the unemployment rate at this time of nearly double the national average: 16.7% compared to the US average of 9.1%. Recent job growth stood at −0.57 whereas the US rate was −0.12% (http://www.bestplaces.net).

These trends raise interesting questions for the interview with the mayor of Lompoc. Furthermore, what if the air force base is closed some day? Is the economy sufficiently otherwise diversified to sustain such a loss? At present, there are 15 wineries in the area and businesses working in the field of entertainment technology. Are there plans in place to further this evolution to a more diverse economic base? At present, Vandenberg is the largest employer with nearly 7,000 jobs; it is followed by the local school system at 1,528, a Lockheed facility at 1,091, a local prison at 743, and a hospital at 500.

Still, with 7% of Santa Barbara County's gross economic output and 8% of its jobs, Vandenberg Air Force Base is critical to the local economy (City of Lompoc, 2012). Construction activities on the base also result in regular construction work for local companies. The base is the source of a constant stream of visitors who help support a thriving hospitality community in and around Lompoc. The base has also helped to attract primary air force contractors to the region, including Lockheed Martin and Boeing, as well as various federal agencies. As a result of the economic diversity in Lompoc, the city's higher education opportunities reflect a similar diversity of offerings. These include Embrey-Riddle Aeronautical University, the University of La Verne, and Allan Hancock University, all of which operate onbase campuses, as well as the nearby campuses of the University of California Santa Barbara and California Polytechnic State University.

Lompoc, California: Interview Declined

Lufkin, Texas

The micropolitan city of Lufkin, Texas has been named the top economy of its size in the state of Texas. It has historically been based on oil production and the manufacture of related equipment but also includes lumber processing and paper production. The Lufkin Paper Mill, for example, has a $150 million payroll in addition to the purchases it makes in the local community. Other large employers in Lufkin include the public school system, hospitals and health care, timber, and retail. The city's website lists government employment as 23% of the total, trade, transportation, and utilities at 19%, manufacturing at 18%, and health care, education, and social services at 29% (City of Lufkin website, 2012).

Perhaps as a result of the economic diversity in Lufkin, the current unemployment rate is about 7.6%, comparing favorably to the national average of more than 9%. Recent job growth is down, however, registering at −0.23% whereas the national average is only −0.12% (http://www.bestplaces.net). Nonetheless, the population of the city has continued to grow, rising by more than 8% between 1990 (30,206) and 2000 (32,709); and again by 2.5% in 2005 (33,522; US Beacon, 2012).

Lufkin, Texas: Interview Declined

Marquette, Michigan

Marquette has suffered through the current recession, (please see Figure 6.36), as have many of Michigan's communities, large and small. At the time of this writing, it has an unemployment rate higher than the national average: 9.6% to 9.1%. Recent job growth is nearly flat at +0.03%, somewhat better than the national average of −0.12% (http://www.bestplaces.net). Reflecting the state's economic woes, Marquette's population has also reflected gains and losses in recent years. Between 1990 and 2000, the base shrunk by 10.54%, from 21,977 to 19,661; but, by 2005 it had regained some of that loss and reached 20,581, an increase over 2000 of 4.7% (US Beacon, 2012).

The closure of Sawyer Air Force Base in the mid-1990s enabled the locality to develop a private airfield that helps to sustain economic growth. As a hub micropolitan city, the retail outlets in the city service a much larger region. This too can be seen as a stabilizing feature in the local economy. Both T.J. Maxx and PetSmart were adding to that retail base at the time of this writing, increasing the retail base by more than 36,000 square feet.

Figure 6.36 The shoreline of Marquette, Michigan. (Courtesy of City of Marquette)

Two areas that should be explored with the mayor are whether timber, mining, and mineral extraction are important to the city's economy today and whether they will be more or less important in the future; and whether the policies of the state of Michigan are helping or hindering economic growth in Marquette. The presence of the university by the same name helps to promote spending and tourism attraction, all of which help drive economic development, particularly in times of economic decline in other industries. The mayor should be asked to describe other ways in which the university is, or will be, involved in helping to develop and sustain the city's economy.

Interview with the Honorable John Kivela, Mayor of Marquette, Michigan

Mayor Kivela explained that the city of Marquette is somewhat of an aberration in the state of Michigan, a community that, according to its mayor, is "doing very well, economically." Marquette is believed to be the only municipality in Michigan where property values have not declined throughout the current recession. Townhouses and condominiums being built in the downtown area are ahead of plan by about three years due to an accelerating demand.

Mayor Kivela attributes the success of Marquette to its extraordinary quality of life and the willingness of the city to protect it, grow and sustain it, and promote it. "Outdoor activities, water sports on Lake Superior, golf, bike paths, and arts and culture help to attract people and business to town." In fact, the mayor states that people have become very creative in how to find work and to be able to work from home just so they don't have to move away from the quality of their lives in Marquette. "We really like the 2-person company, the 5-person company, the 20-person company."

Marquette is fortunate to be succeeding in this way. As a prime example of an isolated micropolitan city, Marquette is a three- to three-and-one-half-hour drive from the next largest city, Green Bay. As the mayor noted, "Other than that, we *are* the big city." This requires the city to provide a full array of services and opportunities for its residents as well as those of the entire region. Thus, the city's plans for further economic growth include the expansion of electrical power capacity because, at present, there is only a 1% excess capacity reserve. Expansion of the seaport and the inclusion of the airport into those activities has meant that international shipment of local goods is much easier and the attraction of new businesses that will want to export their products will have an additional business asset to promote.

As the population grows back to earlier levels, people will buy houses, generating both jobs and additional real estate tax revenues. To attract these new residents/new buyers, Mayor Kivela returns to his interest in enhancing and sustaining the community's quality of life. Because the state of Michigan caps the allowable increase in the taxable valuation of property at 2.9% per year, it is important for the city to maximize the opportunities that present themselves in that area to the fullest extent feasible.

Mayor Kivela is one of the relatively few mayors interviewed as part of this study who have interest in further office. In his case, he was campaigning for a seat in the state legislature at the time of the interview. As a businessman—such is the case for many of his colleagues in this study—Mayor Kivela believes that a businesslike approach to municipal governance is a smart way to work. The result: Marquette has not had a tax increase in six years, and the city has a healthy rainy-day fund. The business sense he possesses has led him to believe that one can, through technology, work smarter and cheaper and still accomplish even more, and that this applies to the public sector as well as to business operations.

A final lesson offered by Mayor Kivela is that one "Needs to listen to everyone very carefully, *especially* those who have differing opinions. The squeaky wheel need not always get the grease. Do what is right for the city and for most of the people."

Marshall, Texas

Marshall has seen virtually no change in the city's population base for two decades. Between 1990 and 2000, the base decreased by about one-quarter of one percent from 23,997 to 23,935. From that time to 2005, it grew by about three-tenths of one percent back to a level of 24,006, just nine residents more than it had 15 years earlier (US Beacon, 2012). At this time, the unemployment rate in Marshall is one percentile point below the US average of 9.1%, and recent job growth is −0.34%, compared to the national average of −0.12% (http://www.bestplaces.net).

The largest employers in the city are Eastman Chemical Company (with nearly 1,500 employees), followed by a variety of much smaller health care and mining companies as well as manufacturing concerns. Several nearby colleges and universities represent significant economic development assets, although there needs to be clarity as to their actual present or future involvement. The presence in and near Marshall of East Texas Baptist University, Texas State Technology College, Wiley College, and Panola Junior College give the mayor an opportunity to explain the roles and potential of higher educational institutions for economic development in micropolitan America's cities.

Marshall, Texas: Interview Declined

Marshalltown, Iowa

Marshalltown has managed to maintain a degree of stability over the recent past although there may be reason to believe that its economic past and future are hindered by the relatively high levels of taxation imposed by the state of Iowa. The local newspaper included this statement in late 2011: "There is a general consensus among state leaders that high commercial property tax rates put Iowa communities at a competitive disadvantage" (*Des Moines Register*, 2011).

This needs to be a topic of discussion for an interview with the mayor of Marshalltown. The city's population base has held relatively constant, first growing by 3.3% between 1990 and 2000, from 25,178 to 26,009; and then declining by about one-tenth of one percent through 2005 to a total of 25,977 (US Beacon, 2012). The economic picture is fairly stable, with an 8.4% unemployment rate that is currently slightly better than the national average of 9.1%; and a current job growth measure of +3.62%, far better than current national performance (−0.12%; http://www.bestplaces.net).

Marshalltown, Iowa: Interview Declined

Martinsville, Virginia

Martinsville, Virginia (please see Figure 6.37) has, at the time of this writing, an unemployment rate of nearly 18% (http://www.bestplaces.net)! This is the result of losing several key industries that were the bases of the economy of this part of the Commonwealth of Virginia including coal, lumber, and textiles. That dated back to the 1970s and the very high level of unemployment has been sustained over the intervening years; the result has been the loss of the population base. From 1990 to 2005, the total population of Martinsville declined from more than 16,000 to less than 15,000. The US census reports of 2010 showed a further decline to 13,821 (US Beacon, 2012).

Figure 6.37 Public facilities in downtown Martinsville, Virginia. (Courtesy of City of Martinsville)

Martinsville is one of the few micropolitan cities in this research that is located on the border of its home state; in the case of Martinsville, that means far southern Virginia. Martinsville is also an isolated micropolitan city, providing retail and services for the residents of the greater region, including areas of North Carolina and Tennessee, which is somewhat farther from the city. It is located 45 miles from Greensboro, North Carolina; 56 miles from Roanoke, Virginia; 100 miles from Raleigh-Durham, North Carolina; and nearly 200 miles from the state capital of Richmond.

The city's largest current employers are all involved in warehousing and distribution or some form of manufacturing, from furniture to food products. This is complemented by the Memorial Hospital of Martinsville and the Piedmont Community Services agency as well as other health care facilities in and around the city. The Patrick Henry Community College is also a significant employer, although not simply in terms of the jobs it houses, but also in terms of programs it can offer to partner with industries in the area to conduct training programs designed specifically for that employer's lines of business.

The interview with Mayor Adkins needs to address plans for resolving some very serious problems: a poverty level of 20% among adults and a relatively undereducated workforce.

Interview with the Honorable Kim Adkins, Mayor of Martinsville, Virginia

Mayor Kim Adkins of Martinsville, Virginia is unlike most of the mayors in this study: she is not a native of the city she leads (although her husband is), and she may indeed have an interest in further office. She and her city face some very tough economic challenges; Martinsville has been adversely affected by NAFTA (North American Free Trade Alliance) and issues of world trade for the past 20 years, first with textiles and later with the furniture industry.

Today, the city and its region still pursue manufacturing but primarily of more advanced types and processes. Mayor Adkins, however, makes clear that such economic diversification does not happen right away. After 20 years, Mayor Adkins feels that her city is just beginning to see the light at the end of an arduous tunnel.

The mayor's professional background is in the area of workforce development. She now manages the local Workforce Investment Board (WIB). She is in a perfect position to understand that the great need in Martinsville is both for training of the existing residents and the attraction of new residents who can accept some of the positions that are currently available but cannot be filled by existing residents due to the present skill mismatches.

As is the case with many of the other micropolitan cities in this research, there has been a realization that Martinsville must collaborate with surrounding Henry County for economic development purposes. The city has only 11 square miles within its borders, and the collective assets become much more impressive to prospective business site location decision makers when there is a regional collaborative outreach effort.

A second lesson Mayor Adkins offers her peers in other micropolitan cities is that "There are no silver bullets. Economic development takes a long time and requires strong leadership. And, that leadership needs to be holistic, including ways to attract new businesses and to sustain the city's existing businesses as well as preparing the labor force and improving the local quality of life. You just cannot put all your eggs in one basket."

Maryland Heights, Missouri

Maryland Heights (please see Figure 6.38) serves as a regional employment hub, with a nighttime population only 42% of its daytime population of 64,955 (Wassmer and Boarnet, 2002). That population base has slowly increased in recent years, climbing from 25,407 in 1990 to 25,756 (+1.37%) in 2000, and again by more than 3% by 2005, to a total of 26,554 (US Beacon, 2012).

Unemployment in the city is marginally lower than the current US standard of 9.1%, sitting at a level of 8.6% in Maryland Heights. Recent job growth, too, exceeds national performance (−0.12%), and presently measures +0.55% (http://www.bestplaces.net).

Maryland Heights is not an old city, having been formally incorporated in 1985. The presence of several attractions, including casinos, an amphitheater, a regional airport, and the hospitality industry to support them, has made the city an attraction in itself. If the local budget is supported primarily by the sales tax these assets

Figure 6.38 Entering Maryland Heights, Missouri. (Courtesy of Sara Berry, City of Maryland Heights)

can generate, then the stability of the tax base and the jobs in Maryland Heights can be regarded as secure.

Interview with the Honorable Mike Moeller, Mayor of Maryland Heights, Missouri

Maryland Heights is a metropolitan micropolitan city. As a suburb of St. Louis, Missouri, Maryland Heights is dependent on the larger metropolitan area economy; however, it does also depend upon its own economic base for the development of its budget and the provision of public services to its citizens. About one-third of the city's $35 million budget is derived from revenues generated by the city's casino. Other revenue sources provide the balance, including a 5.5% utility tax. There is no property tax in Maryland Heights so the economic development plan largely, and quite logically, addresses various means of driving more visitors to the casino.

Mayor Moeller describes the mood in the city as "OK ... people are doing OK ... no worse here than anywhere else. We do have the casino and we do have a new 20,000-seat amphitheater, and 3,600 hotel rooms." That's the good news; the tougher part of economic growth for the city of Maryland Heights has been an area known as the South Heights, which is an older, rundown, 200-acre section of town that is being redeveloped, in part through revenues generated by a TIF program (tax incremental financing). The city has already succeeded in attracting between 1,200 and 1,500 jobs to the South Heights.

Another similar area of Maryland Heights is known as The Bottoms, a 6,000-acre part of town, of which about 2,000 acres can be developed. The city has used gaming revenues from the casino to fund the construction of a highway through The Bottoms in the hopes that the resultant potential customer flow will help start and sustain small businesses along its path.

Mayor Moeller describes two of the lessons that were learned in this process. First, the use of gaming revenues has virtually always been for infrastructure projects. The mayor believes that there would be significant public dissatisfaction with the use of such proceeds for the "routine" operating expenses of the city administration. If, however, residents can see and use the product of those revenues, there will be far fewer concerns raised about the source. Infrastructure projects from which everyone can benefit is the absolute best use of these funds in the mayor's view.

The second lesson learned relates to the nature of leadership. When public officials begin to use terms such as "blight" and begin to exercise the rights associated with eminent domain, the populace naturally becomes skeptical. It is at such times that it is incumbent upon the leadership in a community to manage expectations, both positive and negative, as well as reactions to stated policies. Mayor Moeller was asked how one can do that. "Communicate with residents as often as possible, not just about what you want as outcomes but also about the process itself. How can they learn more? How can they make their feelings known? How can they better understand how the decision will be made as well as what the long-term objectives are?"

As relates to the future viability of micropolitan cities generally, Mayor Moeller thinks it will become increasingly challenging over time. This seems to be a somewhat consistent response from micropolitan cities that exist within larger metropolitan areas (as opposed to those that are more isolated). In St. Louis County, Maryland Heights is one of 91 municipalities, each of which competes for funding, jobs, and attractions. The mayor believes that some may have to merge at least some of their operations in order to be more efficient in the provision of public services and in order to survive. This has begun and the mayor expects some efficiencies to be realized through the sharing of facilities without formal mergers. Again, the mayor intones that "The most important thing is to communicate about what you want to accomplish and how the process of decision making will take place. Ignorance is the greatest enemy of planning. We've worked hard at educating our citizens and it has paid off. We need as much public involvement as possible."

Mason City, Iowa

The population of Mason City, Iowa (please see Figure 6.39) has seen relatively small declines in the past 20 years, dropping slightly from the 1990 level of 29,040 to the 2010 census report of 28,079 (US Beacon, 2012). Unemployment is currently running about 2.5 percentile points lower than the US average (http://www.bestplaces.net).

Mason City has been coordinating its economic development outreach with other cities in the northern Iowa region. Comments in the media and on the website indicate that the collaboration has been effective in creating a greater and more

Figure 6.39   A streetscape in Mason City, Iowa. (Courtesy of Visit Mason City)

impressive array of assets to promote for business relocation and retention. It has also seemed to create a greater likelihood of receiving state resources in the form of incentive programs for the corridor.

This is an area of questioning that should be put to the mayor. Numerous announcements included some form of financial inducement. The issue becomes whether the cost of the incentives are returned in the forms of sufficient growth and tax generation. One example is the incentive granted for the expansion to a Harley Davidson plant that resulted in the retention of 20 jobs and the creation of just six new jobs. Questions for the mayor would include whether the return on the investment is projected to equal or exceed its costs, as well as any reactions from other, existing manufacturing employers in Mason City to the incentives given to Harley Davidson.

Interview with the Honorable Eric Bookmeyer, Mayor of Mason City, Iowa

"Cautiously optimistic" is how Mayor Bookmeyer characterizes the current economic outlook in Mason City, Iowa. The state of Iowa, and northern Iowa in particular, have been rather resilient as the national and global economies have faltered in recent years. As it was never a really high-growth area, Mayor Bookmeyer feels that it will not be likely to experience dramatic swings in its economic fortunes in the future.

Mason City has the geographic advantage of being roughly two hours from Des Moines, Minneapolis, Waterloo, and Cedar Rapids, and is connected by major highways to each of these larger cities. This makes it a hub micropolitan city for both retail and medical services. In fact, the local hospital, Mercy North Iowa, is regularly cited as one of the top institutions in the United States, which is partly the result of being the focus of such a large region's demand for medical services.

Not very long ago, the balance of the employment and economic base of Mason City related to two major cement manufacturers; however, one of the two departed three years ago, and the economic development focus of the city needed to grow to support the growth of the city's population. Advantages for that purpose include the purity of the local water supply. Mayor Bookmeyer notes that the local tap water is better for manufacturing purposes than the bottled water that is sold. This has enabled the city and the region to become a primary location for food processing operations.

Other assets for economic development are clear to Mayor Bookmeyer, who has worked as a corporate recruiter: a strong local work ethic, strong public education systems, and the midwestern values that exist throughout Iowa. One concern for the mayor and the city is the loss of many young people—the so-called brain drain—who depart the region for other experiences and return when they approach middle age or begin families. This means that the economy is deprived of many of its youngest and brightest when they are in their most productive years. They return at a time in life when they are still productive, and are more experienced, but also now have children who need to be educated, thus creating pressure on the municipality's budget resources.

To address this, the city has created a microenterprise program for businesses with less than $500,000 in annual revenues and fewer than nine employees. In this program, the city will return one-half of all the businesses' property taxes for up to three years if the owners take business courses in the city and make their capital purchases locally. Mayor Bookmeyer estimates that those expenditures may get spent and respent within the city as many as seven times over.

The primary lesson that Mayor Bookmeyer offers to others is that the city's public leadership must partner with its private leadership. The latter have knowledge and skills that are useful for the future of the city as well as that of their own businesses. He also notes that, by pooling regional assets for purposes of promotion, smaller cities can present a more attractive picture to their economic development prospects.

Menomonie, Wisconsin

Menomonie (please see Figure 6.40) is, relative to the other micropolitan cities in this study, at the small end of the 10,000 to 50,000 definitional range. In 2000, the city had 14,937 residents, up from the 1990 tally of 13,547. By 2005, the total had risen significantly to 15,244. By 2010, it had increased again to 16,264 (US Beacon, 2012). Unemployment levels were better than the US average, 7.4% to 9.1%, and recent job growth registered slightly worse than the national average, −0.28% to −0.12% (http://www.bestplaces.net).

Figure 6.40   Downtown Menomonie, Wisconsin. (Courtesy of Cedar Corporation)

Press coverage refers to a regional partnership for economic development, the success of which would be a prime topic for the interview with the mayor. Also strong topics for the discussion would be an August 2011 expansion of the local 3M plant and the importance of agriculture both to today's economy and that of tomorrow in Menomonie.

In mid-2011, the state of Wisconsin announced the granting of $770,000 in incentives to the 3M Company to expand its Menomonie facility. The result will be a $28.4 million project that will expand the plant and bring in new technology but will result in only 25 new employment opportunities. The resulting cost of $30,000 per job created is pretty steep relative to other incentive deals of the recent past. This would be a good topic to broach with the mayor: what really is the return on investment for the community or the state?

It is unclear from the coverage in the local press whether other projects were also given incentives to expand in or relocate to Menomonie. For example, in mid-2012, Hidden Valley Industries and Shape Products added 12,000 square feet to its Menomonie plant and predicted another 36,000 square feet to be added in mid-2013. Were they, too, provided financial inducements to remain in the city?

Planning to revitalize and beautify Menomonie's downtown has been the subject of a great deal of local media coverage. A mid-2011 report to the city on this topic resulted in several conclusions that should be food for discussion with the mayor when interviewed (LHB, 2011).

Many of the proposed actions in that study call for collaboration and interaction for economic development purposes with the University of Wisconsin—Stout Campus. Other concepts relate to gateways to the downtown, and improvements to the "walkability" of the downtown area as well as "pedestrian experiences."

Interview with the Honorable Randy K'naack, Mayor of Menomonie, Wisconsin

Menomonie is the primary city within a relatively large region. Sixty miles to the west is Minneapolis and 25 miles to the southeast is Eau Claire, Wisconsin. This establishes Menomonie as the primary location for the purchase of some, though not all, types of goods and services. Those seeking medical services, for example, go to the relatively large hospital in Eau Claire. The local university is home to 10,000 students and a total population of about 15,000, and drives a great deal of local spending.

In the state of Wisconsin, however, sales tax generation accrues to the benefit of the state and the counties. Five percent goes to the state of Wisconsin and one-half percent to the county. This has prompted attention being spent on the diversification of the city's economic base. Mayor K'naack points out that many of the landowners within the city's limits are public entities and thus not required to pay property taxes. This includes the university, the public schools, state offices and institutions, and churches, all of whom directly benefit from city services such as protective services, maintenance, and more. [Author's Note. This is a common concern voiced by mayors whose cities have relatively small areas, much of which has already been developed. Removing properties from the tax base can greatly exacerbate already difficult budgeting scenarios.]

In pursuit of a diverse economic base, the city has promoted its industrial park effectively. It is now home to Cardinal Glass, 3M, a Swiss Miss Pudding plant, Anderson Windows, a Walmart distribution facility, and more. The university has become increasingly effective in spinning off new small businesses around solar panel production, computer parts production, and more. Additional growth can be enabled by the local airport, which is sufficient to accommodate small corporate jets.

The positives, at this point, outweigh the negatives, and Mayor K'naack characterizes the economic mood in the city at present as "pretty positive. We all know we're struggling, but anyone who wants to work at this point can do so."

A high-speed rail connection is a hope that would give direct reach for local employers and residents to Minneapolis and Chicago and would attract employers seeking a lower-cost, safe and pleasant community with ease of access to the big cities. Mayor K'nacck firmly believes that this is one of the greatest strengths of America's micropolitan communities.

Meridian, Mississippi

Meridian, Mississippi was originally settled by the Choctaw Indian tribe and later grew at the confluence of two major rail lines, the Mobile and Ohio and the Southern Railway of Mississippi. Today, it is one of the micropolitan cities that serves as a regional hub for the provision of health and other personal services as well as for its retail requirements. No other city exists within a 90-mile radius of Meridian.

Unfortunately, due to the extended national recession, retail sales are down and jobs in that sector have been lost, leaving the city with a current level of unemployment of 14.8%, compared to a national average of 9.1%. Recent job loss has only been registered at –0.01%, slightly better than the national measure of –0.12% (http://www.bestplaces.net). As a result, the city's population base has declined steadily in the recent past. Between 1990 and 2000, it declined from 43,539 to 39,968, or –8.2%. From then through 2005 it declined again by 3.4% to 38,605 (US Beacon, 2012).

How has Meridian's leadership planned for its economic revival and to what extent have the lost sales tax revenues due to lower spending in the recession hurt the city's budget? What is the strategy for recovery?

Meridian, Mississippi: Interview Declined

Minot, North Dakota

The current economic data on Minot, North Dakota present an interesting question to put to the mayor. The current 4% unemployment rate is low, less than half the national average of 9.1%. Recent job growth is –22.5%, far worse than the US average of –0.12% (http://www.bestplaces). Yet, at the same time, the population base has declined rather precipitously: from 1990 to 2000, from 43,639 to 36,567 (–16.2%); and again from 2000 to 2005, down another 4.3% to 34,984 (US Beacon, 2012). The question then becomes whether people have left the city because jobs were being lost and whether their departure is the basis for the low unemployment rate, thereby potentially masking a greater problem. And, is this out-migration trend one that the mayor would like to reverse or does the city regard it as an acceptable form of "right-sizing?"

The strength of the extraction industries in the region would suggest otherwise: natural resources are not only strengthening the local economic base but are also providing both jobs and tax revenues to the city and to the region. Related occupations also benefit as growth occurs in spinoff businesses and the region's tertiary economy. Reportedly, 800 semitruckloads of material each month must be moved from an oil well. And, the 112 drilling rigs in the area invest about a dollar a second into the local economy (Ogden, 2010).

At least one source suggests that the population of Minot will return to a level of more than 50,000 in the next few years (knext, 2008). What is the basis for this forecast? And, if it is accurate, or even simply desirable, is the city prepared for the housing and infrastructure demands that kind of growth will generate?

Part of the answer to these questions may come from local oil production, or perhaps growth that is expected at Minot Air Force Base. Still, agriculture remains the primary economic driver in Minot and in the region. In 2010, the following North Dakota crops constitute very high percentages of total US production: durum wheat (56%), sunflowers (43%), barley (35%), navy beans (38%), pinto beans (56%), canola (90%), flax seed (95%), lentils (24%), and honey (24%; Minot Area Chamber of Commerce, 2011).

Agriculture and related production today employ nearly one-fourth of the region's workforce. Although productive, these are not typically high employment growth areas so it would be important to ask the mayor for his thoughts about community and economic growth as it relates to agriculture in general.

Revenues from production agriculture, both plant and animal, have been reported as steadily growing for several years. Statewide, farmers in 2009 were reported to have received more than $5.5 billion from agriculture-related revenues (Knutson, 2011). Wholesale trading, warehousing, transportation, and a variety of personal and educational services help to diversify Minot's core economy and to sustain it through the peaks and valleys caused by macroeconomic events.

Minot, North Dakota: Interview Declined

Moline, Illinois

The city of Moline (please see Figure 6.41) sits about 165 miles west of Chicago and has the economic advantage of being on a major interstate highway, I-74. This may be part of the reason that, although not strong, the city's economy is hovering around national averages: an unemployment rate of 8.4% to a national measure of 9.1%; and a recent job growth in the negative at −0.55% whereas the national average is at −0.12% (http://www.bestplaces.net). The city's population has held fairly constant over time, growing by 1.3% between 1990 and 2000 (43,202 to 43,768) and then declining by 2% through 2005 to 42,892 (US Beacon, 2012).

Much of the literature regarding the local economy discusses regional approaches taken by Moline in conjunction with its neighbors in the "Quad Cities:" Rock Island in Illinois and Davenport and Bettendorf in Iowa. This is an interesting approach given that multistate regional cooperation for economic development is

Figure 6.41   The landscape of Moline, Illinois. (Courtesy of City of Moline)

often frowned upon by the two states involved for reasons of tax base generation. This should prove to generate an interesting discussion with the mayor.

The city of Moline is reported to have declined greatly in the 1980s but made a recovery in the next decade, in part by using its riverfront as an economic development attraction. Deere and Company contributed to this effort by smashing its riverfront warehouses in an area on which a civic center is now located. Today, the city is home to several major employers, including Deere, which has more than 5,000 employees throughout the region, and the nearby Rock Island Arsenal, which employs 6,300 people. Trinity and Genesis Health Systems combine for an additional 8,000 workers in the region as well.

Interview with the Honorable Don Welvaert, Mayor of Moline, Illinois

After four years as an alderman and eight years as the mayor of Moline, Don Welvaert will not seek re-election and has no further political ambitions. He is, as are so many other mayors in this study, a native of his city.

Moline is, curiously, one of five cities in the Quad City area that encompasses part of western Illinois as well as eastern Iowa including, most notably, the largest of the cities, Davenport. The city has turned a corner, according to its mayor, but is affected in its economic development outreach by the well-known financial difficulties of the state of Illinois. This is a particular issue for Moline because business prospects who want to be in the Quad Cities area can simply cross the border into Iowa. Still, the city has experienced significant growth in its retail base throughout the recent recession.

Moline is also fortunate still to be able to initiate a process long in planning: the development of an Amtrak station from which employers and employees can travel. In particular, it is hoped that this development will help enable the growth of a nascent technology community. Those jobs are important to the region because so many other jobs have been lost over recent years. The region's pre-1980s mainstays, agriculture and manufacturing, have both diminished substantially in importance since that time. Mayor Welvaert believes that the lessons from that experience were learned well by the leadership in Moline.

Over time, the fortunes of John Deere and other large employers rose and fell but the city is also home to other large employers such as Kone Elevators that continued to increase their employee base throughout the recession. Today, Moline's economy is well diversified with strengths in financial services, health systems, information technology, and tourism.

The mayor is very proud that people have begun to return to Moline's downtown area and he has led the development of strategies to enhance that trend. Parks have been built along with hiking paths; the main drag in town, Fifth Avenue, has been revitalized to bring residents back. Retail on the ground floor of buildings in the downtown with lofts above is very popular in the city now. Mayor Welvaert characterizes these successes under the banner of "build it and they will come!" He also notes that the city is the beneficiary of its geographic location at the conjunction of several major highways and near a strategically placed airport.

Western Illinois University has built a new campus in Moline that the mayor believes will help fuel company development in the city as well as attract tourist dollars. Furthermore, because the dormitories will be developed privately, they will be taxable and benefit the city's ability to provide public services.

The lessons of his tenure as mayor relate to the appearances of cities. "Keep up the attractiveness and cleanliness of the city," he advises. "People want things like our new library, parks, trails, and things to do." Another issue about which the mayor counsels is municipal collaboration to provide public services. Although there is typically resistance on many levels, there are great efficiencies in joint fire districts and school districts. As a beginning, three Chambers of Commerce in the Quad Cities area merged to form a single Chamber which is much stronger; but, according to Mayor Welvaert, it is only the beginning.

Mount Pleasant, Michigan

Initially a logging area, the primary employer today in Mount Pleasant, Michigan is Central Michigan University. Its growth has paralleled that of the community. From 1990 to 2000, the population base grew by 11.43%, from 23,285 to 25,946. By 2005, it had grown by another 1.2% to 26,253 (US Beacon, 2012).

The current economic growth picture in Mount Pleasant is a mirror of the national positions both in terms of unemployment rate (9.1% for both) and the current level of recent job growth (–0.08% in Mount Pleasant, –0.12% across the nation; http://www.bestplaces.net). Yet, with 27,000 students, the university's presence results in job and expenditures throughout the city and the region. It would be noteworthy to hear from the mayor how the university is engaged in economic development programs as well.

The Chipewa River waterfront also represents a potential economic development asset for the city. Once the reason for its location—the transport of lumber—the river and the city's downtown area are topics that should be explored with Mount Pleasant's mayor.

Mount Pleasant, Michigan: Interview Declined

Murray, Kentucky

The population of Murray, Kentucky (please see Figure 6.42) has remained remarkably constant for decades. The 1990 census showed total residents in the city limits to be 15, 058. By 2005 the level had only grown by 450 individuals to a total of 15,538 (US Beacon, 2012). This may be due, in part, to the relative absence of job expansion over that time; the unemployment rate of 8.7% mirrors that of the nation as a whole (9.1%; http://www.bestplaces.net). Regardless, the city's population growth trend continued through the report of the 2010 census, which showed 17,741 people living in Murray.

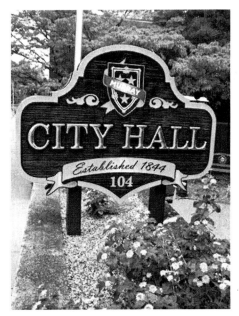

Figure 6.42   A welcome to Murray, Kentucky. (Courtesy of Melissa Taylor)

Murray is an isolated micropolitan city that sits on the western edge of Kentucky and is significantly closer to out-of-state population centers than to those within its own state. Louisville is 226 miles away. Lexington is 267 miles away, and Frankfurt, Kentucky nearly 300. Out-of-state locations to which Murray is more proximate include Memphis, Tennessee (156 miles), Nashville, Tennessee (120 miles), and St. Louis, Missouri (219 miles).

Naturally, Murray markets itself for economic development purposes as being near the geographic center of the United States. One question for the mayor should address whether he feels that smaller cities on the borders of states either are forgotten in the legislature or feel outside the state's mainstream economy. Because the city is the largest community for these distances, it has a substantial catchment area from which to draw labor. This represents an asset to potential employers as they can draw on a total estimated labor pool in 2012 of more than 90,000 workers (Thinkmurray, 2012).

The only recent job growth activity in Murray that could be found through an Internet search relates to the development of 75 new jobs by Pella Windows (Pella Windows, 2011). The mayor should be asked to shed some light on the absence of job growth as well as any plans for new economic development in Murray.

In order to prepare itself to attract business prospects, the city has recently completed the preparation of a 140-acre industrial park. The mayor should be asked to discuss this. Other mayors have indicated that although they would like to implement similar plans, the risk inherent in building something at great expense in order to attract businesses that may not appear for many years is too considerable. The conundrum that results is that without such a park there will be nothing to offer potential business prospects.

Interview with the Honorable Bill Wells, Mayor of Murray, Kentucky

Although Mayor Wells is not a native of Murray, or even the state of Kentucky, he is like most of the other mayors in this research in one respect: he has no interest in higher office. Mayor Wells came to Murray to become the principal of Murray High School, a post he held from 1982 to 1995. While still principal, he won election to the city council and served as a member for 20 years until the previous mayor passed away and he ran for that position. Although designated as a "part-time" office, the mayor, like many of his peers in other micropolitan cities in this research, puts in between 50 and 60 hours in a typical workweek.

Mayor Wells agreed that Murray is an isolated micropolitan city and that there is a need to "remind" those in the rest of the state of their needs from time to time. However, he also notes that the relative isolation of his city makes it an attractive location for outdoorsmen, including those who hunt, fish, or enjoy hiking. "People come to us and that helps the local economy," Mayor Wells said. The need to ensure that visitors return may be part of the reason that, according to Rand McNally (2012),

Murray is the friendliest city in the United States. Mayor Wells also proudly notes that its Chamber of Commerce has been ranked as a leader for US Chambers of its size.

About a decade ago, Mattel Toys left Murray and relocated its factory in Mexico, taking 1,100 jobs with it, as well as those that existed because of those primary jobs. Fortuitously, Pella Windows came to town at roughly the same time and replaced many of those jobs. Clearly, this is the reason Mayor Wells, who was on the city council at that time, emphasizes this lesson: "Never take your success for granted. You simply cannot coast or rest on your laurels."

A clear economic development asset is the presence of Murray State University and its 11,000 students. The university is a primary employer for the region and expects to grow over the remainder of the decade in order to reach a student base of 20,000. This will mean more jobs and greater visitation for the city as well as greater tax generation. The university has also been very effective in establishing partnerships with local businesses, such as Pella Windows. Such collaborative efforts are a hallmark of Murray and other cities its size, according to Mayor Wells. He noted that it must be so, especially when the cities are as isolated as is Murray. He notes the strong levels of collaboration among the city, the business community, and the university in a variety of areas.

The budgetary impacts of growth are of significance in smaller cities, again especially those that are more isolated. Murray has attempted to encourage that growth by not enacting a payroll tax on local businesses. Mayor Wells believes that Murray is the only city in Kentucky not to have done so. This means that the city had been raising the revenues for the provision of public services from automobile license fees ($50 per vehicle) and property taxes.

Recently, the city enacted a "wet" policy. Previously, as a dry city, alcoholic beverages could not be purchased. The new ordinance permits the sale of alcoholic beverages in restaurants as long as total sales remain at least 70% of all food sales and no more than 30% of the revenues come from the sale of alcohol. The city will authorize eight stores to open and will benefit by receiving 8% of all sales. This will enable the city to enhance and sustain its public service offerings.

Indeed, the vote on "going wet" was rather close and Mayor Wells realized that he needed to assuage the feelings of those who voted against the measure. Thus, he explains the benefits of the decision not in terms of tax revenues that will be generated but in terms of the number of new police officers the city is now able to employ. This resonates with all of the residents and has made that particular decision more palatable.

Muskegon, Michigan

As has much of the state of Michigan, the micropolitan city of Muskegon has suffered through economic decline in the current recession as a result of their dependence on the American automobile industry. Although Detroit has been key to their fortunes, Muskegon is actually closer to Chicago at 180 miles (Detroit to Muskegon is about 190 miles). Not surprisingly, the population has declined in the past decades, dropping from 1990 to 2000 by 25%, from 53,453 to 40,105, although by less than one-half of one percent from 2000 to 2005, to 39,919 (US Beacon, 2012).

The jobless rate in March of 2009 stood at 20% (Michigan Unemployment Up Again, 2009)! An overdependence on the automotive industry hurt Muskegon. When General Motors closed its local plants in the early 1990s and the industry declined generally, there were no other employers present in sufficient numbers to help prop up the local economy. What were left were relatively low-paying jobs that generated little in the way of taxes for the city services for which there was a dramatically increasing demand.

At the same time, the labor force, which had strong skillsets, has fled in search of employment, leaving behind a less attractive workforce with which to attract new employers. This brain drain and how to reverse it would be a topic for the mayor. Major employers in the city today include manufacturers of gas turbine components, auto parts, high-grade paper, communications systems, and bowling equipment. Is this enough to serve as a sufficiently diversified base for new economic growth in Muskegon? Are they too at-risk due to the loss of the most well-trained workers in the labor pool?

Muskegon, Michigan: Interview Declined

Muskogee, Oklahoma

In north central Oklahoma, Muskogee serves as a regional hub for both employment and the provision of shopping and cultural opportunities as well as health and other personal services. As a result, retail jobs are reported to be on the increase by 12% over the previous year and, in the current recession, the unemployment rate is at about two-thirds the national average of 9.1%, sitting at 6.3% in Muskogee. Recent job growth is in the negative at −0.06%, a mirror of the national average of −0.12% (http://www.bestplaces.net).

The population base has remained fairly steady, which is a little different from many of the more isolated micropolitan cities in this study. In many cases, the rural residents in the immediate areas have moved into the cities to find work, thereby both increasing the population counts and raising the level of unemployment unless more jobs have been attracted to the communities. This would be a question to pose to the mayor. In Muskogee, the population rose in the decade of the 1990s by 1.6%, from 37,708 to 38,310; and again by 3.8% between 2000 and 2005 to a total of 39,776 (US Beacon, 2012).

The city is also home to industries that are not service providers, including a new Eagle Claw plant that added 175 employees in mid-2010. White-collar jobs constitute 53% of the current employment base and blue-collar jobs are about 29% of the total.

Muskogee, Oklahoma: Interview Declined

Naples, Florida

Naples, Florida (please see Figure 6.43) is located across the southern tip of Florida from Miami. Its population from 1990 to 2000 declined by 34.62%, from 32,081 to 20,976. Such a precipitous drop would need to be addressed with the mayor. Over the next five years, through 2005, it grew by 3.5% to 21,709 (US Beacon, 2012). The 10.2% unemployment rate (http://www.bestplaces.net) somewhat exceeds the national average of 9.1% although one must wonder whether the counts are accurately reflecting the large number of retirees who live in the community for part of each year.

Interview with the Honorable John Storey, Mayor of Naples, Florida

Mayor Storey first describes his city's location: Naples, Florida sits at the southern end of the state across from Miami on the east side; Naples is on the west coast. The city enjoys great beaches and many affluent communities with beautiful Gulf views. It also has some less upscale, older communities in which the houses are smaller and the incomes are lower. The city and the region are very diverse and include many retirees who contribute taxes to the city coffers but are also generous with their volunteer hours. Indeed, Mayor Storey points out that the city's brand is its beaches, landscapes, and buildings; they promote the city's "wow factor."

Tourism is both a prime driver for the economy and a challenge for the provision of city services. The challenge comes because it is seasonal with several months of

Figure 6.43   View of the Gulf of Mexico from Naples, Florida. (Courtesy of Penny Taylor, Vice Mayor)

the year being too warm to attract tourists or even keep residents. This is in contrast with the several months of the year when capacity is "more than 100%" and city services are strained. The challenge is to keep employees year-round and to balance their workload. Much of it is done with overtime in the busy months but the mayor acknowledges that a complementary business sector to fill the slow times would be helpful. One current effort is to promote the medical services sector to attract patients to the area and use the hotel rooms and restaurants during their stays.

The population of Naples in general can also tend to rise and fall as people go to cooler climates during the summer months and then return in the fall. Indeed, the 1990 to 2000 population statistics reflect an interesting anomaly: the city's population declined from about 32,000 to about 21,000 as the construction industry declined dramatically and much of that workforce, many of whom were sharing single residences among several families, departed with it.

Mayor Storey conveyed several points about the city's economic history that may be instructive for other micropolitan communities in the country. Because he possesses a business background, he and other leaders in Naples concluded years ago that the existing one-year plan for budgeting and the one-year plan for capital expenses were inadequate, and moved both processes to five-year cycles. As part of the process, the city began to set aside funds to create larger reserves in case of economic downturns; and this was done during the boom times.

Today, the city of Naples enjoys an undesignated reserve fund of about $50 million, which equates to roughly six months of operating expenses. A second lesson from Naples relates to another form of seasonality: water usage and water treatment. A 20-year integrated plan has been completed that covers issues related to both potable water and storm water management. These have resulted in greater drinking water being available in all seasons as well as improvements in the environment such as the reversal of the steady destruction of the mangroves in Naples Bay.

Natchitoches, Louisiana

Natchitoches (please see Figure 6.44) is located inland in the state of Louisiana so has not been devastated by flooding as was the city of New Orleans. In fact, the city has seen a fairly stable population base, with limited growth over the past two decades. Unemployment in the city is slightly below the national average at the time of this writing (9.1%). Natchitoches presently has an unemployment rate of 8.3% (http://www.bestplaces.net), The city's population base has been on the incline for the past two decades. From a 1990 level of 16,609, it grew to 17,701 by 2005 and again by the census of 2010 to 18,323 (US Beacon, 2012).

The city sits near the confluence of several air, water, rail, and highway connections. Other than public functions, the largest (private) employers in the city include Conagra Poultry with more than 1,000 employees, and Walmart, Willamette Industries, and Alliance Compressors each with between 250 and

Figure 6.44 Downtown Natchitoches, Louisiana. (Courtesy of Chris Post)

500,000 employees. Public sector employers in Natchitoches include the parish school system, Northwestern State University, the parish hospital, and the city itself.

Natchitoches also boasts in its marketing materials that the presence of Northwestern State University is a tool for economic development although there is no clear indication of how the university is actually used to grow, attract, or retain companies or jobs. This would be a topic for the interview with the mayor.

The city's largest private employers are Conagra Poultry, with more than 1,000 employees, and Pilgrim's Pride, Roy O Martin, Alliance Compressors, and the regional medical center, each of which employ between 500 and 700 persons. Weyerhaeuser recently upgraded its local lumber plant, adding 77 new jobs and retaining the 175 workers already working for the company at that location. To secure the deal, the state of Louisiana sweetened the pot with $300,000 of incentive payments to be made over a five-year period.

In total, the workforce of the city is employed in relatively high-paying jobs. Thirty-two percent of those in the total workforce are employed in the areas of education, health, and social services. Another 13% are employed in retail trade, and 10% in the arts, entertainment, and hospitality industries. Only 10% work in manufacturing functions (City of Natchitoches, 2012). Interestingly, these types of jobs are precisely what one might expect in a hub micropolitan city that provides services to a larger region.

Interview with the Honorable Lee Posey, Mayor of Natchitoches, Louisiana

Natchitoches, Louisiana is the oldest settlement in the territory covered by the 1803 Louisiana Purchase. Its existence, which predated that event, means that Natchitoches is, at the time of this writing, approaching the celebration of its tricentennial as a community. Mayor Posey is in his first four months as the mayor after serving for 20 years on the city council. As are nearly all of his peers in this study, Mayor Posey is a native of the area and has no interest in further elective office.

Mayor Posey is also similar to the other mayors in this study in terms of his career: he spent 34 years in business in the community and insists that the experience now enables him to be more effective as he discharges his duties as the mayor of a micropolitan city. "We have the same issues, and the same principles apply: people issues, cultural issues, working together to accomplish something important."

The city has bucked national recessionary experiences of the past few years due to production from a nearby source of natural gas. "Everyone has benefited: hotels, restaurants, retailers." The production is now declining, but the city is in good shape because it used or saved the resultant revenues but did not presume their long-term continuation and did not build those resource expectations into long-term budget planning.

Because Natchitoches' city budget is heavily dependent upon sales tax generation, retail is an important growth focus, as are the overall tourism and hospitality sectors. The city is also home to a large number of retired individuals and has built a small services business cluster around them. All of these growth sectors are built around assets the city has, including centuries-old plantations, a beautiful riverfront area, a number of festivals, waterparks, and a convention center.

The mayor also recognizes the value of repeat customers, a lesson from his business career. As a result, he has visited with all of the businesses in the city to learn about their interests and needs as well as their plans to expand, relocate, or contract. Another city asset for economic development is Northwestern State University, which is home to more than 9,000 students, plus faculty and staff as well as a performing arts center and more. One of the lessons the mayor has learned is to take the best advantage of the assets small cities have. Another is to "Be willing to listen to people. Other people have learned a lot too and you can build upon their strengths and their experiences."

New Bern, North Carolina

The founding of New Bern, North Carolina (please see Figure 6.45) by the Swiss dates back to the very early 1700s. In more recent times, the city's population base has grown significantly, although the 33.2% growth rate between 1990 and 2000 (17,363 to 23,128) is so dramatic as to imply more than in-migration.

Figure 6.45 Sailing on the Trent and Neuse Rivers, New Bern, North Carolina. (Courtesy of New Bern Craven County Convention and Visitors Center)

Perhaps the mayor can reveal whether there were land annexations also involved during that time period. By 2005, the total grew to 24,106, a more normal 4.23% growth rate (US Beacon, 2012).

At the time of this writing, the unemployment rate in New Bern exceeded the national average of 9.1%, standing at 9.7%; however, the recent job growth tallies for New Bern were in the positive at +0.86%, compared to the national average at the time of −0.12% (http://www.bestplaces.net).

Given the numerous historic attractions in and around New Bern, it would be a question for the mayor as to whether there is an effective tourism bureau for the city, the extent to which growth of the hospitality industry is an important part of their overall growth strategy, and how important transient occupancy (hotel) taxes are to the city's budget. In addition to the tourist attraction possibilities, New Bern is also home to a number of well-known businesses, including Weyerhaeuser, Hatteras Yachts, SBH Home Appliances, and Moen Faucets. A local community college is also a potential asset for further economic development.

The employment breakout for surrounding Craven County shows the predominant sectors to be services (7,912 jobs), retail (6,670), and manufacturing (4,725; City of New Bern, 2011). Within the manufacturing sector, Naval Air Depot (NADEP) dominates with 4,000 people making aircraft engines and parts, followed by Hatteras Yachts and Moen Fixtures, both with approximately 1,000 jobs. However, the local BSH plant recently contracted its production schedules and laid off about 100 people who had made home appliances, out of a total labor force of 730. Has this been sufficient diversification to sustain New Bern through the current recession?

A further discussion to hold with the mayor relates to the tax base losses from a reduction of 100 workers; how does that affect city revenues and public services?

Interview with the Honorable Lee Bettis, Mayor of New Bern, North Carolina

New Bern's mayor is unlike most of the other mayors in this study. He is not a native of the city he leads. In fact, Mayor Bettis landed in New Bern as the result of an intentional search to find where he wanted to live. As a lawyer in New York, the attacks of 9-11 caused him and his family to seek a different environment. They settled on New Bern, which recently celebrated its 300th anniversary and has beautiful vistas that appealed to him and his family. Given his background and expertise in financial areas, he observed problems with the city's financial management practices and became involved because he felt he could help redirect his adopted hometown.

Mayor Bettis is not apologetic about having made numerous tough decisions, including several necessary employee dismissals, in order to set the city administration on a different track. "You can't worry about those things; you just have to do what is right. If you have to walk into Walmart and face people every day, you accept the challenges needed to improve the situation."

One of the positive outcomes of those decisions is that the city's budgetary reserves, hovering around 2% when Mayor Bettis took office, are now at a much more comfortable 22%. An increase in the local bond rating to AA will save the city millions of dollars over the coming years. Furthermore, the mayor believes that the improved financial stability of the city is not lost on existing or prospective employers, and that such prudent management represents an asset for economic development marketing.

In terms of lessons that he has learned as mayor, he notes that "Change is sometimes painful, but if you have a clear vision, the trouble is worth it. Sometimes, you'll get it wrong. Then, you apologize and try something else. Identify what you want to do and be honest about it. You will certainly be held accountable in a small town." A second lesson: "The most important thing the council does is to hire the city manager. Do it carefully and get the best."

Newberry, South Carolina

Newberry, South Carolina (please see Figure 6.46) has had a relatively steady population over the past 20 years with a 2010 reported level of 10,277 (US Beacon, 2012). This makes Newberry one of the smaller micropolitan cities to be included

Figure 6.46 Opera house, Newberry, South Carolina. (Courtesy of Michael Moore)

in this research. Its current unemployment rate of 9.3% exceeds the national average of 8.6% (http://www.bestplaces.net).

One of the primary drivers of economic growth in the city must be Newberry College although there is no press coverage to explain how the institution is being, or can be, used. This would be a topic of discussion for the mayor. There was some coverage of a new branch of the Piedmont Technical College opening in the area, and that should be an additional economic development asset worthy of discussion with the mayor. That campus enrolls about 600 students, an increase over time. This is something that has been mentioned relative to other micropolitan cities: as recessions deepen, college enrollments tend to pick up as jobs become scarcer and people attempt to gain new and marketable skills and credentials. For example, this institution's enrollment increased between 2008 and 2010 by more than 22%.

At present, Newberry County's largest employers include Kraft Foods, the Georgia-Pacific Company, Newberry College, the hospital, Caterpillar, Walmart, and Komatsu. Numerous other manufacturers appear to give the economy some diversity, as do the presence of seven foreign-owned companies (all in the manufacturing sector). Caterpillar's 2010 plant expansion created 500 new jobs to manufacture generators. A question for the mayor would need to be whether they generate sufficient employment opportunities and tax revenues for the city.

Interview with the Honorable Foster Senn, Mayor of Newberry, South Carolina

The area around Newberry, South Carolina, like much of the southeast, was initially built on an agricultural base. The city itself resulted from the growth of the textile industry and was ultimately home to three mills, all of which closed in the 1970s due to the much lower labor rates that could be found overseas.

Mayor Senn describes how the town needed to "regroup," and did so by rebuilding its historic Opera House, which had slipped into disrepair over time. The Opera House had been built in 1882 and was home to traveling shows and vaudeville productions that had attracted many visitors to town for many years. Following the demise of the traveling shows, the theater remained in use for a time for moviegoers and was ultimately converted to an office building. In 1998, the leadership of Newberry decided to restore the building to its former luster and began to attract performers; today, 100 shows appear in the Opera House annually. This has, in turn, led to the creation of seven new restaurants and more upscale shops in the immediate area. Moreover, points out Mayor Senn, it has led to a revival of the community's pride in its downtown.

Complementing the revitalization of the downtown, Newberry has begun to climb out of the recession, although it still remains in the lower third of South Carolina's counties in terms of its unemployment rate. A Caterpillar plant that manufactures large industrial generators and a Komatsu plant are in town and help to stabilize the economy. There is also a Kraft plant that prepares and distributes turkey meat.

Higher education is another asset for economic development in Newberry. Newberry College and the Piedmont Technical College both partner with the city, although Mayor Senn is intent upon increasing those levels of collaboration. "We have been a town with colleges. We need to be a college town," the distinction being in the degree to which working together more will increasingly benefit all.

Small towns have both advantages and disadvantages, according to the mayor. They don't have all of the same resources and opportunities enjoyed by larger cities, however, a small town can "pull together" and rally around projects such as the Opera House. Mayor Senn encourages his constituents to "shop locally; it will help our local merchants succeed."

Indeed, in terms of lessons learned, Mayor Senn states that collaboration has to be the focus. A $20 million project is underway to convert an old mill to college dorms. This is a joint effort of the university, the county, and the town. The town has also devoted resources to cleaning up much of the area adjacent to the new dormitories. Another project—at the cost of $8 million—will convert an old

Walmart store into a technical training school. The second lesson: "In small towns, you have to work at it all the time. The watchwords are constant and active collaboration, not just cordial collaboration. We're just too small not to work together."

New Castle, Pennsylvania

New Castle sits in an advantageous geographic position for economic development, about 50 miles from Pittsburgh and 35 from Philadelphia. Its population has declined over recent years. Between 1990 and 2000, it dropped by 12%, from 29,849 to 26,309; and it declined by another 5% between 2000 and 2005, to 25,030 (US Beacon, 2012). The city's relative cost of living (18.4% below the national average) makes it an ideal bedroom community for the two larger cities. However, that could cause problems for the city's budget, depending upon how municipal budgets derive their revenues in the state of Pennsylvania. Certainly it is an apt topic for an interview with the mayor. Unemployment at 9.8% is slightly above the national average of 9.1%, and recent job growth is reported at –1.46%, also worse than the national average of –0.12% (http://www.bestplaces.net).

New Castle, Pennsylvania: Interview Declined

Nogales, Arizona

Nogales, Arizona is a border town. Much of the literature found in an Internet search addresses issues related to Nogales in that context: the relationship with the Sonoran state in Mexico. Given the location, the population of Nogales is a blend of the American, Mexican, and Native American cultures. This fact, as well as the city's location in the Sonoran Desert, creates opportunities for tourism and a range of educational endeavors.

Of course, its location as a major border crossing also creates challenges. The requirements for transportation and other infrastructure development and maintenance are significant. More people cross the Nogales Port of Entry than go through either Los Angeles International Airport or O'Hare Airport in Chicago per day (City of Nogales, 2010). It is possible that the need to provide service to these through-travelers is the reason for the significant job growth between 1990 and 2000 from 19,489 to 29,676 (52.3%), however, the level reflected in the 2010 census is only 20,837. This is an area to explore with Nogales' mayor.

The issue is also reflected in the rate of growth of Nogales' civilian labor force in the growth years of the 1990s: from 8,403 to 8,698, which is an increase of only 3.4% (City of Nogales General Plan, 2010). The current unemployment rate stands at 15% against a US national average of slightly over 9%. The current job growth rate at the time of this writing was also further into the negative in Nogales than the national average, –2.73% versus –0.12% (http://www.bestplaces.net).

But the primary issue relates to cross-border difficulties. Sonora on the Mexican side is reported to be the site of considerable drug-related criminal activity, including attacks by "hit squads." The violence has caused New Mexican and US officials to crack down on border crossings. Some of those retail store owners interviewed in a recent article (Bauge, 2011) said that as much as 80% of their sales come each year from Mexican residents who come to Nogales to shop. In a city that derives 100% of its revenues from sales taxes, this is not a good situation.

The impact of border crossings extends to the produce business quite notably. The city's website (Nogales USA, 2012) notes that in the winter months approximately 136,000 trucks carry Mexican produce to 70 Nogales-based warehouses where it is picked up for further distribution by 200,000 American trucks. "Nogales is the gateway for 50% of all fresh fruits and vegetables shipped into the United States from Mexico.

The budget issues are further exacerbated by the need to hire additional law enforcement officers. Perhaps the mayor can provide an answer about how to resolve the problems as they relate to the Nogales budget and can explain the effects on the state's resources as well.

Nogales, Arizona: Interview Declined

Ossining, New York

Located in Westchester County, situated along the banks of the Hudson River, Ossining (see Figure 6.47) is essentially a bedroom community for the city of New York. From 1825, the home of the infamous Sing Sing Prison, Ossining has a reputation not befitting the beauty of its setting. Its population has been relatively stable

Figure 6.47 Downtown Ossining, New York. (Courtesy of Ingrid Richards, Village of Ossining)

over time: it declined between 2000 and 2005 from 24,010 to 23,547 (–1.9%), but that followed the decade of the 1990s during which it had grown by 6.3%, from 22,582 (US Beacon, 2012).

As jobs in New York are often the objective, employment in Ossining tends to be service-oriented and retail, and the numbers tend to be fairly constant. Current unemployment rates are 6.3% in Ossining and 9.1% nationwide. Recent job growth has been in the negative at –1.73% whereas the US average is somewhat better, although still in the negative at –0.12% (http://www.bestplaces.net).

A 2008 consultant's report of the demand drivers for economic growth in the downtown indicated that the issues to be addressed by the village were a shortage of residential units in the downtown, a growing demand for workers, and a need to develop the waterfront areas more fully (City of Ossining Market Analysis, 2008). It was felt that one area of opportunity would be "downsizers" and Manhattanites seeking an alternative lifestyle. These conclusions led to others, including the need for convenience stores and personal services, themed restaurants, fitness clubs, family activities, and more.

Given the above descriptions and conclusions, topics for the interview with the mayor should include the use of the riverfront area for further economic development and the revitalization and preservation of the downtown area. Housing costs and housing shortages may also prove to be interesting topics.

Interview with the Honorable William Hanauer, Mayor of Ossining, New York

The New York village of Ossining, as is the case with many of the municipalities in the Empire State, suffers from the imposition of difficult tax policies by the state. The legislature imposed a tax cap on municipalities, said Mayor Hanauer, then promoted the notion that although they, the state legislators, had capped taxes, it is the local elected bodies that have reduced services.

Mayor Hanauer asserts that it is the tax revenues that were cut by the state that enabled the village of Ossining to provide public services to its residents, businesses, and visitors. Such policies by the legislature have meant that economic development has become an increasingly important area for the village of Ossining. An economic development staff person was recently engaged, although not at the expense of other tax-funded public services. Instead, the village was able to use some of the revenues it generated from the sale of waterfront properties along the Hudson River. Over the recent past, the economic mood has brightened somewhat and the outlook has become a bit more positive.

The mayor characterizes opportunities in the village as significant because it is "under *re*-developed." Old industrial space along the beautiful Hudson River is now being planned for high-end housing. The village sits on a train line that deposits riders at Grand Central Station in just 42 minutes. The mayor also notes that higher-end housing also has the benefit of having fewer children to be educated in public schools and thus lighter demands for public services. On the flip side, Mayor Hanauer is a strong advocate for the inclusion of the affordable housing that enables workers of all levels to live in Ossining. Today, any residential developer that builds at least six units must set aside 10% of their project for affordable housing.

In the downtown area, retailers are currently being sought to parallel the housing growth. Upscale retail helps to attract the high-end residential users who have greater expendable income. In turn, this generates sales tax revenues and helps to pay for public services that accommodate the growing residential population.

The lessons offered by Mayor Hanauer include the following: "Don't be bullied into doing something that isn't in the best interest of the village" (a reference to the state-imposed tax cap). As soon as possible, get someone to focus on redevelopment issues and opportunities. Beware of promising and not carrying through on those promises, "Lip-service benefits no one." Money spent on investments can yield benefits in the future. This comment is a reference to investments the village made on a water purification plant that will generate income for the village as well as reduce the expenditure made by the village to procure drinking water from New York City. Said Mayor Hanauer: "There are things communities can—*must*—do, even in the worst of times. You cannot let people begin to think, 'We cannot do this.' If it must be done, do it!"

Ottumwa, Iowa

Ottumwa's population has remained around the 24,000 range for many years: 24,488 in 1990, up 2.1% to 24,998 in 2000 and then down by −0.8% to 24,798 in 2005 (US Beacon, 2012). The cost of living in Ottumwa may be helping to sustain the population base, despite the city's economic trends: the cost of living in Ottumwa is more than 20% less than the US average. The current unemployment rate, however, is 8.1% (the US average is 9.1%); and the recent job growth numbers are in the negative at −0.22%, compared to the national average of −0.12% (http://www.bestplaces.net). The unemployment rate in Ottumwa today is reported to be the highest of any micropolitan city in the state of Iowa.

The loss of several manufacturing plants beginning as early as the 1960s spelled economic disaster for this micropolitan community. This was exacerbated by floods that damaged crops and chased away many residents from the region. Today's economic issues may also center around the regulations imposed on the economy and its municipalities by the state of Iowa. Numerous articles reference the need to ease up on the environmental regulations and rules that "interfere with Iowa's economic growth" (Newman, 2011).

Health care for the larger region provides many jobs as well. Ottumwa Regional Health Center accounts for 850 jobs. Its employees, by spending their salaries on goods and services, generate millions in tax revenues for the city. This is typical of many hub micropolitan cities. Ottumwa is located more than 80 miles from the next largest city, Des Moines; Cedar Rapids is over 100 miles away, and Omaha and Kansas City are both 220 miles distant. The catchment area for the city's businesses and other service providers includes a 10-county region. Within a 30-mile radius, there are more than 100,000 residents and, within a 60-mile radius, there are nearly 350,000 (City of Ottumwa, 2011).

Ottumwa, Iowa: Interview Declined

Owatonna, Minnesota

In this community, Owatonna, Minnesota (please see Figure 6.48), the population base is growing at a fairly strong pace. Between 1990 and 2000, the city grew from 19,386 residents to 22,434, or by 15.72%. Over the next five years, through 2005, it grew again by 7.57%, to 24,133, and again by the 2010 census to 25,599 (US Beacon, 2012). Good news for the local economy came in late December 2011, when a local business announced an expansion of its current operations, agreeing to lease an existing 141,000-square-foot facility and create 100 new jobs. Thus, the current unemployment level in Owatonna is 7.7%, less than the national average of 9.1%, although current job growth is down by –2.4%, perhaps reflecting a lack of momentum created by the earlier announcements (http://www.bestplaces.net).

Owatonna serves as a hub micropolitan city, providing retail and health care for a larger region. The closest large city is Rochester, Minnesota, which is nearly 40 miles away. The city's primary employers include manufactured glass products, electrical components, and metal working. Insurance carriers, retail, and public sector jobs round out the list.

Figure 6.48 A park in Owatonna, Minnesota. (Courtesy of Owatonna Area Chamber of Commerce and Tourism)

Interview with the Honorable Thomas Kuntz, Mayor of Owatonna, Minnesota

As a micropolitan city mayor, Thomas Kuntz has a relatively long tenure: nine years as mayor and a newly approved additional four-year term. However, as with many of his colleague mayors in this study, he is a lifelong resident of his city. The mayor left Minnesota for six years to serve in the US Air Force and returned to spend a 30-plus-year career, culminating as the head of the city's public utilities department. As do many of the others, Mayor Kuntz believes that his private sector experience gave him the skills needed to be successful in the public sector.

The economic mood in Owatonna is strong, according to the mayor, who characterizes the city as having been "blessed with a strong set of entrepreneurs back in the 1940s and 1950s who started a wide variety of businesses that were very diverse and that have become very successful." These include automotive tools manufacture, musical equipment and band risers, windows and window hardware, large-scale glass manufacture, and more. That diversity continues today in Owatonna and that has sustained the city through the recent recessionary periods.

The city has experienced difficult times for its budget during the current recession. Sales taxes are collected by the state of Minnesota and redistributed to the localities based on current relative need. Thus, although the economy of Owatonna is doing relatively well, the point-of-sales taxes are not benefiting the city as much as they had in the past. Recent revenues from that source are down from over $5 million to less than $2.5 million annually. As a result, the fiscal year 2013 budget for the city is at the same dollar level as that of fiscal year 2007. The city has had to freeze vacant positions and work smarter to continue public service levels.

Economic development targets for the city are, to a great extent, the businesses that are presently housed within the city limits. Mayor Kuntz places great value on growing the community's existing businesses. Often this has been done by connecting various resources in the city to one another. One such example is that of Cybex, a manufacturer of cardiovascular workout equipment. The company was encouraged to keep its 300 employees in Owatonna rather than relocate when the city and a private owner made a building available to the company at reduced costs. Such arrangements are important to the city because competition with other states that give land or cash incentives for economic development is, by the mayor's assessment, very intense.

Land is in short supply in Owatonna. Still, the city attempts to keep significant acreage free within the industrial park to accommodate a large user if one becomes interested. This points to the need to build teams in micropolitan cities that incorporate all relevant interests: "You need to know who in your community has connections, and make them all part of the team."

Figure 6.49 Enjoying the Tennessee and Ohio Rivers in Paducah, Kentucky. (Courtesy of City of Paducah)

Paducah, Kentucky

Paducah, Kentucky (please see Figure 6.49) has been losing its population base although not at alarming rates. Between 1990 and 2000, the base declined from 27,256 to 26,307, or 3.5%. From that point to 2005, it declined by another 2.8%, to 25,575 (US Beacon, 2012). The current level of unemployment is slightly greater than the US average of 9.1%, and now stands at 9.6%. On a positive note, although the US average of recent job growth has been in the negative at −0.12%, it is in the plus range in Paducah, at 2.5% (http://www.bestplaces.net).

With a range of manufacturing operations and a significant health care sector, Paducah's largest employers include Ingram Barge, Lourdes Hospital, and the county and city school systems. This diversity should be a topic of discussion for the mayor. The city has planned for its strategies looking forward 15 years, in a document available online entitled "Choices 2025." Several references to the need for a balance between economic development and other planning goals require follow-up with the mayor, as do statements regarding the need for greater coordination between various organizations within the city. Finally, Murray State University has a campus in Paducah so it would be of interest to see how they are involved in the economic development planning and programming.

The riverside location of Paducah helps to drive the city's overall economy. More than 90 million tons of cargo on 8,000 vessels pass by the city annually along the inland waterways. Paducah sits at the convergence of four rivers: the Mississippi, the Ohio, the Tennessee, and the Cumberland. This also gives Paducah immediate access to numerous major US cities, including the Port of New Orleans. Does the city take the best economic development advantage of these assets and their riverfront location? Do the Paducah Campus of the University of Kentucky and the West Kentucky Community and Technical College play roles in training people for relevant careers?

Sectors targeted for economic development outreach are stated as chemical manufacturing, maritime, and big-box retail. Does the mayor feel this will generate a sustainable and sufficiently diverse conomic base for the Paducah of the future?

Interview with the Honorable Bill Paxton, Mayor of Paducah, Kentucky

Although Paducah, Kentucky has seen "no home runs yet; we have been hitting singles and we have a very positive mood now," said its mayor, Bill Paxton. The city waterfront provides a strong economic development asset and has resulted in 24 riverboat companies located in Paducah. Mayor Paxton estimates that about 5,000 men and women are employed in river-related industries. Coupled with the recent purchase of a building in the city's industrial park by American Electric Power, the outlook is strong.

An additional asset in Paducah is the nation's sole remaining uranium plant, which now employs roughly 1,200 people directly and supports thousands more in the support economy. Paducah identified collaboration between the public and private sectors as a strategy for the promotion and acceleration of economic growth. Mayor Paxton proudly relates that the effort has been successful and that local senior business executives are actively engaged in city planning and policy discussions. "We're all on the same page," he said, "the economic development group, the city, the business community, and our residents."

The economic development organization in Paducah is a public–private joint venture into which the city invests $600,000 and the private sector the balance of a $1.5 million budget. In addition, the state and the county invest more resources in the form of various economic development incentive programs to attract and retain businesses.

Mayor Paxton also noted that Paducah's success in diversifying its tax base has led to stability in the quality and quantity of public services for the community. Payroll taxes and a 2% sales tax provide the basis for most general fund expenditures, bolstered by a property tax which has, during Mayor Paxton's 12-year term, been reduced from the level of $.40 per $100 of assessed value to $.25.

Paducah is a hub micropolitan community, serving as the center for health services and retail for a wide region that reaches toward Nashville and Memphis to the north and St. Louis to the south. This is why medical services are strong in Paducah, which has two large hospitals employing a total of 6,000 to 7,000 people. These have helped to offset the loss of jobs in the 1960s at the uranium plant as a result of issues related to the union. The city had to recover and diversify its job base to avoid such extreme dislocation in the future.

As is the case with many of the other mayors in this research, Mayor Paxton is a former businessman with 30 years of experience as a bank executive. He firmly believes that this has helped him be more effective as the mayor of Paducah, a post he accepted (again, like many of his peers) simply to "do some good" in his community. Perhaps another outgrowth of not being a professional politician, Mayor Paxton sees his role as that of a "servant of the public." Still, he believes that a mayor need not be overly cautious before doing what he believes is the right thing to do. "You don't have to put your finger up to test the political winds before making decisions. Just do what is right." This works better if one follows Mayor Paxton's second admonition: "Hire strong professionals and let the city manager be the CEO. Think of the council as the board of directors and the mayor as the chairman of the board."

Another lesson Mayor Paxton has learned is to collaborate whenever possible. Paducah and the surrounding county are considering the creation of regional government operations. "It would give us additional clout in Frankfurt (Kentucky's capital) and in Washington, DC." When asked what else Paducah required to sustain its economic growth over time, the mayor indicated that being a right-to-work state would heighten their comparative advantage when speaking to potential businesses. Today, the neighboring states of Indiana, Tennessee, and Georgia have that competitive edge for business attraction.

A final lesson learned by Mayor Paxton is that a lean city government staff can still get the job done. Thirty-two positions have been cut from the city rolls but the provision of public services has not suffered and, in fact, Paducah has recently been assigned an AA bond rating, enabling the city to save millions of dollars. This, in turn, has enabled the city to add a performing arts center in the downtown area, new parks and trails, and more.

Paramus, New Jersey

Paramus sits on the banks of the Hudson River looking across at the upper west side of Manhattan. As a bedroom community to New York City, its own local economy can be vibrant if the source of the city's budget is income taxes. If, however, the primary source is from the real estate tax base, economic growth can be based on services that support the businesses in the city that want or need to be close by but seek out the lower lease rates of New Jersey. The assumption must be made that there are many services businesses in Paramus that support the needs of Manhattan because the daytime population is significantly higher than the nighttime population, which is in the mid-20s. By day, the city is host to an estimated 52,645 people (National League of Cities, 2011). These would be good discussion points for the mayor.

Population growth in the city has been steady but fractional. Between 1990 and 2000, the base grew by 2.67%, from 25,067 to 25,737; and between 2000 and 2005 it grew by 3.14% to a total of 26,545 (US Beacon, 2012). The unemployment rate follows that of New York more closely than it does that of the nation. At this writing, the national average stood at 9.1% and it was 7.3% in Paramus. Recent job growth was in the negative at −0.78%, somewhat less than the national average of −0.12% (http://www.bestplaces.net).

Paramus, New Jersey: Interview Declined

Picayune, Mississippi

Picayune (please see Figure 6.50) is at the low end of the population range to qualify as a micropolitan city. Its population base in 2010 of 10,878 is just slightly greater than the reported level of 1990: 10,633 (US Beacon, 2012). At the time of this writing, the national unemployment rate sat at 8.6% and the rate in Picayune went into double figures at 10.6% (http://www.bestplaces).

The city of Picayune derives more than 50% of its tax base from sales taxes. One would assume that economic development in Picayune is planned to attract retailers and others who generate sales taxes for the city as well as jobs for its residents.

Interview with the Honorable Ed Pinero, Mayor of Picayune, Mississippi

Although Mayor Ed Pinero is not a native of Picayune (he grew up as a "service brat"), he moved to the city as a teenager and attended the city high school, and has now lived there for 36 years. Mayor Pinero, as are most of the other mayors interviewed

Figure 6.50 Historic downtown Picayune, Mississippi. (Courtesy of City of Picayune)

herein, is not a career politician and has no interest in "higher" office. Possessing a PhD in international development, he has worked as a public servant as well as an adjunct faculty member throughout his professional career. He believes that, by not being a career politician, and because he has no further political objectives, he can be more effective as mayor of Picayune. It enables him to do what he believes is best for the city and its people. "I don't need to worry about votes or the next election."

The city is located in close proximity (a 45-minute drive) to a variety of economic development hot spots, including New Orleans, Hattiesburg, and the Stennis Space Flight Center. It is also widely reputed as "the first high and dry ground" coming from New Orleans. This gives the city a great advantage for residential construction. It has also prompted some commercial growth; a new manufacturing plant will employ 300 people, new restaurants and retailers have announced locations near the site, and the city has recently completed a new $70 million hospital center.

The economic development planning for the city focuses on taking maximum advantage of these proximate assets. Much of the planning is conducted in conjunction with Mississippi State University, which has finished several needs assessment studies for the city and, in itself, represents a strong and well-acknowledged economic development asset for Picayune.

Much of the economic development focus for the city going forward centers around the Stennis Space facility, and includes businesses involved in various areas of aeronautics, polymer production, and hospitality. The latter is advantageous for the city because it has a 7% sales tax and a 1% tax on all restaurant and hotel sales that accrue to the city coffers, and represents more than half of the city's budget revenues. In fact, the city recently annexed additional contiguous parcels equating to more than five square miles in order to enhance its tax base from the sales tax revenues in that area. Twenty businesses thus became resident within the city limits of Picayune.

After being mayor for more than three years (Mayor Pinero did not previously serve on the city council), he is able to offer several lessons for other micropolitan mayors. "First, invest in the infrastructure. I campaigned on the promise to pave all the city's streets, not just those in some neighborhoods. And we did all of them in the first year. Companies looking for manufacturing sites don't want to dodge potholes and they don't just drive through their downtown or in certain neighborhoods. They drive the back roads, too." And, most of the water infrastructure has also been updated.

A second lesson from Mayor Pinero echoes one heard from several of the other mayors in the study: "Never make a decision because it helps you get re-elected; only do things on the basis of what's good for your city."

Placentia, California

Placentia, California was first settled in 1837 but remained a small community in terms of area until the 1960s when the annexation of surrounding land increased both the size of the city and its population. In that decade, the city grew from about 5,000 to 25,000 inhabitants. From 1990 on, the population base grew again: first, by 12.7% between 1990 and 2000 (41,259 to 46,488) and then again over the next five years by 7.1%, to a total of 49,795 (US Beacon, 2012). A point of inquiry for the mayor is whether that growth is expected to continue and whether the infrastructure and amenities are in place to support further growth, and whether the budget can also grow sufficiently to accommodate it.

The current employment situation in Placentia appears sluggish but, at least by national standards, is in relatively good shape, although the current unemployment rate is at 8.1% (the national average is 9.1%) and the recent job growth is registered at –1.04% (the national average is –0.12%; http://www.bestplaces.net).

Placentia's labor force must be considered a strong economic development asset as 82% of the adult residents of Placentia have a college diploma or greater. Perhaps as a consequence, the rate of poverty is comparatively low at only 8.5%. Agriculture, particularly citrus crops, is an important part of the local economy and is complemented by nearly 40% of the employment base being in management and professional positions and nearly 29% in sales.

Placentia, California: Interview Declined

Plainfield, New Jersey

Plainfield, New Jersey is a typical bedroom community, in this case to New York City. As such, its fortunes are, at least to some extent, tied to the city it "serves." This may help to explain recent trends in the population base of the city. Between 1990 and 2000, Plainfield's population, which is approaching two-thirds black, rose by more than 2.7%, from 45,567 to 47,829. However, from that point until 2005, the population base declined by nearly 4% to 47,642 (US Beacon, 2012).

Unemployment in Plainfield at the time of this writing has exceeded 14%, which is more than 50% higher than the national average of 9.1% at the time. Furthermore, recent US job growth had been reported as –0.12% whereas that of Plainfield had declined about two and one-half times faster (–0.31%; www.bestplaces.net).

Plainfield, New Jersey: Interview Declined

Plattsburgh, New York

The micropolitan city of Plattsburgh, New York sits right on the US border with Canada. Its population base registered a significant decline between 1990 and 2000, dropping from 28,012 to 18,816. That trend reversed itself from that time through to the census report of 2010, which shows Plattsburgh's population as 19,989 (US Beacon, 2012). The mayor should be asked to explain why the decline occurred as well as the reversal in that trend.

Local press coverage suggests that economic development needs Plattsburgh to include downtown revitalization projects, particularly along the city's waterfront; the development of affordable housing of various styles and price levels; and a variety of infrastructural improvements. The closing of the Plattsburgh Air Force Base in the fall of 1995 damaged the local economy but left a property with facilities and infrastructure that could be marketed by the city through a redevelopment corporation. This represents an economic development asset that can be used to advantage. Another potential asset for economic growth is Plattsburgh State College, which is a branch of SUNY (the State University of New York) and which may be engaged in the economic development program. Again, this should be raised with the mayor when interviewed.

Plattsburgh, New York: Interview Declined

Ponca City, Oklahoma

Ponca City sits in the heart of Oklahoma's oil industry. Over time, the city's fortunes as well as its population base have reflected the trends of the day in that sector. Between 1990 and 2000, that meant a decline in the residential base of about 3.3%, from 26,359 to 25,919, and again through 2005 to 25,070 (US Beacon, 2012). The unemployment rate at the time of this writing stood at 7%, compared to the national average of 9.1%. And, current job growth was at −5.0%, a far greater measure of job loss than the national average of −0.12% (http://www.bestplaces.net).

A very interesting topic for discussion with the mayor would be the extent to which a further diversification of the economic base is being pursued. There is some indication that such is the case. As Ponca City is concerned, the experience with Conoco exemplifies the economic history. In the 1980s, Conoco had about 5,000 employees working in and around Ponca City. By 1993, the number was down to 1,400, still a large number, and the $40 million payroll sustained the city's economy. In 2002, Conoco merged with Phillips Petroleum and many of the jobs departed for Houston. Today, the city's website cites the local employment as 860.

There are references in the press about the effects on the city's psyche. Perhaps the mayor can enlighten readers as to how a city can recover from economic impacts that are so strong that they not only mean job loss but a loss of collective pride and drive. Another element of the latter impact has been, in other cities, a return to the past. That is, residents preferred to return to a solely oil-based economy. This is what they know. Did this happen in Ponca City and, if so, how were expectations managed and how were new targets developed?

There is some evidence in the local media of other business sectors emerging. Oklahoma State University may play a role in that economic growth and diversification. In 2007, Dorada Foods completed a 180,000-square-foot facility, adding $200 million to the economy over 10 years and creating 350 new jobs. Still, the city's largest employers are responsive to economic development rather than creators of growth in primary economic sectors. They include the public school system (800 employees), a medical center (460 employees), Walmart (400 workers), and the city itself (384 employees). What industries will the city pursue as part of its future growth?

Ponca City, Oklahoma: Interview Declined

Portsmouth, Ohio

Portsmouth, Ohio, among the micropolitan cities in this study, has experienced one of the higher rates of population decline over the past generation. The city's population had peaked in the 1950s (at about 34,000) but that base declined as foreign competition forced the local steel plant to shut down in the 1980s. The population declined by nearly 8% between 1990 and 2000, from 22,676 to 20,909; and by another 4% by 2005 (20,101; US Beacon, 2012). The population levels of the past 20 years do not fully reflect the losses of this community. The population of Portsmouth in the 1950s was more than 36,000.

Despite having fewer workers in the labor pool, the unemployment rate in Portsmouth is currently nearly 12%, far higher than an already high US average of 9.1%. The rate of recent job growth is a stunning −1.72%, far worse than the national average of −0.12% (http://www.bestplaces.net).

Like many cities of all sizes, when the jobs leave, the best of the workers also leave. They are the ones who have the requisite skills to be in demand elsewhere. Those left behind have fewer skills, fewer jobs, and less pay, and that translates into a declining tax base to provide the public services that are suddenly in greater demand than ever. Unemployment and poverty often give way to increased rates of crime. In Portsmouth, an underground trade in drug trafficking has emerged and has given way to a steady rise in accidental deaths from overdoses. Nearly 10% of last year's newborns countywide (Appalachian County) tested positive for drugs (Tavernise, 2011). What can the mayor do to improve such conditions and to improve the perception of the city among site location decision makers?

The city does have two evident economic development assets: a riverfront area, which brings river cruises by the town and thus represents a potential tourism draw; and a university, Shawnee State. However, much of the city is reported to be suffering from the deterioration of various properties. A topic for the mayor would be whether there are plans for how those sites can be cleaned up and used for the future economic development of Portsmouth.

Portsmouth, Ohio: Interview Declined

Pottsville, Pennsylvania

Pottsville's (please see Figure 6.51) population base has been in steady decline for the past 20 years. The 1990 level of more than 16,600 was reduced to slightly more than 14,300 by the 2010 census reports (US Beacon, 2012).

Figure 6.51   Nestled along Sharp Mountain in Pottsville, Pennsylvania. (Courtesy of City of Pottsville)

In the early part of the twentieth century, Pottsville's "... coal boom had brought a wave of immigration from Poland, Germany, Lithuania, and Ireland. Now almost 30% of Pottsville's population is made up of first- and second-generation Americans" (Fleming, 2007).

Interview with the Honorable John Reiley, Mayor of Pottsville, Pennsylvania

John Reiley has been the mayor of Pottsville, Pennsylvania for 12 years, having succeeded his son in the post. He, like many of his colleague mayors in micropolitan cities, is a native of Pottsville and has no intention of running for "higher" elective office.

Pottsville sits at the gateway to the Keystone State's anthracite region and because it is 66 miles from its closest neighbor (Scranton), it is a hub micropolitan city. Pottsville is an old city with aging infrastructure and little land available for additional development. Once the mines were closed, Pottsville and the state began trying to reclaim some of the land for additional new development but the city is bordered by Sharp Mountain which, according to the mayor's description, is too steep and unstable (although some of the mines have now been filled in) to allow actual development. Access roads up the mountain have been cut in switchback patterns and resemble bobsled runs.

Within the city limits, narrow streets and narrow lots mean that the only way new construction—either residential or commercial—can take place is by first tearing down existing structures. Nonetheless, a 45,000-square-foot medical arts building was recently completed and construction on a 12,000-square-foot office building will begin soon. These additions are vitally important to the city as it derives its budgetary revenues from real estate taxes as well as various user fees and assessments.

In situations like this, cities such as Pottsville must depend heavily on volunteerism. The Volunteer Fire Department not only protects the city but also raises its own funding. Mayor Reiley notes that, "If we had to pay for that, we'd be broke." The city, at one time, served as the regional shopping hub for the greater region but has lost that role to malls and big-box retailers located outside the city limits. It is now serving a similar function, however, for banking needs and health care services. Several public sector employers, including a jail and two prisons (one federal and one state) help to diversify the economy as well as provide job opportunities for the residents of Pottsville.

Reaching a conclusion about lessons learned in his experience was easy for Mayor Reiley. "You have to get the citizens involved. Volunteers keep us going and keep the costs down. And, they do a great job." Volunteerism in micropolitan communities must also be seen to include contributions from local business owners. One local business picked up the tab for the city's recent bicentennial celebration: Yuengling Breweries is a homegrown business and does much for the city while getting "not nearly enough credit for it!"

Poughkeepsie, New York

Poughkeepsie possesses several assets for economic growth. Perhaps as a result, this upstate New York micropolitan city has also seen modest population growth. Between 1990 and 2000, the city's base grew by 3.6%, from 28,844 to 29,087. By 2005, the total rose by 1.62% more, to 30,355 (US Beacon, 2012). Still, the unemployment rate currently sits right at the 9.1% national average, and recent job growth is in the red at −1.48%, compared to the national average of −0.12% (http://www.bestplaces.net).

As Vassar College is located in the city, perhaps the mayor can address how an institution of such great reputation is involved in the economic development efforts although, given the level of unemployment, a side issue will be the question of a brain drain from the city and the region. Another topic for discussion with the mayor would be the extent to which the riverfront is used for economic development purposes.

Finally, given the press coverage of the relatively high tax position of the State of New York, the mayor's perspective on whether being in the Empire State is a help or a hindrance when it comes to attracting and keeping companies in Poughkeepsie should be enlightening. The Federal Reserve Board of Buffalo issued a recent report that noted that "… an important long-term trend shaping the region's economic conditions and prospects is the significant out-migration of the population over the past three decades … represents a self-reinforcing trend that is gaining momentum and exerting a drag on upstate New York's economy and growth potential." (Abel and Dietz, 2008)

Poughkeepsie, New York: Interview Declined

Pullman, Washington

Pullman, Washington (please see Figure 6.52) has seen a steady growth in its population base over the past 30 years. The 1990 level was 23,478; by 2000, the level had risen only to 24,675. However, by 2010, the base had grown to 29,799 (US Beacon, 2012). Questions for Mayor Johnson should focus on why the increases occurred and how the city and the region have accommodated the resultant marginal costs of providing public services.

Current unemployment levels are running about two-thirds of the national average (6.9% versus 9.1%; http://www.bestplaces.net). The majority of the relevant press coverage of business or economic growth in Pullman relates to retail outlets and restaurants. This raises the question of how the city builds the municipal budget. If sales taxes are a critical portion of the whole, these efforts are logical economic development strategies. This should be covered in the interview with the mayor.

One article describes the local attitudes toward development as "blasé" (Nicolau, 2008). The argument is made that the community and many of its key citizens are so intent upon relying on agriculture as the primary economic driver that they are reluctant to allow the growth of retail opportunities in the city. Notably, this was written before the onset of the current recession (in the summer of 2008). Perhaps Mayor Johnson can shed some light on more current attitudes toward economic development.

Figure 6.52 Downtown Pullman, Washington at night. (Courtesy of Robert Hubner)

Finally, the region is home to two universities, Washington State University and the University of Idaho, just across the border. Jointly, they employ more than 10,000 people. In most micropolitan "college towns," this level of academic presence both sustains the economy through difficult macroeconomic times and contributes to thought leadership in the community as well as supporting business growth through training, retraining, and technology transfer and company start-ups. The question for the mayor of Pullman should be whether and the extent to which this has happened in and around Pullman.

A final area of inquiry should focus on the positive and negative attributes of existing in a multistate region.

Interview with the Honorable Glenn Johnson, Mayor of Pullman, Washington

To some extent, Pullman, as have many other micropolitan cities, has found its municipal budget negatively affected by the recession as much due to state actions as to local economic stress. The state has cut back on appropriations to Washington's 281 cities and has made legislative decisions that have had further negative impacts on the localities and their ability to provide public services to their residents. One example is the decision to sell the state's liquor stores to private vendors. Although the move provided one-time revenues for the state, it cost the localities, which derived some of their revenues from the taxes generated by the state-owned operations.

Pullman's mayor, Glenn Johnson, understands these impacts as well as anyone; he has served as the chairman of the state's association of cities. He explains that Pullman and the others must rely on growth in the private sector to generate additional revenues. As the budget is based primarily on real estate and sales taxes, the attrition of both primary businesses and retailers is critical.

But, Pullman, Washington has an additional advantage in sustaining their local economy, Washington State University. In addition to attracting visitors and generating jobs, the university contributes to the tax base. State law dictates that, unless a building is dedicated to either research or bioscience, the university must pay real estate taxes on it, even though Washington State University is a state institution.

Moreover, the university is a generator of new businesses. Perhaps the best example is Schweitzer Engineering Labs. The company makes protective relays for electrical utilities and is a spinoff from the university. Today, with 1,900 employees, it has its thirteenth building in Pullman under construction, and has "grown right through the recession." Another WSU spinoff is Decagon Devices, which manufactures moisture detection meters that are used in everything from food service operations to the Mars Rover.

For many years, Mayor Johnson expressed, students from the university would graduate and leave the area for jobs in California. They have now begun to return to Washington to enjoy the benefits of life in a smaller town. Although this trend is favored by the mayor and the city, it means additional demands for public services at a time when budgetary pressures are substantial. Again, the state of Washington has made matters more difficult for its municipalities by enacting a law that permits cities to raise the local real estate tax by no more than 1% annually. This does protect property owners, but it hampers the ability of local governments to provide education and other critical services to their residents, especially at a time when state allocations are declining and sales tax revenues have declined.

Mayor Johnson is a little different from many of his peers in this research in that he is not a native of the city he leads. He came from California to teach at the university and stayed because he likes the slower pace and the relatively low crime rates in Pullman. He is similar in that he has no interest in statewide elective office, although he has been asked. This is more typical of micropolitan city mayors than of their counterparts in larger conurbations.

When asked about what lessons he has learned having been mayor since 2004, he notes the need to diversify the local economy and to help new enterprises grow and become successful. He also stresses the need for smaller cities such as Pullman to diversify their revenue streams to the extent possible. That, however, is limited to those revenues and the limits allowed under state legislation. Mayor Johnson also mentions the need to ensure that the infrastructure is in place to support business growth as it occurs and to have strategic plans that look well into the future.

Quincy, Illinois

Named in honor of America's sixth chief executive, John Quincy Adams, this micropolitan city (please see Figure 6.53) lays claim to another bit of the nation's history: it was the site of an 1857 Lincoln–Douglas debate. And, although there is much Civil War-era history in the region as well, one of the defining demographic characteristics of Quincy is its homogeneity: in 2010, nearly 93% of its residents are characterized as white. Less than 1% of the population of the city is Hispanic and only about .7% is Asian. More important in demographic terms is the fact that about 40% of the adult population of Quincy possesses less than a high school diploma. The total population base has remained somewhat steady over time, climbing from the 1990 level of 39,681 to 40,366 by 2000, but shrinking back to 39,841 by 2005, and returning to a level of 40,633 in the 2010 census (US Beacon, 2012).

Recent job growth is reported as being not only negative, but significantly more negative than the US average for recent job growth. Furthermore, despite the fact that more than 83.5% of the city's jobs are categorized as being white-collar positions, per capita income in Quincy is reported as being substantially lower than the US average, at $21,623 and $27,067, respectively (http:www.americantowns.com/il/quincy 2011).

Figure 6.53 A park in the middle of downtown Quincy, Illinois. (Courtesy of Travis M. Brown)

The Mississippi River overflows its banks periodically and that has caused significant damage to both the physical plant of the city and the local economy. A 1993 flood, for example, displaced 16,000 residents, closed more than 300 businesses, and left 10,000 people without work. The damages exceeded $600 million and deprived the city of an estimated 40% of its sales tax base. It is hard for a city to recover from such devastation and it is hard to recover the will of the populace to rebuild. These should be interesting topics for discussion with Mayor Spring.

Interview with the Honorable John Spring, Mayor of Quincy, Illinois

Mayor John Spring of Quincy, Illinois is a pragmatist. He regards the economic mood in his city as improved from the previous year or two but he also acknowledges that much of his city's resiliency is based on a diverse economic base that includes manufacturing, professional services, and retail. Reductions in force in the numerous manufacturing companies had lifted the unemployment rate in Quincy to the fifth highest in the state of Illinois.

In the last two years, two new companies have come to town and helped to lower the unemployment rate. The city has done its share as well by implementing reductions in force through early retirements, position freezes, and mandatory furloughs of city employees. The city's budget has suffered as a result of lost income and sales taxes. Yet Mayor Spring reports that the city has managed to reduce the tax burden on residents over the past two years in order to help them manage their own financial situations.

Quincy has an advantage for economic development in that it serves as a regional hub for an area that includes part of Illinois as well as northeastern Missouri. As the only sizable municipality in the greater region, Quincy has become the retail and financial hub as well as the medical services center for the population of both the city and its environs. Like other micropolitan communities, Quincy has capitalized on this position through outreach to other nearby communities and by encouraging a regional collaboration with them. Mayor Spring noted that the city and the region learned the necessity for doing so following severe flooding in 1993. The "great dialogue" that resulted from that experience has been embraced ever since.

The diversification of the city's economic base is a strong factor for stability as cited by Mayor Spring. Older manufacturing companies have been converting to more advanced forms of manufacturing; there are 26 trucking companies that operate out of Quincy, and there are technology research interests in the city. There are railroads and related businesses as well as two daily Amtrak routes to and from Chicago. The various transportation connections have spawned new businesses in Quincy as well as enabled its residents to travel easily to employment opportunities elsewhere. It has also enabled students to travel to the many colleges and universities that are located along that route. Finally, the local airport runs six daily flights to and from St. Louis, about 120 miles away. In fact, 7% of the city's working residents leave Quincy each day for work and about 30% of the jobs in the city are filled by in-commuters.

But, Mayor Spring is aware that there is work still to be done. The loss of manufacturing jobs has resulted in residents taking jobs with local retailers in positions that generally do not pay as well. The Quincy experience underscores the problems of underemployment in micropolitan communities. The loss of a single employer or a single industry, if substantial enough, can mean that the situation can be somewhat misunderstood: although residents are reported as fully employed, their diminished expendable incomes affect not only local retailer and service providers but the local tax base as well. Mayor Spring agrees, noting that what Quincy needs is "more head of household jobs."

Another missing asset in Quincy is sufficient housing that can be afforded by young people at the beginning of their careers. He feels strongly that the attraction and retention of young people with technical skills is a requisite for sustained economic growth. Related to this is his perceived need to improve public education at a time when state expenditures are being reduced. This and other intercommunity issues have led Mayor Spring to the strong belief that collaboration with leaders outside Quincy is vital and this includes communities in Missouri and Iowa as well. As he put it, "We need to be sure that what is good for Quincy is also good for Keokuk." This, too, is a recurring theme in the interviews with the mayors of America's micropolitan cities.

Mayor Spring is not unusual in another respect. Like many of his peers around the country, he is only the seventh mayor to serve a second term since the city was incorporated in 1840. As many of these cities are not like the municipalities within major metropolitan areas, neither are the mayors full-time nor paid well enough to allow people to serve as full-time officials. Mayors in these communities tend to do their civic duty and get back to their own businesses or professions and to helping support their families.

When discussing the future of micropolitan communities, Mayor Spring joins his colleagues in noting that these locations, because they can be relatively isolated, tend to have something for everyone. Furthermore, there is the same range of opportunity as in major metropolitan areas to engage in leadership positions, but with fewer people. This makes their futures bright as many people want the traditional values and the closeness of relationships that can be found in the micropolitan communities of America.

Roanoke Rapids, North Carolina

The economy of Roanoke Rapids, North Carolina benefits from its natural advantage: its location on Interstate Highway 95 about midway between New York and Florida. However, although the regional economy has grown to provide services to travelers, the impact on the city may tell another story. This would be an interesting topic for the mayor to discuss.

Within the city of Roanoke Rapids, population has declined in recent years. Between 1990 and 2000, the population increased by nearly 8%, from 15,727 to 16,957, but between 2000 and 2005, it declined by nearly 3% to 16,458 (US Beacon, 2012). The economy, however, has been somewhat less stable, reflecting a current unemployment rate of 12%, exceeding the national average of 9.1% by a third. Recent job growth is in far greater decline than the national average of −0.12%. In Roanoke Rapids, it has been −2.85% (http://www.bestplaces.net).

In a region that 76,000 people call home, Roanoke Rapids has become more of a retail center and less of a residential community. This could be OK with city leaders, depending upon how their local budgets are constituted; if they are largely based on sales tax revenues, they could be very pleased with these trends because they were collecting the tax revenues and not having to provide more public education and other services to their residents. If, however, the tax base is more dependent upon real estate taxes, they may have a significant problem. This would serve as an interesting topic of discussion with the mayor.

The growth around the city provides both challenges and opportunities. Growth of a nearby regional airport would be an opportunity to bring more people to shopping in the city. However, retail centers generally attract the types of big-box retailers that make it difficult for the smaller "mom and pop" shops to survive. The mayor will be able to shed light on that issue as well. This density of retail may be regarded locally as a positive, however, sprawl throughout the region may have become a resultant issue for Roanoke Rapids. This would be an interesting topic for discussion with the mayor as well, as sprawl is more generally thought of as a problem in major metropolitan areas rather than micropolitan communities.

The city is not, however, without expansions. An early-2011 announcement resulted in the addition of more than 500 jobs at one local food production plant. The press reported the reaction of the elected officials in the community and the state as hopeful that the expansion would have trickle-down effects, creating additional jobs in the secondary and tertiary economies' jobs as well as additional tax revenues for the city.

Roanoke Rapids, North Carolina: Interview Declined

Rolla, Missouri

Rolla, Missouri (please see Figure 6.54) has enjoyed steady and significant population growth over the past two decades, growing from the 1990 census level of just over 14,000 to its 2005 level of 17,392. The 2010 census report showed the city at a level of 19,559 (US Beacon, 2012). Over the course of the current recession, Rolla has managed to keep its unemployment rate low (7.9%) relative to the 9.1% US average (http://www.bestplaces.net).

The Missouri University of Science and Technology, with more than 6,000 students, is located in Rolla and has recently created a business park, although it is unclear from the media coverage whether the park exists for companies grown within the university itself or simply exists as a commercial office park owned by

Figure 6.54   Connections to Rolla, Missouri. (Courtesy of Scott Grahl, City of Rolla)

204 ■ *The Economic Viability of Micropolitan America*

the university and available to outside tenants. This is a topic for elaboration by the mayor.

There is evidence that Rolla serves as a hub micropolitan city by providing the retail and health care needs of the larger (south-central Missouri) region. This has prompted recent growth in the facilities by, and the employment of, both Phelps County Regional Medical Center and St. John's Mercy Healthcare System. That growth has been timely because it has helped to offset the loss of thousands of manufacturing jobs in the region, including the 1,100-position loss at the local Briggs and Stratton plant in late 2007.

Nearly one in four jobs in Rolla and the surrounding counties is in the public sector. A topic for discussion with the mayor would be whether that represents a comfortable balance in the employment base or whether that is a cause of concern. Current primary employers in Rolla include the Phelps County Regional Medical Center, with 1,500 employees, the Missouri University of Science and Technology, with nearly 2,000 jobs, and a Walmart distribution center that employs about 1,000 people.

Fort Leonard Wood, and its nearly 70,000 soldiers, is located in the larger region and the city may benefit from its proximity, particularly in terms of the opportunities that creates for the hotel, restaurant, and hospitality industry, but that would have to be reviewed with the mayor to evaluate.

Interview with the Honorable William Jenks, Mayor of Rolla, Missouri

After six years as the mayor of Rolla, Missouri, Bill Jenks is more convinced than ever that micropolitan cities benefit from having people serve in elective office who have backgrounds in the business community. "They understand cash flow, making payroll, and job creation." He attests that it has enabled him to better serve the people of Rolla.

Rolla, he believes, has survived the recession "fairly well." The economic base both benefits and suffers due to the significant number of public sector institutions in the community. These include a major regional hospital, a facility for the US Geological Survey, an office of the US Forestry Service, and the US Army's Fort Leonard Wood. Although the facilities are not liable for taxes themselves, their employees do pay taxes and spend their salaries in the local economy. They also help sustain revenue levels for the city and that enables the ongoing provision of public services at a constant level.

The Rolla budget has remained flat during the recent recessionary years. Position freezes have helped the city to avoid significant layoffs caused by the flat budget and generally rising costs. Real estate revenues are helpful but the city cannot raise the annual rate by more than $1 per year without going to a referendum, which has not occurred during Mayor Jenks' six-year tenure. Furthermore, real estate taxes represent only about $1 million of the $26 million in the annual budget, whereas 54% of the city's revenues are derived from sales taxes.

Thus, the city is interested in new retail openings including, most recently a Kohl's department store, but has enjoyed perhaps more impressive success in spin-off businesses from the University of Missouri/Rolla. One such business is Brewer's Scientific, which has created 250 jobs and now holds three-fourths of the world's market for miniaturized semiconductors, according to the mayor. In another example, a university professor has commercialized his technology that enables automobile rearview mirrors to switch from day to night driving more readily as well as glass beads that are presently being used in such widely varied applications as treating cancer to improving night-vision goggles. These jobs—based in newer technologies—are a positive improvement over the types and salaries of the jobs lost due to competition from outside the United States, notably China. However, the numbers do not represent a complete recovery.

When asked about lessons learned, Mayor Jenks notes that the attraction of retail businesses is a very competitive process. The companies want land and development concessions that sometimes appear to be unreasonable in light of the trade-offs. However, the citizens need these amenities and often will support deals that are not advantageous enough for the community. Retail is particularly important to Rolla and cities of its size that are as isolated as is Rolla: two hours from Springfield, Missouri, two hours from St. Louis, and nearly that to Jefferson City. People in the community need to have shopping available.

Ruston, Louisiana

Population growth in Ruston, Louisiana (please see Figure 6.55) has continued although the rate of the growth has slowed in recent years. Between 1990 and 2000, the city grew from 20,027 to 20,546, an increase of 2.6%. From that point to 2005, the increase was only by 0.6% to 20,667 (US Beacon, 2012). The population loss is being driven by an economy that is also on the incline. The unemployment rate in Ruston, at the time of this writing, had reached 9.2%, slightly higher than the national average of 9.1%, but recent job growth was well into the positive range at +1.54% whereas the national average was in decline, losing jobs in the recent period at a rate of −0.12% (http://www.bestplaces.net).

One key ingredient of recent job growth has been growth of the programs at Louisiana Tech. The university has created an Enterprise Center and business incubator to facilitate the growth of spinoff technology companies in the community. The community, which is also home to Grambling University, has the dual benefits of the impacts of their hiring and spending as well as the opportunities to use both in their economic development planning. It should be a key element of the discussion with the mayor to assess how these universities are engaged in economic development and whether there are unique programs that might

Figure 6.55 Strong partnerships in Ruston, Louisiana. (Courtesy of City of Ruston)

be emulated by other micropolitan cities with higher education institutions in their midst.

Following the decline of the oil industry in the 1980s, the city of Ruston needed to seek other employment opportunities for its residents. Efforts to diversify the economy, including serving as the entire region's source of health services, retail, and other services, while still benefiting from the presence of the two universities, would be another topic for discussion for the mayor, as would be the need for, and success of, regional efforts to attract economic growth in a relatively isolated area such as Ruston.

Furthermore, a regional airport serves the community and supports tourism efforts, creates jobs, and generates tax revenues. Other expanding industries include timber (Weyerhaeuser), poultry, and cattle farming. Numerous manufacturing concerns help round out a diverse local economy. Health care is large and growing regionwide and Ruston serves as a retail hub for a region with 423,000 residents in north-central Louisiana and southern Arkansas (City of Ruston website, 2011).

Interview with the Honorable Dan Hollingsworth, Mayor of Ruston, Louisiana

Dan Hollingsworth has been mayor of Ruston, Louisiana for 13 years, in which time his greatest accomplishment in economic development has centered on the inclusion of Louisiana State University and Grambling University in city and regional efforts. Because of LSU's presence in the city, the mayor uses the term "blessed" to explain that Ruston has not suffered in the current recession to the same extent as other micropolitan cities.

Another reason he cites for the fairly stable recent experience of his city is the fact that, several years before the recession began, in the "good times," Ruston embarked upon a program to improve the local infrastructure, which had the effect of attracting new retail shops to the downtown area. This, in turn, generated additional property and sales tax revenues that enabled the city to improve the quality and quantity of its services. Along with the practice of hiring municipal employees who have experience working in the private sector, Mayor Hollingsworth feels that the city became a more efficient service provider. Furthermore, the retail outlets are important because, in Louisiana, 1.75% of the sales tax receipts go the municipal government in which they were generated (these are known as point-of-sales taxes).

Retail growth is also important to the city of Ruston and the region because the city is somewhat isolated, sitting in a parish of 150,000, thirty miles from Monroe and sixty miles from Shreveport. Despite these distances, the city benefits by sitting on or very near (e.g., one mile) major arterials. These retail operations also helped to replace the jobs lost when the local timber industry declined and the state of Louisiana was forced to make cuts in its spending on higher education. As LSU is the city's largest employer by far, this had quite an impact on local jobs, support economies, and spending. The mayor feels that the city has been fortunate to have broken relatively even in terms of total job numbers.

The key lesson, however, according to the mayor, relates to the strong collaboration he has established between the city and the university. The university is entrepreneurial in nature and has recently collaborated on a successful appeal for federal funds to build a research park that is between the campus and downtown Ruston. The city has begun to build sidewalks between the three locations and this has led to further interaction and mutual support.

Mayor Hollingsworth attributes this strong relationship to "communication, *seeking* projects of mutual interest, and a basic mutual respect." He is quick to point out that he once lived in another university town and had observed other cities where these close relationships, which are seemingly self-evident in terms of their potential economic development and other types of value, do not always occur. The mayor's recommendation for other micropolitan cities with colleges or universities: do not allow them to become constrained by land use practices around them; ensure that those uses are consistent with what the university is trying to accomplish generally.

In a recent strategic planning exercise, the entire community was engaged. This resulted in the Ruston 2020 Plan, which includes emphases on what the residents want to see in their city in the future: higher K–12 standards, preservation of the city's unique "feel," preservation of the cosmopolitan nature of the city that comes from being a college town, and a revitalized downtown. "Include the citizens," intones the mayor. "Establish trust and treat them as customers."

Salina, Kansas

In the mid-1960s, the economic base of Salina, Kansas suffered as the result of the closure of Schilling Air Force Base. The base had brought many to the community who stayed at the conclusion of their service because of the opportunities that existed at that time in manufacturing as well as the relatively low cost of living, reported today as being more than 15% below the national average (http://www. bestplaces.net). When the base closed, many of the manufacturers in the area lost some or all of the demand for their services and many of the jobs in the community that were not directly related to the base, but supported by the spending by its personnel and their families, were no longer in demand either.

In the decades since, Salina has managed to establish new employment opportunities for its residents, largely in manufacturing operations but in other areas as well, including university employment and health services. The manufacturing component of the local economy has become increasingly diverse and now includes such areas as frozen foods (including a large frozen pizza plant), automobile batteries, aircraft parts, electronic equipment, cabinets, turbines, and more. This economic diversity, even though it is within the manufacturing category generally, has provided stability to the region. In the current recessionary period, the unemployment rate in Salina is 7.0%, far less than the 9.1% national average, although recent job growth (−1.62%) has been further into the negative than the national average of −0.12% (http://www.bestplaces.net). Still, the population has grown consistently over the past generation, climbing from 42,303 in 1990 by 8.0% to 45,679 in 2000, and again by 6.1% to 45,956 in 2005 (US Beacon, 2012).

Salina, Kansas: Interview Declined

San Luis Obispo, California

San Luis Obispo (please see Figure 6.56) was incorporated as a city in the state of California in 1856. Its great appeal then remains one of its greatest assets today: the coastal location affords beautiful views that help attract residents and visitors alike, and can be used to attract business locations as well. However, the local economy—once soundly supported by health care, construction, and advanced manufacturing—has experienced some struggles in recent years as have many of the local economies throughout California. Sluggish growth statewide, coupled with state policies that have been perceived as not being "business-friendly" and difficult macroeconomic times, have affected the city's ability to sustain the vitality of its economy over the past decade and have contributed to higher than normal unemployment and less than moderate projections for short-term job growth.

Population growth in San Luis Obispo has been relatively flat for more than 20 years. The 2000 population of 44,750 was fractionally lower than that of 1990 (44,948; San Luis Obispo Chamber of Commerce, 2012), and the growth rate

Figure 6.56 The beautiful geography of San Luis Obispo, California. (Courtesy of SLO Chamber, David E. Garth Photography)

between 2000 and 2005 actually declined by 1.5%. By the 2010 census, the level had risen once again to 45,119 (US Beacon, 2012).

But, growth (or decline) of the population is not the only standard by which one can measure the future receptivity of a local economy for growth or enhanced vitality. Workforce preparedness is of far greater concern to potential incoming employers. The resident labor pool in San Luis Obispo (2009) includes one in nine individuals who do not have a high school diploma. However, about one in five (19.3%) has a bachelor's degree (San Luis Obispo Chamber of Commerce, 2012), and there is a higher than typical number of PhDs in the labor pool because of the presence of California Polytechnic State University (Cal Poly).

In terms of the largest existing employment sectors, San Luis Obispo has a decidedly strong presence of public employers although it was also noted by a local newspaper reporter that "The county does not have enough private sector, *head of household* jobs," meaning higher-paying employment opportunities (Lynem, 2011).

An examination of the largest industry sectors reflected in the city's economy, as listed in the local Chamber of Commerce's website, bears out her point. The largest segments of the economy are government employment and accommodations and food, both of which represent just under 13% of the total employment. That is followed by education and health services at 11%, state government (as distinct from federal and local) at just under 10%, and professional and business services at 8.5%. No other single category exceeds 5% of the city's job base.

The same source lists the top employers (by numbers of jobs). The absence of primary sector private employment in San Luis Obispo becomes clear when viewing the listings. From the largest employers to the smallest, it reads as follows: university, hospital, hospital, gas and electric company, college, prison, hospital, social welfare organization, public school system, and a medical center. That's the top 10; a hotel places at number 11, a department store at number 15, and a bank at number 23.

In November 2009, the unemployment rate for San Luis Obispo was reported at just under 9%, representing 12,000 men and women out of work. The critical question is whether this type of economic base is right for San Luis Obispo and whether it can thus sustain long-term economic viability.

A study of targets of opportunity for the city's job growth was funded as a public–private collaboration. It identified six potential industries as growth opportunities for San Luis Obispo (Lynem, 2011):

- Building design and construction
- Health services
- Knowledge and innovation services
- Specialized manufacturing
- Promotion of local foods, wines, and recreational attractions
- Green energy

Can the city of San Luis Obispo successfully attract and grow businesses in these sectors? Its assets in doing so are cited by Moody's Analytics (Moody's Analytics, 2012) as its coastal location, the presence of Cal Poly, and a general increase in demand for wine. Moody's Analytics also cites San Luis Obispo's weaknesses: housing costs, long-term water supply issues, and the high costs of energy. And Forbes.com adds as weaknesses the crime rate (30th on its list of "The Best Places for Business and Careers") and subprime mortgages (27th on the Forbes.com list). In terms of the costs of doing business in general, SLOs ranking of 143rd and the overall cost of living (ranked 177th) are not positive portents of success in business attraction.

As the population has stabilized and the job base declined, the state of California also experienced reduced revenues, which have meant diminished transfers to local governments and smaller local tax bases from which to pay for city services. The local press has noted the impact: "Government will continue to downsize until it meets its new budget goals …" (Lynem, 2011). In other cities across the United States, this has created a doubly difficult situation: fewer resources to provide the very public services that would support the growth of the business base that is needed to support further public services and growth.

In late 2010, a report was issued (Economic Vitality Corporation, 2010) that summarized the economic development strategic visioning process that had taken part in San Luis Obispo County. What is noteworthy is not so much the conclusions as the description of the process itself (italics added): "*For the first time, more than 100 of San Luis Obispo County's business leaders have agreed to work together—and with partners in government, education, and community sectors …*" Although this was a reference to the county rather than the city, the theme of collaboration should be an important one for the interview with the mayor.

Interview with the Honorable Jan Marx, Mayor of San Luis Obispo, California

San Luis Obispo was first founded as a mission in 1742 and formally established as a city 160 years ago. The Honorable Jan Marx became mayor of San Luis Obispo approximately one year before the interview, although she had served as a member of the city council for several years prior to that. When asked why, in the heart of the nation's worst recession in the past 80 years, she would want the job, she replied that she loved the city and its people and that "difficult times call for people to pitch in."

The issue of economic vitality for Mayor Marx is predicated upon the revenue sources for the local budget from which city services are provided. As noted earlier in this book, if the primary source is real estate taxes, one needs commercial space to help pay for residential services. However, if a critical source is income taxes, residential growth is the source of enhanced funding to support public services. In the case of San Luis Obispo, the revenue sources are distributed over a number of categories and, given the nature of these sources, the current employment sectors that are strongest in the local economy seem to be the most appropriate. This is especially important in California where, as the mayor points out, Proposition 13 still restricts the permissible growth in tax increase imposed by local governments.

As there are no local income tax levies in the state, sales taxes remain the dominant revenue source for San Luis Obispo. When added to a one-half cent city sales tax and a transient occupancy (or hotel) tax, it is logical that the establishment and growth of hotels, dining, and cultural and retail opportunities are given great importance by the city's leadership. And these areas are supported by the mayor and council as they look to the future.

The interview with Mayor Marx revealed an interesting mix of concern for the environment with an acceptance of the need for growth as long as it is conducted within the framework of the expectations the city has established. The council is in the process of preserving a greenbelt around the city and annexing properties that will enable the city to grow both eastward and to the south. The latter will provide the housing seen as necessary to support the workforce employed by local businesses. Mayor Marx noted that the nighttime population is about 45,000 whereas the daytime population exceeds 120,000. Still, the city has self-imposed an annual 1% growth cap and does not even reach that.

San Luis Obispo has a large employment base in public sector entities as well. This includes hospitals, universities, a prison, a National Guard office, an airport, and the district office of the California transportation agency (CalTrans), as well as others. In addition, notes the mayor, there are numerous nonprofit organizations that are affiliated with government agencies. All of this creates a situation potentially susceptible to the rise and fall of public expenditures. However, Mayor Marx is not overly concerned. Cal Poly is an "economic engine" for the entire region, supporting the local hotels, restaurants, and retail outlets. The relationship with the city is strong and partnerships exist in the support of an incubator, an arts center, the commercialization of research, and in the establishment of mentor programs designed to keep young graduates in the region. These are not the things that concern the mayor most.

What does concern Mayor Marx the most are the macroeconomic impacts on their San Luis Obispo. For example, if the economy quickly recovers, there could be greater pressures on the leadership to grow too quickly, thus perhaps causing San Luis Obispo to lose its unique character and become more like a "typical southern California city." On the other hand, if the recession deepens, there will be budgetary pressures on San Luis Obispo, which is now quite accommodating to homeless individuals. However, the people of the city are "very emotionally invested in the community" and very entrepreneurial in spirit. The mayor believes that their "can-do attitude" will sustain them through even the toughest of times.

The various perspectives of Mayor Marx are as different from those of many of her colleagues as is San Luis Obispo different from other parts of the United States. This made her thoughts about the economic future of micropolitan cities in general most interesting. She strongly maintained that the micropolitan cities have a greater "sense of place" and greater cohesion in the community than is found in larger metropolitan areas. "People know people in a great many different ways—there are these interlocking networks—in a smaller community. Without that kind of community spirit, small cities can be disasters. Here, people pitch in; they volunteer through service clubs and nonprofits. It's the real America."

Finally, Mayor Marx maintained that economic growth may not always be the most important issue for a micropolitan community. "The imperative of growth is questionable. What is really important is making the community more vital and making people's lives better. Growth is a means to an end."

Sedalia, Missouri

Sedalia (please see Figure 6.57) was founded in 1860 as a railroad town. In recent years, Sedalia has grown its population base very marginally. From 1990 to 2000, it increased from 19,800 to 20,339, a jump of about 2.7%. Through 2005, it grew again, but by less than one-half of one percent, to 20,430 (US Beacon, 2012). Current economic measures are running pretty close to national averages, with

Figure 6.57   State fairgrounds in Sedalia, Missouri. (Courtesy of Missouri State Fair)

an unemployment rate of 8.6% (US average is 9.1%). Recent job growth measures −0.39% whereas the US average is −0.12% (http://www.bestplaces.net).

One point of discussion with the mayor would be whether the strategy of working hard on economic development in the good times has paid dividends in the current recession. The numbers could, of course, be much worse, as they are in many of the other micropolitan cities researched for this book. A recent quote recorded from a county commissioner in the area states the case: "I think that right now, when the national economy is in trouble, this really shows the value of the dollars we spent on economic development locally. If we hadn't been very aggressive years ago, we wouldn't be sitting where we are today. We would be looking at the same problems we are nationally" (AllBusiness, 2011).

Sedalia can thank geography for its relatively stable economy through the recessionary times. It serves as the hub for shoppers throughout the region. Columbia and Jefferson City do not effectively draw the region's shoppers away from Sedalia. But the city has a finite amount of land, 13.1 square miles, and needs to maximize that land for commercial uses.

Sedalia has enjoyed some recent successes in expanding the employment base. In mid-2012, the local Tyson's meat plant expanded, creating an additional 200 positions in Sedalia over a two-year period, on top of the pre-existing 1,450. Notably, the press coverage reported that the immediate jobs were not the only benefit of the expansion: "Annual pay for the complex for Fiscal Year 2011 was more than $46.3 million; total family farmer pay to grow chickens for the complex was approximately $27.4 million" (Sparkman, 2012).

Another company, ProEnergy, reported in 2011 that it would expand its Sedalia facility, making a capital investment of more than $25 million, and creating 300 new jobs over the following three-year period.

Especially in smaller towns such as Sedalia, where one or more prominent industries represents a large component of the economy, the direct and indirect spinoff economic benefits can be quite considerable. Regrettably, this most often means that, as a company departs from the city, the impacts are immediately and widely felt in the tax base and public services, throughout local organizations that are in part dependent upon charitable contributions, and other parts of the community. Fortunately for Sedalia, this has not been the case.

Interview with the Honorable Elaine Horn, Mayor of Sedalia, Missouri

As the population of the city of Sedalia, Missouri grows, its mayor believes that the city has a bright economic future and characterizes the present economic mood as "very good." Sedalia, she maintains, has not felt the sting of the current recession as deeply as have other small cities throughout Missouri. The unemployment rate has not been as low and several new businesses have recently either opened or expanded.

Much of this she attributes to the skill levels of the local workforce. To further that asset, the local community college secured a grant from the state of Missouri to train people to work for a local facility that converts methane gas into energy that is being used to power facilities at the college. A wire manufacturer helps to further diversify the local economy and recently was expanded as the company's other facilities were shut down and rolled into the plant in Sedalia. Mayor Horn believes this is a reflection of how the company views the capabilities of the local workforce.

As do many of the other micropolitan cities included in this study, Sedalia serves as the regional hub for an area many miles in all directions, providing primary retail and health and other personal services. Sedalia lies roughly one hour from Kansas City; 70 minutes from Columbia, the state capital; and two and one-half hours from St. Louis. Retail success is also important because "the majority of the city's budget comes from sales taxes."

One puzzle piece Mayor Horn believes would facilitate further economic growth is less expensive means of connecting the railroads (Union Pacific) to businesses on new spurs. The costs would have to be borne by the businesses as they can be quite steep. In terms of the economic future of micropolitan communities, Mayor Horn considers it to be bright because small towns have "a different feel than larger cities." Many of her friends who left Sedalia returned when they started families because they wanted their children to enjoy the same lifestyles with which they grew up. She does admonish, however, that smaller cities need to have everyone working together as a team in order to survive. "People here make a commitment to our community."

Figure 6.58   The historic Bridge Walk reenactment in Selma, Alabama. (Courtesy of B.J. Smothers)

Selma, Alabama

At the time of this writing, the unemployment rate in Selma, Alabama (please see Figure 6.58) was stated as exceeding 16%. The national average, also high, was nearly half that of Selma, at 9.1%. Recent job growth in the city was negative at –1.66%, compared to the national average of –0.12% (http://www.bestplaces.net). With fully one in four of every job in the transportation and materials moving sector, economic growth is a serious challenge and the city leadership faces serious challenges in pursuing growth.

Thus, it is not surprising that the population of Selma is, and has been for some time, declining. Between 1990 and 2000, the loss was from 23,755 to 20,512, or by nearly 14%. From 2000 to 2005, a further decline to 19,401, or 5.4%, was registered in Selma (US Beacon, 2012).

What has happened in Selma as a consequence of too few jobs accompanied by population losses is not atypical of cities, large or small, with these forces at play. Those who can leave, do. This leaves behind those who are unable to leave because of low skills or education levels and who now are unable to find even low-skilled, low-wage employment. Much of this decline started as far back as 1978, when Craig Air Force Base was closed, resulting in the loss of many manufacturing jobs that were related to the needs of the base.

At present, the city is left with insufficient employment opportunities and a rapidly declining tax base to pay for public services at the very time when demand is increasing at a breakneck pace. In many cases, this leaves poor people without any resources. In these conditions, many cities record concurrent rises in crime rates across the board. Today, manufacturing dominates the business base. The largest employers include International Paper, American Apparel, Hanil E-Hwa Interior Systems, Bush Hog, Honda Lock, and others. And, more recently, Zikha Biomass Fuels added 52 new jobs in a wood pellet plant, while adding more than $45 million more to the local economy.

Selma, which was incorporated in 1820, does have a number of historic sites and stories on which to build an increased tourism trade. These include Civil War sites (Selma was captured near the end of the war, in 1865); the Tuskegee Institute, founded by Booker T. Washington in 1881; and landmarks of the 1965 Selma-to-Montgomery civil rights march. The city's leadership has developed a comprehensive plan that focuses on some of these historic sites as part of a broader revitalization of the downtown area. This may be seen as an opportunity to increase tourism and to grow jobs related to visitor services (e.g., retail, restaurants, and hotels). Perhaps the mayor would be able to shed some light on whether this has indeed been regarded and treated as an opportunity. The city has three office parks that are marketed as economic development assets. This, too, would be a point of discussion in terms of the successes realized in attracting employers to those parks.

Interview with the Honorable George Evans, Mayor of Selma, Alabama

Mayor George Evans is a native of Selma, Alabama who, after leaving to attend college in Kansas, returned to become an educator and coach and later entered politics. His affection for his hometown and its evolution through bad times and good is almost infectious. He is also, however, realistic in his economic expectations for Selma.

Mayor Evans characterized the economic mood of his city as "better." Two years ago, he explained, the unemployment rate climbed into the low twenties. At the time of the interview, it had come down to less than 15%, still high but improving. One of the reasons seemed to be a great source of pride for the mayor: "People who live here are spending their own money to invest in the downtown." New retail establishments have opened, financed locally. This has helped the city to revitalize its downtown shopping area and to improve the general appearance of the city.

Retail growth is important to Selma, which relies heavily on sales taxes to constitute its local $17 million budget. Another significant component of the city's budget comes from the hotel tax, of which half (4%) goes to the city and half to the state. Hotels in Selma are able to attract visitors to the various historic locations and activities in the city. This includes most notably the Bridge Walk Jubilee, held each March to commemorate the 1965 bridge walk for civil rights. The mayor explains that this and other events are intended to attract visitors and to keep them in the city for a few extra days when they do visit.

To complement these events, the city has begun to work on the development of other attractions, especially along the riverfront where there are plans to build a zoo, a river walk, an amphitheater, and bike and walking trails. Water Avenue is, to Mayor Evans, the key to getting people interested in living and working in Selma.

When asked about the future of Selma and cities of its size, the mayor noted that partnerships and collaboration with the private sector and other communities throughout the region is essential. "We must realize that we must act regionally. We need to share our successes. In our city, a lot of this has to do with family. We all pull together. You get that here in Selma and in other small cities."

One advantage of larger metropolitan areas that Mayor Evans points out is that they receive a lot of federal funds for redevelopment that are based on entitlement formulas, whereas Selma is too small for entitlements and therefore must collaborate with others in the region to submit "shovel-ready" projects. In the greater numbers, they can garner greater attention. "We must grow together," repeated the mayor.

Shelby, North Carolina

Shelby, North Carolina, first settled in 1540 by the Spanish, was named for a Revolutionary War figure, Isaac Shelby. The city has grown in recent years due more to annexation than from natural growth or in-migration. Between 1992 and 2002, the city added 2,500 new homes and 6,500 new residents through numerous annexations. It also added approximately $400 million annually to the city's budget. What was the purpose for doing this? Has it been successful?

As a result of this practice, the city's population jumped between 1990 and 2000 by more than one-third (14,669 to 19,477) and again by more than 9% between 2000 and 2005, up to a total of 21,263 (US Beacon, 2012). Regardless of the purpose and or initial successes of these actions, Shelby has suffered in the current recession. Its unemployment rate presently approaches 12%, far higher than the 9.1% national average. Recent job growth figures register a loss at –3.81% in Shelby, compared to national averages of –0.12% (http://www.bestplaces.net).

Many of the area's manufacturing jobs had been in various textile operations; those jobs went offshore in the 1980s and 1990s. By the mid-1970s, the city was producing fewer than 2,000 bales of cotton, compared to the 1948 peak production of 83,000 bales (History of Shelby, 2012). The types of jobs currently in and near the city today are primarily in manufacturing, data centers, and call centers. The combination of more people and fewer jobs is not a good one. It usually depletes local government's budgets and the ability to provide enhanced levels of public services at the very time that the demand is increasing.

There have been some positive announcements. In early 2011, Baldor Electric Company announced their investment of $17 million in Shelby. Clearwater Paper Corporation expanded its facility in 2010 and, in the process, added 250 new jobs that pay well over the area's average wage. Of course, for a small community such as Shelby, these represent more than just jobs and a tax base; it also means validation of the community as a good place to do business.

Another economic development asset that exists in Shelby is Gardner-Webb University, however, it is unclear from a web search the extent to which, and how, it is or will be involved in the economic development of the city. This would be a good topic for discussion with the mayor.

Shelby, North Carolina: Interview Declined

Shelbyville, Tennessee

Shelbyville is one of the fastest growing micropolitan cities in this study, increasing in population by 14.6% between 1990 and 2000, from 14,049 to 16,105; and again by 15.8% by 2005 to a total of 18,648 (US Beacon, 2012). Part of the reason for these increases is the cost of living, which is about 16% less than the national average. Recent job growth has been positive at +1.33, compared to a negative national average of −0.12%, but the current unemployment rate stands at 10.8%, higher than the national level of 9.1% (http://www.bestplaces.net).

Several articles in the local press made references to issues of high rates of dropouts from the public school system and a downtown that is greatly in need of revitalization. These should be topics for discussion with the mayor of Shelbyville.

These matters would be difficult to address, however, in light of other topics being covered, including budget reduction exercises by the city. How can a city with these types of serious issues find a way out? What tactics have shown some positive results? And can they be replicated in other micropolitan cities? Can the current manufacturing sectors (food products represent about 44%, plastics 27%, and transportation 19%) be enhanced or expanded (http://www.city-data.com, 2012)?

Some recent hope that such could indeed be the case may be found in some recent announcements: SMW (an automotive supplier) has made a $26 million investment in Shelbyville to build a 131,000-square-foot plant that will result in an estimated 170 jobs over the next five years. A recent decision by Walmart will also add to the food distribution sector in the city with a 400,000-plus-square-foot facility. And Century Mold expanded its Shelbyville factory to the tune of more than $4 million in early 2012, creating 58 new jobs in manufacturing in the process.

Shelbyville, Tennessee: Interview Declined

Sierra Vista, Arizona

In the 1970s the population base of Sierra Vista increased dramatically. It is unclear whether this was the result of in-migration, natural growth, some combination of the two, or the annexation of additional areas by the city, which is, like many micropolitan cities, a regional hub existing somewhat alone in a greater region.

The city of Sierra Vista was incorporated as such in 1956. Between 1960 and 1970, the population more than doubled from 3,121 to 6,689; however, between 1970 and 1980, that total quadrupled, reaching 24,937 (Sierra Vista, 2012). It is also possible that the growth of the population during that timeframe was tied to growth at nearby Fort Huachuca. By 1990, Sierra Vista had grown to 42,220 residents, however, that number was reduced by 2000 to 37,775, a loss of more than 10%, which was recouped by 2005 (41,908), and increased again by the 2010 census count (43,888) (US Beacon, 2012).

Fort Huachuca generates a significant amount of visitors which, in turn, has helped to establish the hospitality industry, including hotels, restaurants, and retail. The presence of the fort has also helped to attract jobs in companies that provide goods and services to the units housed there. This also helps to explain the relatively high education levels of the Sierra Vista labor force: in 2000, it was reported that more than 90% of adults possessed at least a high school diploma and more than one-fourth possessed at least a bachelor's degree (Sierra Vista, 2012). These facts certainly help to explain the relatively low rate of unemployment: 5.2% against the national average of 9.1%, as well as a positive current job growth rate of +0.75% at a time when the national average stood in the negative at −0.12% (http://www.bestplaces.net).

Still, even a relatively thriving micropolitan city, with numerous assets for additional economic growth, must exist within a state. The state of Arizona has not enjoyed economic stability through the current recession. In 2009, reports indicate that the GDP of the state of Arizona declined over the previous year by more than 4%. And the state's economic issues are not the only problems confronting its communities. That economic decline translates directly and immediately into line-item budget losses that, in turn, mean fewer and fewer public services for residents and fewer transfer dollars from the state's coffers to cities like Sierra Vista.

Another issue that is plaguing Sierra Vista in terms of its ability to attract companies, and even to retain its existing businesses, is its image. Perceptions (and they may be either real or inaccurate or some combination of the two) are strong factors where businesses locate themselves and their employees and their families. Sierra Vista has gained a reputation for having troubles with immigration and border protection. This is exacerbated by the perception (again, real or not) that there is significant drug activity coming over the border from Mexico. Clearly, this needs to be addressed, both in terms of the realities and the external perceptions.

Sierra Vista, Arizona: Interview Declined

Starkville, Mississippi

Starkville, Mississippi (please see Figure 6.59) experienced a population boom between 1990 and 2000, growing by 18.5% from 18,458 to 21,869, and again by

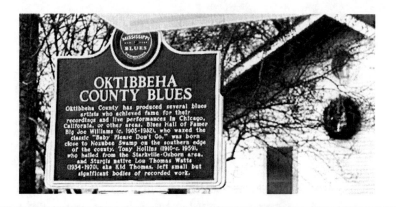

Figure 6.59 Cultural attractions of Starkville, Mississippi. (Courtesy of City of Starkville)

1.2% through 2005 (22,131), and yet again by the census count of 2010 to 23,888 (US Beacon, 2012). How does a relatively small town maintain its economic stability with this kind of consistent population growth over time?

A 2011 survey of the local residents in Starkville resulted in a finding that more than 70% of respondents felt the region was "competitive" and an additional 21% felt it was "very competitive" (Nalley, 2011).

Starkville has a strong economic development asset in the form of Mississippi State University, which has an enrollment of about 17,000 and a faculty complement of 700. The university's website boasts a number of research institutes relevant to local industry segments as well as programs designed to promote the growth of entrepreneurial businesses. Among these are the Raspet Flight Research Laboratory with 90,000 square feet of lab space, office space, and hangar space. It also provides precision machine equipment aircraft assembly rooms and testing areas. Its impressive client list includes Honda, Westinghouse, DuPont, Bosch, and others. It has also incubated a number of aerospace companies. To support and accelerate the growth of the industry in the region, the state offers numerous incentive programs for potential employers.

A similar cluster exists around Department of Defense technologies and also includes university programs and state incentive programs. An additional cluster is the automotive cluster, which is supported by the Mississippi State University Center for Advanced Vehicular Systems in which research is conducted on electronics, manufacturing and design, computational simulations, and ergonomics. Its client list boasts such well-respected companies as International Truck, Flexible Flyer, Northrop Grumman, Nissan, and others. Similar clusters and university support and state incentive programs have been built around clean energy research and production and biomedical businesses. It would be interesting to hear how these programs have helped Starkville to develop its local economy as well as to diversify its employment base.

Interview with the Honorable Parker Wiseman, Mayor of Starkville, Mississippi

The mood in Starkville, Mississippi regarding the economy is, according to Mayor Parker Wiseman, "Pretty good, all things considered." He explains that the city, although not immune from recessionary forces, is relatively safe from their impacts. The presence of Mississippi State University, the city's largest employer, makes the difference: between 2008 and 2012, its student body grew by about 15%, creating new demands for student housing, various city services, and more schools in the Starkville system. Fortunately, the demand has not yet greatly exceeded the local supply, so the result has not been costly.

Complementing the university-based employment and any spinoffs is the presence of some older manufacturing facilities that are still in operation including a wire cable manufacturer, and others in paper production and furniture design and building. A city research park has also seen positive growth in recent years, including a silicon carbide wafer manufacturing facility. A major hotel and conference center is planned and will require $80 to $100 million in investment. This will be the result of a public–private partnership between Mississippi State University, the city, and a private developer.

The mayor expressed some concern that, as the city and the region move forward to attract more advance manufacturing concerns, it will need to assure employers that it has an adequate supply of people with relevant skills in the labor force. He feels that this is not an uncommon problem in university towns where the educational attainment levels tend to be skewed higher. To be able to do so, the region must work together to assemble a workforce with the necessary numbers to satisfy employers' demand. In the three-county region around Starkville, there are 150,000 residents and that makes a better impression on economic development prospects than that of Starkville by itself. Today, there are already major employers present in the area, including a steel mill with 400 jobs, a truck manufacturer with 1,000 jobs, and a solar panel manufacturer with more than 1,000 jobs, as well as others.

Because the real estate taxes that are generated by such operations comprise large shares of the municipal budgets, regionalism is sometimes a challenge to promote. Micropolitan communities can have bright futures, says Mayor Wiseman, but they must begin making efforts in regionalism as soon as possible.

Steven's Point, Wisconsin

Steven's Point saw some population growth between 1990 and 2000, from 23,006 to 24,551 (6.7%), but had a marginal decline of about 1% to 24,298 by 2005 (US Beacon, 2012). The unemployment rate is now at 7.5%, a good bit below national averages of 9.1%, and the recent job growth parallels the national rate at −0.08% and −0.12%, respectively (http://www.bestplaces.net).

Steven's Point is roughly in the geographic center of the state of Wisconsin. As it sits 70 miles from its closest neighbor, Wausau, it is something of a regional retail hub although it is a relatively small, sparsely populated region. It also serves as a regional site for numerous recreational activities.

A local branch of the University of Wisconsin represents a further economic development asset but it would require the mayor to explain how that campus is being incorporated into the city's outreach for business attraction, retention, and start-ups. Other topics for discussion with the mayor would be the importance of the regional airport to economic development and any plans for its expansion as well as the relative importance of agriculture to the overall economic development plan going forward.

Prerecession economic sectors included education, manufacturing, and tourism. In the surrounding Portage County, prerecession strengths also included manufacturing, agriculture, financial and personal services, and public sector employment. The mayor could illuminate the effects of the recent recession on these sectors.

Steven's Point, Wisconsin: Interview Declined

Stillwater, Oklahoma

Stillwater, Oklahoma continues to grow, reaching a population in 2005 of 40,906, up by 4.7% over the 2000 level of 39,065, which in turn was up by 6.5% over 1990s level of 36,676 (US Beacon, 2012). The economic picture is extremely positive, with a current unemployment rate of 4.2%, healthy by any standard and less than half the national average of 9.1%. Furthermore, the recent job growth reports indicated growth at a +1.19% pace whereas the nation shows a loss at the rate of −0.12% (http://www.bestplaces.net).

The presence of strong economic anchors in the community explains this situation to some extent. Oklahoma State University (OSU), with an enrollment approaching 25,000, both spends and generates a lot of money in the city and in the region. It would be interesting to learn from the mayor whether and how Oklahoma State is engaged in generating new employment opportunities in the region as well. OSU also contributes to the city's position as the regional retail hub, with many of the students and their visitors contributing to the sales revenues. This has been a recurring theme in many of the interviews: colleges generate visitors and visitors spend money, thereby contributing greater amounts to cities' tax bases than the value of what they require in public services.

Universities have also been cited by mayors as being a stabilizing force in the economy because their spending is countercyclical. Oklahoma State University, for example, saw a rise in enrollment in the 2001 to 2003 recessionary period of about 1,800 students (Spears School of Business, Oklahoma State University, 2008). A 170-acre technology park also adds to the potential for further growth in Stillwater. The park is a joint effort of the city, the university, and a private developer.

Other large employers in and around Stillwater include Mercury MerCruiser, the medical center, the city and the public school systems, and Walmart. And wire product manufacturer National Standard brought in 75 new jobs and $13 million dollars of new investment to Stillwater in the height of the current national recession, in the spring of 2011 (Woodruff, 2011).

The city has been ranked consistently high on lists of nice places to live and that, too, has helped generate economic growth, yielding a diverse economy, including construction, financial services, health services, food services, retail, mining, and educational services. Just how all that came about in Stillwater would be the primary topic of discussion with the mayor.

Stillwater, Oklahoma: Interview Declined

Texarkana, Texas

Texarkana, as the name suggests, sits on the border between Texas and Arkansas, and is in a growth corridor that encompasses a large portion of northeastern Texas. From 1990 to 2000, Texarkana saw its city population grow from 31,656 to 34,782, or by nearly 10%. Over the next five years, it grew by another 2.8% to 35,746 (US Beacon, 2012). Its recent job growth has declined by –.37%, but that decline is only slightly in excess of the national average of –0.12%. On the plus side, the city's unemployment rate of 8.0% is lower than the reported national average for that period of 9.1% (http://www.bestplaces.net).

Texarkana's strategy can account for part of that population growth as the city and the region promote themselves as retirement destinations with outdoor activities and the relative cost of living (more than 15% below the national average) as prime features. This raises the question pondered by other communities regarding the marginal costs of public services (recreation, health services, and more) for retirees who may spend less and contribute less to the city's tax base than other residents. This tends to be a matter of how local budgets are built in Texas. It would certainly be a point of discussion with the mayor.

Texas A&M (formerly East Texas State University-Texarkana) has 56 faculty and more than 1,500 students, adding revenue-generating sources to the city's economy as well as attracting visitors and establishing a potential asset for further economic growth. These would be good areas to investigate with the mayor.

Other economic activities in the Texarkana economy include timber, dairy, and food processing and distribution as well as oil, natural gas, and coal, giving the city and the region enough diversity in the economic base to predict stability despite rises and falls in macroeconomic trends that are beyond the city's control. An obvious question to pose to the mayor of Texarkana would cover the relationships with others in the region, especially inasmuch as that region of about 60,000 residents cross the border between two states.

Texarkana, Texas: Interview Declined

Tifton, Georgia

The city of Tifton, Georgia (please see Figure 6.60) is near the small end of the population range that defines micropolitan cities. The level has increased steadily over the past 20 years (1990 to 2010), from just over 14,000 to more than 16,000. At the time of this writing, the level of unemployment is much higher than an already high US average (12.2% versus 9.1%; http://www.bestplaces.net).

Recent successes have brought a significant number of jobs to the city, as reported in the local press (Young, 2012). Construction sites for Publix, a retailer, and Premiere Transportation, herald the attraction of new jobs in the range of 1,000. Furthermore, a scan of recent news coverage indicates that the city has a few positive assets on which to base an economic rebound. The Tift Regional Medical Center reports (*Tifton Gazette*) that its economic impact on the city and the region exceeds $400 million. It is also Tift County's largest employer with approximately 1,700 positions.

Another recent success that was reported in the local press (Thompson, 2012) involves American Textile's plans to initiate operations in a distribution facility and hire 50 people immediately and an additional 70 individuals over the next five years. The announcement of the initial 50 openings generated more than 700 applications.

The University of Georgia has a branch campus located in Tifton that includes the College of Agricultural and Environmental Sciences, which contributes research and products to the local farmers as well as providing jobs and revenues to the local tax base. Questions for Tifton's mayor should focus on how these two institutions can help play strategic, as well as tactical, roles in planning the economic growth of the city going forward.

Figure 6.60   City Hall, Tifton, Georgia. (Courtesy of City of Tifton)

Interview with the Honorable J. G. "Jamie" Cater, Jr., Mayor of Tifton, Georgia

Tifton mayor Jamie Cater describes his city as one recovering from the loss of jobs in the local textile mills that resulted from the North American Free Trade Agreements (NAFTA). "When those industries went outside of the United States, we lost hundreds of jobs; more than 550 in just one such decision." Happily, some new jobs in similar fields have come in but the numbers are far less (e.g., American Textiles' pillow production factory) with 50 or 60 positions.

Mayor Cater discussed the importance of locations in a small town the size of Tifton that may seem insignificant to others but are very important for a hub micropolitan such as Tifton. A recent example of this was the opening of a Publix store that was greatly needed in the community. He also noted the vital importance in micropolitan cities (particularly those that are either somewhat or substantially isolated) to have buildings ready to be occupied. Communities cannot hope to compete if there are not facilities in place, with the infrastructure ready to go. Thus, Tifton has several buildings ready to be occupied.

Mayor Cater stated that companies looking for sites know that communities want and need them, so they ask for a lot in return. On the other hand, he noted, they do bring in jobs and the people they hire then spend money in the stores and around the community, and that helps sustain others as well. Construction jobs are particularly effective in that way, and local projects to refurbish a historic theater in the city as well as build an apartment building for seniors and to renovate the building that will one day house the city hall cause those kinds of contributions to occur.

The mayor of Tifton is a businessman who, like many of his peers across the country, regards that background as a reason for his success in municipal governance. His service as mayor has a current tenure of four years and follows on five years as a city commissioner. As such, Mayor Cater regards his citizens as clients. "Being mayor is being a servant of the people. The people are my bosses." His lessons come from that perspective: "Don't just grow to get big. Grow so you can have jobs for people today and for their kids tomorrow."

In economic development terms, his key message is "Don't put all your eggs in one basket (i.e., textiles). You never know what the economy is going to do so you have to be diverse. Finally, it is never a good idea to spend a lot of the city's money when people are suffering. And, if you have to do it, do it gradually. Always think first about the people."

Tupelo, Mississippi

The city of Tupelo, Mississippi (please see Figure 6.61) has been experiencing significant residential growth in recent years and has retained a fairly stable economic position to accommodate that growth. From 1990 to 2000, the city's population

Figure 6.61   City Hall, Tupelo, Mississippi. (Courtesy of Daphene Hendricks)

grew by 11.5% from 30,685 to 34,211, and again by 4.3% by 2005 (US Beacon, 2012). Although the unemployment at this writing stood at more than 10%, exceeding even the relatively high national average of 9.1%, recent job growth was reported as a very healthy +3.9%, comparing most favorably to the national average of −0.12% (http://www.bestplaces.net).

Between 1983 and 1991, the surrounding county added an average of more than 1,000 manufacturing jobs per year and totaled 9,297 for that entire period. However, the unemployment rate today is higher than even an already high national average. What economic activity does exist reflects a relatively strong diversity. The economic base of Tupelo today includes electrical, furniture, and plastics manufacturers as well as a tourism outreach program built around Civil War history, the city's Indian heritage, and the birthplace of Elvis Presley.

The employer base in Tupelo is heavily based on the public sector and manufacturing interests. Other than the local healthcare system and the public school system, Tupelo's top employers include Lane Furniture Industries, Cooper Tire and Rubber Company, and MTD Products. Much of the job growth in the city and the region come from the expansion of existing plants, including the 2010 investment by Lane Home Furnishings of $36 million to expand its current plant in the city.

Recent announcements of closings of chain retail stores are indicative of a problem for cities of this size. Although cities such as Tupelo may be thriving and attracting many shoppers from a large catchment area, chain stores often make decisions about national operations or regional operations on the basis of overall performance rather than one of two successful areas. In any event, this has added to Tupelo's woes. Presumably, the mayor would be able to explain whether he believes that the economic base is vital enough to support the job needs of the current and future population. Further plans for industrial diversification and visitors' services would also be apt topics for discussion with the mayor.

Interview with the Honorable Jack Reed, Mayor of Tupelo, Mississippi

Tupelo has a "strong mayoral system," meaning that Jack Reed is the chief executive of the city and occupies a full-time position. The seven-member city council holds the city's purse strings and approximately half of the Tupelo budget is derived from sales taxes (another 38% comes from property taxes). It is not surprising, therefore, that much of the focus of the economic development program is on retail opportunities.

That is not, however, the whole picture by any means. The generation of sales tax revenues is enabled by the fact that Tupelo is the primary city in the larger region, 100 miles from Memphis, 150 from Birmingham, and 200 from Nashville. This makes Tupelo the shopping center of choice and explains the presence of America's largest regional hospital, Northern Mississippi Health Services.

This locational fact also explains much of the stability in an economy in the county once noted as "the poorest county in the poorest state in America." And, as Mayor Reed indicated, it's a good thing because, despite the general misperception of all of the state of Mississippi as fertile soil for planting, Tupelo is in the hills and is suited for dairy farming but not planting. Some of the earlier (50 years ago) mainstays of the local economy, such as apparel manufacturing, have gone to other, lower-wage countries, leaving Tupelo in need of alternative employment opportunities. A 2000 communitywide study group decided to seek industries for which the city had strengths and which would be unlikely to go offshore. It settled on automobile manufacturing and food processing. A three-county collaboration produced a site that ultimately attracted a Toyota plant that will someday employ 2,000 workers and support the employment of another 1,500 in support industries within a 50-mile radius.

In terms of tourism attraction, one popular site is the birthplace of singer Elvis Presley. However, although as many as 40,000 people visit the home each year, they are typically just day trips from Memphis, the location of Presley's Graceland mansion, only 100 miles away. The challenge for Tupelo is to package several sites in order to retain visitors for at least one night's stay.

The enhanced tax revenues from these economic development efforts are vital as the city's population has grown substantially in recent years, much of which has come from people leaving the surrounding rural communities in search of employment. As this has occurred, and as manufacturing operations such as the Toyota plant have become more sophisticated in their operations (e.g., advanced robotics), the assets Mayor Reed believes the city is in the greatest need of is "educated human assets." As the lower-skilled operations have gone offshore, the replacement industries are manufacturing at a higher level and they require skills more advanced than many people possess. This, coupled with the loss of some of Tupelo's best and brightest, combine to suggest the need for an increasing number of jobs in advanced technology and in the services sector.

Tuskegee, Alabama

Tuskegee, Alabama (please see Figure 6.62) has gained renown for two historic reasons: it is the site of the Tuskegee Institute, an early (1881) all-black university founded by Dr. Booker T. Washington, and it is the origin of the famed Tuskegee Airmen. The Airmen constituted an all-black Air Force squadron that fought with great distinction in the Second World War.

Today, Tuskegee is a micropolitan city with a population in decline. The 1990 census reported Tuskegee with a population base of 12,257. By 2005, the city's residential base had declined to 11,741 (US Beacon, 2012). The unemployment rate among the city's working adults at the time of this writing exceeded the national average of 9.1% by a wide margin at 13.2% (http://www.bestplaces.net). The general decline continued through 2010 when the level dipped below that which is necessary to be considered a micropolitan city, hitting 9,865 (US Beacon, 2012).

The city sits in the center of the state of Alabama and is the seat of Macon County. Its major employers today include the Central Alabama Veterans Health Care System, with 1,300 employees, and the university, which employs more than 1,000.

Two important questions to discuss with the mayor would be how the university is engaged in the city's economic development efforts, and how the city uses its historic events to attract visitors and promote tourism.

Figure 6.62 **Beautiful architecture in Tuskegee, Alabama. (Courtesy of Tuskegee University)**

Interview with the Honorable Omar Neal, Mayor of Tuskegee, Alabama

Omar Neal became the mayor of Tuskegee, Alabama four years prior to the interview but without having first served on the city council. He had served previously on the county commission so his perspective is somewhat broader than the city alone. As soon as one hears Mayor Neal's voice, his career as a radio talk personality becomes evident. He, like many of his counterparts, feels that his business background has been a major help in his municipal service.

Although the mayor shares some similarities with his fellow mayors, his city is somewhat different. First, there is little in the way of diversity: 96% of the city's residents are African-American. It is the home of at least four historic places, the most prominent of which include the birthplace of Rosa Parks, the origins of the famed Tuskegee Airmen, and the university that was founded by Dr. George Washington Carver and which shares the city's name. Mayor Neal, however, says that the city has not made a sufficient effort to build its tourism attraction program to take advantage of these sites. Rather, it has focused its economic development attraction efforts on retail outlets with stores of a higher quality than those currently available. The city's declining population base concerns the mayor, who believes that such amenities as shopping, restaurants, and activities will help bring people back to Tuskegee.

Retail also makes sense as an economic development target for the city both because the city's budget is heavily dependent upon the resultant sales tax generation and because Tuskegee serves as a regional hub micropolitan city that can attract more residents of the greater region into the city to shop if more attractive retail opportunities exist there. In preparation for the payoff of this strategy, Mayor Neal notes that the city is now "priming the pump." Although Tuskegee University does not spin off businesses through programs of technology transfer, Mayor Neal states that "People are drawn to college towns because there is so much to see and do, but there is a distinct difference between a 'college town' and 'a town with a college.' We need Tuskegee to become more of a college town." The college has 3,000 students at any given time and about 1,000 staff and faculty on campus. The mayor notes that the college can be more but that it is held back by the lack of development of the town itself. Mayor Neal further notes that this is not uncommon: "HBCUs (historically black colleges and universities) are located often in places that are not well-developed."

As he promotes his vision for the future, Mayor Neal feels that people are beginning to feel an "increase in spirit" about their economic futures. Thus, his first lesson offered to other mayors in other micropolitan cities about how to grow or regrow their local economies is that "People need to be able to start dreaming again. It helps them to be part of the planning and visioning process. There is a difference between managing people and leading them. Leadership has to do with creating buy-in."

Figure 6.63   The Snake River Canyon in Twin Falls, Idaho. (Courtesy of Bill Nichols, Blip Printers)

Twin Falls, Idaho

Of the micropolitan cities in this research, Twin Falls, Idaho (please see Figure 6.63) is among the leaders in population growth over the last generation. From 1990 to 2000, the city grew by 25%, from 27,591 to 34,469; and from 2000 to 2005, it grew again by more than 12% to 38,630 (US Beacon, 2012).

Perhaps in part due to that growth, the unemployment at the time of this research was 9.3%, compared to the national average of 9.1%, but recent job growth indicates a reversal of the higher rates as the national average is −0.12% and the rate in Twin Falls is positive: +2.18% (http://www.bestplaces.net).

In recent years, much of the northwestern and southwestern United States benefited from companies fleeing California. Whether this is part of the reason for the recent job growth would be a good topic for discussion with the mayor.

A cluster exists in the region around research into alternative fuels. Another topic for discussion is the extent to which the city and the state are seeking to provide additional assets to that cluster as well as any incentive offerings that are being made available to companies in that space. The sectors within alternative energy sources being examined in the area include hydroelectrical power, wind power generation, ethanol, biothermal, and methane.

This is a positive sign for a community which, in the 1980s, lost roughly 600 manufacturing jobs when Tupperware and E.F. Johnson moved away. That out-migration continued through the 1980s. The need for job creation and attraction grew when many people who had lived in the surrounding rural areas moved into the city limits in search of employment opportunities.

Twin Falls is a somewhat isolated community, meaning that the city is able to grow one economic sector around personal services for the entire region. The city lies approximately 125 miles from Boise and 120 miles from Pocatello. Its rugged geography and its isolation have given rise to a strong and growing tourism industry. Coupled with agriculture, Twin Falls has two relatively stable and potentially countercyclical revenue generators that provide employment stability and a tax base.

Interview with the Honorable Don Hall, Vice Mayor of Twin Falls, Idaho

Twin Falls exists in south-central Idaho, approximately 90 miles in opposite directions from both Boise and Pocatello. This geographic position has helped to make Twin Falls the region's hub for retail services. That explains the presence of Lowe's, Costco, Home Depot, and others. The retail catchment area for Twin Falls includes roughly a quarter million people, according to Vice Mayor Hall.

This would be a great economic development asset if only that accrued to the benefit of the city's budget in an equitable manner; however, it does not. Sales taxes in Idaho are distributed not on the basis of the point of sale but rather on the basis of a formula that redistributes those revenues to cities throughout the entire state of Idaho.

Vice Mayor Hall notes one consequence of that policy is that Twin Falls builds its city budget for public services largely on the back of real estate taxes, although there are other fees and sources that also contribute. As a result, the city's economic development plan seeks buildings and plants that will contribute to the tax base that enables the city to provide services.

Happily, the city has had some recent economic development success. This came, however, despite federally imposed regulations concerning the clarity of the local water supply. The solution cost the city $30 million but enabled it to demonstrate to a major employer that it was interested and flexible enough to invest in its own future, thereby encouraging the company to want to invest in Twin Falls as well.

In early 2010, the New York-based yogurt company, Chibani, selected a site in Twin Falls and committed to a quarter billion dollar investment that will produce a one-million-square-foot plant. The community was also able to demonstrate its flexibility to the company by arranging for the local community college, the faculty of which includes the vice mayor, to provide directly related training programs as well as temporary space. This was an important part of the recent attraction of a Dell Computer facility as well. One of the lessons Vice Mayor Hall points out for other micropolitan communities is that they can be more flexible than their larger metropolitan cousins. This represents a clear competitive advantage in economic development marketing.

Uvalde, Texas

Fluctuations in the population of Uvalde, Texas (please see Figure 6.64) in the last 20 years would be a topic for conversation with the city's mayor. From 1990 to

Figure 6.64 Downtown Uvalde, Texas. (Courtesy of Olga Charles, City of Uvalde)

2000, the number of residents grew from 14,729 to 16,441, but then declined in the 2010 census count to 15,751 (US Beacon, 2012). At the time of this writing, the city's unemployment rate was slightly higher than the US average of 8.6%, and stood at 8.9% in Uvalde (http://www.bestplaces.net).

The city's website states that future growth sectors are expected to include services, transportation, health care, construction, and border control. The latter reflects the city's proximity to the border with Mexico, only one hour to the south. The city is less than six square miles in area but the surrounding county, also Uvalde County, covers an area of nearly 1,600 square miles.

The city's economic potential is likely tied to its location on two major highways, US 83 and US 90, the two longest highways in the United States. There are also good rail connections in Uvalde, and San Antonio is 90 miles to the east, leaving Uvalde to serve a large region as an isolated micropolitan city. The mayor should be asked to indicate whether these factors will have the potential to drive the local economy forward over the foreseeable future.

Interview with the Honorable J. Allen Carnes, Mayor of Uvalde, Texas

Mayor Carnes characterizes Uvalde as being "fortunate" in terms of the local economy. As a rural Texas town with a strong agricultural base, the city has struggled a little through the current recession but "never really experiences either a real boom period or a real bust time." He does note that balancing the city's budget has been a little more challenging in recent years, particularly because there are some infrastructure projects—notably sewer and water—that must be completed. Still, there is a large oil play south of Uvalde which helps grow the job base and income levels.

Sales revenues from the city's merchants have increased by 17% in 2011 and by 6% more in the first half of 2012. The city's budget does not benefit only from those sales, however, as it derives between 35 and 40% from the *ad valorem* tax and another like percentage from various utility fees.

Although rural, Uvalde's greatest economic development asset is possibly its location. The two longest highways in the United States (Interstate Highways 90 and 83) intersect in Uvalde. Thus, shipping, warehousing, distribution, and related services are a natural for the city. Uvalde's rural location also establishes it as a hub micropolitan city in which the retail, health care, education, recreation, and cultural opportunities for the larger region can be found. The nearest larger city is San Antonio, which is 75 miles away.

The downtown of Uvalde is also an attraction in that it is home to a surprising number of old and large trees, many of which sit in the middle of the streets that pass through the city. The missing ingredient, as defined by the mayor, is a pool of resources that could be used to promote the city for visitors.

Uvalde's mayor, as are many of his micropolitan counterparts, is a lifelong resident of the area, who felt that the elected officials in his town needed to be better listeners. Mayor Carnes pointed out that, in small towns, leaders are needed (both elected and appointed) who will take the long-term view because things take resources and time to accomplish. This means that they must intend to stay in the community for a long time. These cities need a "face" that will be active and help make them competitive well into the future.

Another observation Mayor Carnes made was that, in Texas, there are two types of rural communities: those that are sitting still, losing the younger population to larger metropolitan areas, and being left with the older established population with less income or spending potential; and those that are moving forward by creating opportunities for employment, education, retail, dining, recreation, culture, and more, and are more generally moving ahead. In these latter communities, there is always a plan that looks forward 10 or 20 years to create a vision of the future that everyone can understand even if they don't fully agree.

Valparaiso, Indiana

Valparaiso, Indiana (please see Figure 6.65) was originally purchased from the Potawatomi Indians in 1832, and has grown in population over the recent decades, increasing from 24,414 in 1990 to 27,428 in 2000, a growth rate of more than 12%. Over the ensuing five years to 2005 it grew again by more than 6% to 29,102 (US Beacon, 2012). Today's unemployment rate in Valparaiso is 7.3%, below the national average of 9.1%. Although this is a good sign, especially in light of the increases in the population base and the workforce, recent numbers are not as encouraging with recent-period job growth in the negative at −1.06, lower than the US average of −0.12% (http://www.bestplaces.net).

Figure 6.65 Memorial garden in Valparaiso, Indiana. (Courtesy of Valparaiso Park Department)

Although the mayor should elaborate on the relative economic stability of Valparaiso, it is likely that its location is a key factor. The city sits 50 miles from Chicago with several major interstate highways within easy reach.

The Chamber of Commerce website lists the primary employers in Valparaiso today as Porter Health Systems (nearly 2,000 employees), Valparaiso University (more than 1,000 employees), the public schools and county government agencies (more than 1,500 positions), and 23 other employers with at least 100 employees. Many of these are in the types of employment areas that support a bedroom community, including business and personal services and public sector agencies. Mayor Costas could help describe whether those business sectors are strong contributors to the city's budget. This will depend in large measure on what the state of Indiana permits its cities to collect and retain and what goes to the capital and gets redistributed.

Interview with the Honorable Jon Costas, Mayor of Valparaiso, Indiana

Valparaiso, Indiana has the considerable economic advantage of being the hub for service providers in a larger township (approximately 55,000) and a greater region with more than 150,000 residents. After a glowing description of how well Valparaiso is doing, Mayor Costas was asked why the city was faring so much better than much of the rest of the rust belt. "Valparaiso University has a profound and positive impact on the local economy. It not only creates jobs and spending but it brings in visitors and gives us a lot of intellectual power. Many of the university people serve on local committees and lend their brain power to their adopted community."

Coupled with a strong public school system, Valparaiso has been successful in attracting and sustaining some larger employers, including Emerson with about 350 jobs, the local hospital with about 1,000, and Valparaiso University, which employs about 1,500 people, all of which is complemented by a strong nonprofit sector.

Mayor Costas explains that, over the past decade, the city has concentrated on improving its appearance and its infrastructure. "The roads and infrastructure were in pretty bad shape. The downtown was on life support. The city was borrowing money for its operating expenses. It was not a pretty picture."

Most important, the university, which was seen as the city's greatest economic development asset, was entered by traveling through a part of town that had dilapidated structures and was unsafe. The leadership of the day prepared a series of five core values relating to how the city would move forward and continue to exist. This became the basis for the city's first strategic plan, which provided general long-term direction for the city staff and residents. Because everyone was involved, everyone knew where they would be heading. This eliminated further discussions about "what" and allowed the planning thereafter to address "how."

The resulting efforts to achieve the plan's objectives were public–private partnerships. These efforts enabled the city to beautify the areas leading to the university and to tear down old shopping centers and replace them with student housing projects, including 400 new units initially with another 150 under way. Key to the plan were improvements to downtown Valparaiso. Said the mayor, "If it's not healthy, the whole city suffers." An old downtown parking structure came down and was replaced by a park with a performance pavilion. This created ripples and the buildings around the park are attractive and new.

One of the key principles espoused by Mayor Costas has been frugality. The city has now developed a $6 million rainy-day fund; this represents about one-fourth of the city's annual budget level. But, says the mayor, frugality must be paired with common sense principles. Some money needs to be invested in the new facilities and infrastructure that will serve as an investment in the future of Valparaiso and attract the next generation of employers as well as enable today's businesses to succeed and grow. In this way, Mayor Costas is echoing the words of other city mayors, from micropolitan to metropolitan, that the best way to grow a business base is to create an environment that is conducive to their growth.

Another key lesson from Mayor Costas is that building partnerships in the community is a key part of his job. "Good planning is a necessary investment; and you don't do that alone."

Vicksburg, Mississippi

At the time of this writing, as the national unemployment rate stood at 9.1%, that of Vicksburg, Mississippi was 17.3%. Recent job growth exceeded the national average in the negative column, at −0.64% compared to −0.12% (http://www.bestplaces.net). Between 1990 and 2000, the city's population base jumped by 26.3%, from 20,908 to 26,407. However, the economic decline leading up to such high levels of unemployment resulted in a 2.5% decline in population to 25,752 (US Beacon, 2012).

This is a reflection of a simple and disastrous fact for many micropolitan cities in economic despair: those who are able to leave and find jobs elsewhere will do so, leaving behind a more needy group of people with a diminished ability to pay for the public services that are in greater demand than ever before. Certainly, a topic for discussion with the mayor would be how a city like Vicksburg can cope with these devastating and conflicting trends.

There are some positive attributes on which Vicksburg's planners can build: the cost of living is more than 17% below the national average (http://www.bestplaces. net). Furthermore, the city's and the region's Civil War history provide strong, if not consistent, attractions for tourism promotion. Four casinos in the area are also sources of tax revenues but it is not clear whether they accrue to the benefit of the state or go directly to the municipality's coffers. This would be another good topic to discuss with the mayor. Finally, agriculture has a role: can it be expanded or otherwise enhanced?

Vicksburg, Mississippi: Interview Declined

Walla Walla, Washington

Walla Walla (please see Figure 6.66) appears to enjoy a significantly diversified city and regional economy. Performance through the current recession, however, has mirrored national trends. The current level of unemployment in Walla Walla is 8.9% and the national average is 9.1%. Recent job growth in the city stands at –0.05% whereas the US average is –0.12% (http://www.bestplaces.net).

The residential base of the city has grown slowly but steadily. Between 1990 and 2000, the base grew by nearly 1% from 29,437 to 29,680. Through 2005, it grew again to 30,989, an increase of 4.4% (US Beacon, 2012).

Figure 6.66 Welcome to Walla Walla, Washington. (Courtesy of City of Walla Walla)

Wineries in the region have had great success and are primary components of the economy, representing 8.3% of current jobs held by city residents. It raises the question of what the city is doing to advance and promote the growth of the indus-try. For example, are assets being added that support the cluster? Is the local community college providing training for those in the industry? Are local businesses providing the goods and services required by the wineries? Are there relevant local associations and other connections? One illustration of this can be found at the Walla Walla Community College, which provides courses to support the wineries, fields, wine laboratories, tasting rooms, and tourism elements, and has opened a $4 million enology school. Sixty-nine of the eighty-four graduates to date have been employed locally in the wine industry (Hollander, 2012).

A 2007 report (EMSI, 2007) noted that the wine industry in Walla Walla now supports nearly 1,100 jobs and generates total annual earnings of nearly $47 million. It further forecast the percentage of all local jobs by 2017 that were in the sector to be 16% of all local employment. And, of course, these jobs represent only those directly engaged in the industry and its current local supply chain. There will be more that are unrelated but indirectly dependent upon the cluster and are supported in the community as well.

Wineries are not the only active sector in Walla Walla. A 2007 report noted that 13% of residents held jobs in paper mills, 13% in higher education, 11% in other agricultural operations and mining, and 10% in the public sector (EMSI, 2007). Of course, 2007 was prerecession so it would be interesting to discuss with the mayor what happened in those industries as a result of the recession and how the city has reacted.

Interview with the Honorable Jim Barrow, Mayor of Walla Walla, Washington

Given the recent high prices of wheat, Walla Walla, Washington has weathered the recent recession well. This fact, coupled with a well-diversified business base that includes a growing penitentiary sector (about to add another 400 jobs) and a significant public sector presence in the form of the US Army Corps of Engineers, helps to sustain the city's economy in difficult times. During the current recession, no large employers have gone out of business or left for other locations.

Mayor Barrow explained that the city's budget is derived primarily from sales taxes, complemented by hotel taxes and fees. Because the sales tax is so important in providing the budgetary resources for public services, Walla Walla seeks to attract both residents and tourists to local establishments.

A recent boom in the local wine-growing business has benefited the city in two ways: wine sales are taxed, and tourists come to the region for wine tastings and winery tours. At present, there are as many as 200 wineries within five miles of the city's center. The state of Washington imposes an 8.7% sales tax, a large portion of which is returned to the communities that generated the taxes. To promote the growth of the industry further, Mayor Barrow notes that the enology program at the local college trains and retrains students and workers in the art of wine-making.

Walla Walla also benefits from being rather distant from other cities of greater size. Spokane is about three hours away and the much smaller Tri-City area is about one hour away by automobile. This enables city retailers to generate sales and taxes from the entire region, including communities in neighboring Oregon, only five miles away.

An additional asset that benefits business and business attraction in Walla Walla is the higher education community. Three colleges and universities call Walla Walla home: Walla Walla University, Whitman College, and Walla Walla Community College. These three institutions provide the range of training needed in the immediate community, from nursing to social work and from the liberal arts to horticultural training.

Lessons learned by Mayor Barrow and the city of Walla Walla may be instructive to other micropolitan communities. These include: (1) be fiscally conservative; involve the citizenry in public planning and programs; be open to new and different possibilities; and (2) never blindly rely on past performance to predict future possibilities.

Warren, Ohio

Warren is one of the fastest declining (in terms of population) micropolitan cities in this study. Between 1990 and 2000, the city's population base declined by 30%, from 66,538 to 46,832. Over the next five years, it registered another loss of 2.2% to a total of 45,796 (US Beacon, 2012). Unemployment in Warren, even with fewer people in the labor pool to compete for the jobs, is still in excess of the 9.1% national average, standing presently right at 10%. The situation has recently deteriorated even further as the reports of recent job loss against a national average of –0.12% are at –1.13% in Warren (http://www.bestplaces.net).

Warren competes regionally for employers with cities that are within reach, including Dayton, Pittsburgh, Cleveland, and Akron, but those other cities are significantly larger and have more jobs as well as more educated and skilled workers. What are the advantages of such a location? Can Warren use that for business attraction in a variety of sectors?

At present, 19% of those who work are employed in manufacturing functions, 17% in health care and social assistance, and 16% in retail, all of which are typically lower-paying occupations. Could this foretell a greater role for local colleges or universities, including Youngstown State?

Warren, Ohio: Interview Declined

Watertown, Wisconsin

Watertown (please see Figure 6.67) has an advantageous geographic location, sitting roughly midway between Madison and Milwaukee. That is likely part of

Figure 6.67 The Octagon House, Watertown, Wisconsin. (Courtesy of City of Watertown)

the reason for the city's consistent population growth. During the decade of the 1990s, Watertown grew by nearly 13% from 19,142 to 21,598, and again by 5.6% to boast a 2005 population of 22,816 (US Beacon, 2012). The city's unemployment rate at the time of this writing was the same 9.1% as the US average. Recent job growth, however, was a little farther into the negative at –1.15% to –0.12% (http://www.bestplaces.net).

The city is well served by multimodal transportation networks, including highways, rail, and the Rock River. Although agriculture is an important component of the local economy, the city's largest employers are Trek Bicycle, Watertown Memorial Hospital, the public school system, and Bethesda Lutheran Homes and Services, all of which are reported to employ between 500 and 1,000 people.

The nearby city of Dodge and the county in which it resides, Jefferson County, seem to be likely partners in economic development outreach. It would be interesting to hear the mayor's take on both economic diversification and regionalism for economic growth in micropolitan cities such as Watertown. This is especially true in light of a recent (June 2011) survey that reported 53% of the city's employers expected to begin adding positions over the ensuing 12 months (Taschler, 2011). Why is confidence up in Watertown when it is still in decline in other American micropolitan cities?

Interview with the Honorable Ron Krueger, Mayor of Watertown, Wisconsin

Watertown, Wisconsin, notes Mayor Krueger, represents the only green space in the southern part of the state, giving the city a substantial competitive advantage for purposes of economic development. This may be due to the fact that Watertown is also the largest Wisconsin city of its size not to be connected to a four-lane highway, a distinction that will soon be removed when the highway currently under construction is completed. These advantages, coupled with the city's location 40 miles from Madison and 45 miles from Milwaukee, set it up to be a growing hub for services and retail, particularly grocery shopping and medical services.

A small local Baptist college provides the retailers in the city with a pool of part-time workers and the local hospital also plays an important role in the city's economic development planning and outreach. However, sales taxes in the state of Wisconsin are sent to the capital and then redistributed to localities on the basis of an established formula. Ultimately, sales taxes represent about one-third of the city's annual budget. The other two-thirds come in similar proportions from the real estate tax base and various fees.

Because the state of Wisconsin has no local income tax, the attraction of more retailers and the generation of additional sales taxes are not as critical to the city as the attraction of revenues from new construction. For example, a Walmart Superstore and car dealerships are more important to the community because they provide needed goods and services as well as jobs, but the tax impacts are greater on the real estate side than in terms of the sales taxes they generate.

In terms of future economic development objectives, Mayor Krueger notes that Watertown is home to about 50 small and midsized manufacturers, and cites interest in working with both the city's economic development program and the regional partnership to attract more of such operations. He is quick to note, however, that the support for, and the retention and expansion of, existing employers must be the first priority for the city and the region.

In terms of lessons to be learned from the Watertown experience, Mayor Krueger notes that the city has four active TIF areas in which tax increment financing is applied. He firmly states that, although TIFs can be effective, they must be established very carefully and must be based on a very solid financial plan.

A second suggestion aligned very closely with the writing on clustering (see the work of Michael Porter [1995, 1998, and 2003] and others). Mayor Krueger noted that the city is home to 50 or more manufacturers but that the connections between them are not very strong. A subsequent partnership in the form of a manufacturers' consortium among themselves as well as between them and the city has increased their collective purchasing power and the extent to which they buy goods from one another. There is also new collaboration between them to attract relevant suppliers to the community to support their collective growth.

Local trails and agricultural areas give the region a sense of openness and green space that need to be preserved as the city continues to grow. Watertown is within a one-hour drive of 70% of Wisconsin's population, making outdoor and recreational activities and related tourism important to the local economy as well.

Waynesboro, Virginia

Waynesboro is part of a larger and rather lengthy growth corridor in Virginia that extends along the path of Interstate Route 81. As such, there is no surprise in the population growth of recent years: from 18,549 to 19,520 (+5.23%) between 1990 and 2000, and again by 9% (to 21,269) by 2005 (US Beacon, 2012). This growth has been comfortable for the community as the unemployment rate was less at the time of this writing than the national average (7.9% versus 9.1%) and recent job growth is in positive figures at +.79%, compared to the national average of –0.12% (http://www.bestplaces.net).

In 2009, the city announced that its total economic product had, for the first time, exceeded $400 million. This is a testament to strong leadership as the city passed from being a manufacturing-based economy built around such corporate giants as General Electric, DuPont, and Compton Mills, to alternative economic bases. A 2011 announcement by the aerospace company, PPI/Time Zero, to invest more than $1 million in Waynesboro, creating between 60 and 100 new manufacturing positions will add to the stability as well as the diversity of the Waynesboro economy. The question of how a micropolitan community could accomplish that feat would be fodder for the discussion with the mayor.

The Waynesboro downtown has also been reported as an economic development issue in terms of its need for revitalization, as has been the question of competition with the neighboring micropolitan city of Staunton. These, too, would be good topics for discussion with the mayor.

Waynesboro, Virginia: Interview Declined

Wilson, North Carolina

Wilson, North Carolina derives its economic drivers from its location right on Interstate Route 95 which runs from New England along the entire Atlantic coast to Florida. As traffic has grown along the highway, so has the city's population. In the decade of the 1990s, it increased by more than 20%, from 36,930 to 44,405, and again from 2000 to 2005 by 5.8% to a total of 46,947 (US Beacon, 2012). Perhaps due to the pace of the population growth, the unemployment rate is rather high at the time of this writing: 10.9% as compared to the national average of 9.1%. Recent job growth is in the positive range at +0.61%, which is better than the national performance level of –0.12% (http://www.bestplaces.net).

Wilson has many of the services that one would imagine to appeal to travelers along Route 95, however, it does also have some manufacturing, including many household names such as Bridgestone, Alliance One Tobacco, Merck, Saint Gobain Glass, and Kidde Aerospace. Still, most employment opportunities can be found in the service sectors, including health, hospitality, and food service.

One question for the mayor would relate to how the city builds its budget. If it is based on sales tax revenues, there should be joy in Wilson. If it is property tax-based, there could be a problem. Another topic to explore with the mayor would be how Wilson Community College is engaged in support of the city's or the region's economic development.

Wilson, North Carolina: Interview Declined

Winona, Minnesota

Winona, Minnesota (please see Figure 6.68) presents an interesting conundrum: the population first grew and has more recently held fairly steady at the same time jobs were being lost. This would normally imply a high unemployment rate. Although the rate at the time of this writing was a bit high at 7.1%, it is substantially less than the average national rate at the time of 9.1%. Recent job growth was registered at a very high −4.43% against a national average of −0.12% (http://www.bestplaces.net).

The city's population grew by 6.6% between 1990 and 2000, from 25,399 to 27,069. Although the ensuing five-year period saw it decline to 26,587 that represents not even a 2% loss (US Beacon, 2012).

The composites cluster in Winona is quite strong and services a wide range of industry applications from aerospace and agriculture to appliances and automotive to furniture and medical applications. Why is this cluster still thriving and growing and others in the area have faltered? And what are the city and the region doing to support the further growth of this cluster?

In the city, primary employment sectors include manufacturing, trade, transportation, and education and health services. Winona's major private employers are listed

Figure 6.68 Winona, Minnesota, situated along the Mississippi River. (Courtesy of City of Winona)

as Fastenal, Benchmark Electronics, Wincraft, and Peerless Chain. Public sector employment is also large and includes Winona Health, Winona State University, St. Mary's University of Minnesota, and the Winona Area Public Schools. Mayor Miller should be asked to indicate whether he feels that this business diversity is sufficient to sustain economic growth for the city well into the future.

Interview with the Honorable Jerry Miller, Mayor of Winona, Minnesota

Mayor Jerry Miller is bucking a trend when compared to the other mayors interviewed in the course of this research: he has been in his part-time office for 16 years. Winona, which has a city staff complement of 175, has a professional city manager who administers city service provision and reports to the mayor and the other six members of the city council. The city is also somewhat unique in its composition. Due to the presence of St. Mary's University, with its 10,000 students, as well as the presence of a technical school, the demographics of the city break out fairly evenly: one-third each, students and faculty, retirees, and others.

The city is also different from many represented in this research by virtue of having survived the current recession without significant economic upheaval. At present, there are more than 100 manufacturers in Winona and they represent a variety of types of manufacturing, most notably in composites. Interestingly, Mayor Miller points out that most of the primary employers in Winona are from the city and the region, including the large and renowned Fastenal.

The city has not experienced the type of brain drain that others have. In fact, the mayor is interested in annexing more land from surrounding areas because the last available commercial land in the city limits is about to be absorbed. Mayor Miller wants to ensure that the next generation of entrepreneurs, which he firmly believes are already living in Winona, will have a place to grow their businesses. By way of example, he offers his own family business in which his sons are currently the fourth generation of managers.

Micropolitan communities, he says, echoing the similar sentiments of other interviewed mayors, are small enough to have a safe and peaceful family life, big enough to have a university with social and cultural opportunities, and close enough to major cities that other options are readily available. And although these cities do have some of the negative issues that cities of all sizes must deal with, including drugs and crime, it is on a more manageable scale. "Small communities have big advantages. All we have to do is to figure out how to use them."

In terms of lessons for other micropolitan cities trying to cope with economic challenges, the mayor notes that change is always difficult. The way to deal with problematic issues is to sit down with all the parties concerned and offer them the opportunity to resolve their concerns rather than letting the city decide on something that will satisfy perhaps no one. This can be done more readily in smaller communities where everyone knows everyone else.

Figure 6.69 Downtown Winter Haven, Florida. (Courtesy of Potthast Studios)

Winter Haven, Florida

The leisure and hospitality industry in central Florida has, for many years, provided Winter Haven (please see Figure 6.69) with a stable economic base. In fact, it has typically represented about 3.5% of the local economic output of the city and is followed by professional and technical services. Prior to the recession, the city's and the region's population bases grew consistently over time. Between 1990 and 2000, the city's population grew from 24,725 to 26,487, an increase of more than 7.2%. By 2005, it had grown again to 29,501, an additional increase in just five years of more than 11%. Additional growth occurred by the 2010 census count of 33,874 (US Beacon, 2012). One of the more curious demographic data points is the relatively high median age in Winter Haven of 44 years, perhaps reflective of the large number of retirees in the city and the region.

The current recession has clearly affected the vitality of the local economy. As tourism declined to the local and regional sites, the hospitality and retail sectors suffered dramatically. The city's unemployment rate in mid-2007 had been a mere 4% but began a steep increase in mid-2008 and reached more than 12% by mid-2011 (Central Florida Development Council, 2011). It was also reported that crime statistics were on the rise in 2009 by about 15% over the previous year, not an unusual occurrence in cities during periods of recession (Godefrin, 2009). One bit of good fortune appeared in the form of 1,000 jobs in a new Legoland park starting in late 2011, with the unemployment rate dipping in October to just over 11%.

Other sectors in the economy are also being pinched by the current recession: construction is down to near zero activity, as measured by the number of single-family home construction permits awarded. For purposes of comparison to prerecession levels, the high of 8,000 permits issued was reached in 2005; the 2009 and 2010 annual totals were less than 800. This may be turning around, however, as recent coverage shows downtown occupancy rates up and building permits up in mid-2012 (Little, 2012). The local development council acknowledged that, as is so often the case in situations of high unemployment and little positive news, "Consumer confidence continues to languish near the all-time low for the index ..." (Central Florida Development Council, 2011).

Interview with the Honorable Jeff Powell, Mayor of Winter Haven, Florida

As of this writing, the micropolitan city of Winter Haven, Florida has begun to boom again, largely as a result of a recently announced decision to construct a new theme park, Legoland, Florida, within the city limits. The addition of 1,000 new jobs will help both to lower the city's unemployment rate and generate tax revenues to support city services.

This announcement followed another large economic development win, the attraction of a CSX facility that will house 2,000 workers and will generate tremendous tax benefits for the city of Winter Haven. These 3,000 new jobs will spin off as many as another 6,000 to 9,000 in the area's secondary and tertiary economies.

Often one of the challenges for micropolitan cities with this level of growth is the availability of housing that workers can either rent or buy. Mayor Powell indicates that this will not be an issue for Winter Haven because there are a number of homes on the market at this time and because many of the new positions will be filled by people who already live within commuting distance. This represents a competitive advantage over micropolitan cities that are more isolated than is Winter Haven.

Polk State College, now a four-year institution, serves as an economic development asset for the city and is complemented by Corporate College, which designs its instructional curricula in conjunction with specific employers to match the skillsets they require to be successful. Mayor Powell notes that Polk State College will likely grow in size and renown and will thus become an even greater economic development asset for the city but, until that happens, the absence of a "major" university represents an asset gap. That is not to say that the city markets itself and its colleges as its only assets.

Economic development is seen as a city function as well as a regional function, both of which are complemented by the state of Florida. Prospects that the city cannot accommodate are referred regularly to other cities within Lakeland County. Still, local budget growth is a key focus, and it is derived largely from property taxes. This means that business relocations to, and expansions within, Winter Haven are key economic development concerns.

Mayor Powell believes that the key lesson learned as a result of years of economic development programs in Winter Haven is that cities cannot sit back and wait for the business to come in; it requires an aggressive effort. And that effort must include a willingness to go the extra mile for the business. The city's efforts to welcome Legoland, Florida included trips to visit their executives in Carlsbad, California to determine their needs and to express the city's willingness to be supportive and flexible. "One cannot just sit idle," said the mayor, "and, in economic development, you have to give a little to receive a lot."

Wooster, Ohio

Perhaps Wooster, Ohio's greatest economic development asset is its location. It is easily accessible from several major cities: Cleveland is 50 miles away; Youngstown, 60; Columbus, 90; Pittsburgh, 96; Toledo, 105; Detroit 125; and Cincinnati, 180. Does Wooster, then, serve as a regional hub in the same way that many other micropolitan cities do? Can it establish further economic stability by serving as a center for services to those working in these larger cities? Or is Wooster merely a bedroom community for their workers? And is that OK, given how municipal budgets are constructed in the State of Ohio?

The population of the city has grown substantially: from 1990 to 2000, the base grew by 11.8%, from 22,191 to 24,811, and again by 3.45% between 2000 and 2005, to a total of 25,668 (US Beacon, 2012). At the time of this writing, the level of unemployment in Wooster was less than the 9.1% national average, but still high at 8.3%. Recent job growth, however, was further in the negative than the −0.12% national average, at −0.56% (http://www.bestplacesnet).

The economy of the state of Ohio is suffering and that must surely be hurting Wooster and other cities. "Ohio has lost more than 500,000 jobs in the past decade, most of them well-paying manufacturing jobs. Only Michigan has suffered more from the national industrial decline" (Gauchon). Neither will this be turned around overnight. "It's a long-term strategy. It's how states like Ohio must transform themselves. We don't have any other choice" (Gauchon, 2011).

Nonetheless, there are long-term manufacturing operations that remain successful in Wooster, such as LuK, which started operations 35 years ago and now employs more than 1,000 people in Wooster. Why have they survived and thrived whereas so many others in Wooster have closed their doors?

The city has other assets that need to be explored with the mayor as well, including a tradition of agricultural output that also contributes strongly to local economic growth. Also, Wooster College represents an economic development asset that is worthy of discussion with the mayor.

Wooster, Ohio: Interview Declined

Yankton, South Dakota

The population of Yankton, South Dakota has experienced significant growth over the past generation, increasing in the decade of the 1990s from 12,703 to 13,716, and again by 2010 to 14,454 (US Beacon, 2012). The city's unemployment rate at the time of this writing was a very strong 3.6%, compared to the national average of 8.6% (http://www.bestplaces.net).

The city's website lists its largest employer as Avera Sacred Heart Hospital, with more than 1,000 employees. This may be due to the relatively isolated position of the city and its serving as a hub for medical services to a large geographic region. This may also explain the second largest employer being the state Human Services Center, which employs 625 people. Other large employers include Hy-Vee, the city school system, Kolberg-Pioneer, Walmart, Sapa Extrusions, and Vishay Dale Electronics.

The city has a great economic development asset in its proximity to the Missouri River. Interstate Route 29 provides another link to other areas and to economic development. Regional growth opportunities are thus marketed and include Yankton, Sioux Falls, and Watertown. Industry sectors included in this region are electronics, information technology, financial services, life sciences development, energy, agribusiness, and advanced manufacturing. Activities in most of these sectors involve manufacturing operations.

The asset needs identified to support the growth of businesses in these sectors represent the list of asset needs to be developed over time and constitute a laundry list of topics for discussion with Yankton's mayor. These include workforce attraction and preparation, incubators and research parks, infrastructural developments, and risk capital for investments. Clearly, there is a growing role for the colleges and universities in the I-29 corridor (i.e., South Dakota State, the University of South Dakota, and Dakota State University), each of which has different areas of strengths, as well as the various public school systems.

Yankton, South Dakota: Interview Declined

Zanesville, Ohio

The population of Zanesville (please see Figure 6.70), as has that of many rust belt cities, has declined in proportion to the loss of employment opportunities. From 1990 to 2000, the city lost residents at a rate of 4.5%, declining from 26,778 to 25,586. Over the next five years, the decline was 1.3% to 25,253 (US Beacon, 2012). Today's rate of unemployment in Zanesville is at a very high 12.5%, higher than the national average of 9.1%. Recent job growth is not encouraging either, sitting at −1.43% versus the national average of −0.12% (http://www.bestplaces.net).

Figure 6.70   The Muskingum River and Zanesville, Ohio by night. (Courtesy of Kris Bates)

In 2008, the early phases of the current recession caused the closure of manufacturing facilities in and around the city, resulting in the loss of more than 1,000 jobs. However, the city was fortunate to recover some ground when Time-Warner established a facility that houses 350 jobs, and Avon developed a distribution center. But, these are not the entire answer. The poverty rate in Zanesville today is a very high 19+% (the US average stands at just under 8%). Education levels are lower than in nearby competitive cities. And vacant and abandoned buildings cost the city money, are the sites of a great deal of criminal activity, and present an unattractive view to potential business site location decision makers. More than 11% of all the fires in the city are located in these unoccupied structures (Zanesville Summary, 2011).

How can a location attract, or retain, employers in these circumstances? What is being done to change them? These are interesting topics for the discussion with the mayor. After all, Forbes.com has named Zanesville "America's Seventh Most Vulnerable City."

Interview with the Honorable Jeff Tilton, Mayor of Zanesville, Ohio

When questioned about Zanesville's economic mood, Mayor Tilton explains that the recent storms and power outages will stall the economic growth that had been under way. Much of the hopes for growth in this community rest on the potential for the current oil and gas exploration wells to come in. The results will not be known for about six to twelve months.

Fortunately, there have been some other positive announcements in recent months. Haliburton brought nearly 300 new jobs to the city to serve the oil and gas crews. Mayor Tilton is positive about the ability of businesses in his city to support the oil and gas crews regardless of whether the long-term decisions are to drill in Zanesville or elsewhere in the region.

Zanesville derives much of its local budget from a 1.9% income tax, whereas real estate taxes accrue to the county. For this reason, the city's economic development focus is not just on more jobs, but higher-paying jobs.

A discussion about the mayor's background is quite similar to that of mayors in other micropolitan cities who have been interviewed as part of this research. Mayor Tilton served on the city council for eight years before being elected mayor. He has no interest in further elective office; he has lived his entire life in the area and simply wanted to help make things better. He credits his background in the private sector with his understanding of processes, but has learned that, in public life, things typically take longer. "In the public sector you just have to be patient."

Cooperative approaches that incorporate the interests and the voice of the business community are also critical to success in Zanesville. "They know how to get things done. We manage the process."

Chapter 7

What Has Been Learned?

America's micropolitan cities may be broadly categorized into three types. The distinctions begin with their geography but spread to economic and social descriptors as well. The first type includes those cities that are suburbs of much larger cities and regions. The second grouping represents cities distant enough from larger cities to serve as hubs for retail, medical, educational, cultural, and other needs for the wider region. Generally speaking, it is safe to conclude that the greater the isolation of the micropolitan community, the greater the emphasis needed on rail lines, road networks, regional air service, and telecommunications infrastructure.

The final category includes those cities that are so isolated from other conurbations that they must not only serve the greater region but must be almost totally self-sufficient in doing so. I refer herein to these three groupings as *suburban micropolitans, hub micropolitans, and isolated micropolitans*, respectively.

Micropolitan Cities by Type

Metropolitan Micropolitan Cities in the Study

Chelsea, Massachusetts
Clinton, Iowa
Covina, California
Culver City, California
Denison, Texas
Doral, Florida
Fremont, Nebraska
Holyoke, Massachusetts

Kokomo, Indiana
LaGrange, Georgia
Littleton, Colorado
Lompoc, California
Maryland Heights, Missouri
Moline, Illinois
Muskogee, Oklahoma
Naples, Florida
Ottumwa, Iowa
Paramus, New Jersey
Placentia, California
Plainfield, New Jersey
Stillwater, Oklahoma
Valparaiso, Indiana
Warren, Ohio
Watertown, Wisconsin
Winter Haven, Florida

Hub Micropolitan Cities in the Study

Adrian, Michigan
Ardmore, Oklahoma
Athens, Ohio
Bangor, Maine
Baraboo, Wisconsin
Bartlesville, Oklahoma
Beckley, West Virginia
Blytheville, Arkansas
Bowling Green, Ohio
Brigham City, Utah
Brookings, South Dakota
Burlington, Vermont
Carbondale, Illinois
Chambersburg, Pennsylvania
Chillicothe, Ohio
Clovis, New Mexico
Coeur d'Alene, Idaho
Concord, New Hampshire
Cookeville, Tennessee
Danville, Virginia
Dodge City, Kansas
Douglas, Georgia
Durango, Colorado

Elmira, New York
Findlay, Ohio
Galesburg, Illinois
Helena, Montana
Hutchinson, Kansas
Jamestown, New York
Jasper, Wyoming
Kearney, Nebraska
Kerrville, Texas
Kinston, North Carolina
Kokomo, Indiana
Laramie, Wyoming
Marshall, Texas
Marshalltown, Iowa
Martinsville, Virginia
Mason City, Iowa
Menomonie, Wisconsin
Mount Pleasant, Michigan
Meridian, Mississippi
Natchitoches, Louisiana
Newberry, South Carolina
New Bern, North Carolina
Nogales, Arizona
Owatonna, Minnesota
Paducah, Kentucky
Ponca City, Oklahoma
Portsmouth, Ohio
Pottsville, Pennsylvania
Poughkeepsie, New York
Pullman, Washington
Quincy, Illinois
Rolla, Missouri
Ruston, Louisiana
Salina, Kansas
San Louis Obispo, California
Sedalia, Missouri
Selma, Alabama
Shelby, North Carolina
Shelbyville, Tennessee
Staunton-Waynesboro, Virginia
Steven's Point, Wisconsin
Tifton, Georgia
Tupelo, Mississippi

Twin Falls, Idaho
Uvalde, Texas
Vicksburg, Mississippi
Wilson, North Carolina
Winona, Minnesota
Wooster, Ohio
Yankton, South Dakota
Zanesville, Ohio

Isolated Micropolitan Cities in the Study

Aberdeen, South Dakota
Bangor, Maine
Blackfoot, Idaho
Bozeman, Montana
Elko, Nevada
Eureka, California
Hays, Kansas
Hobbs, New Mexico
Lufkin, Texas
Marquette, Michigan
Mason City, Iowa
Minot, North Dakota
Murray, Kentucky
Muskegon, Michigan
Picayune, Mississippi
Plattsburgh, New York
Quincy, Illinois
Roanoke Rapids, North Carolina
Sierra Vista, Arizona
Texarkana, Texas
Twin Falls, Idaho
Walla Walla, Washington

Economies in each of these types of micropolitan communities can be successful (or not) if the basis for local tax revenue generation—and thus, the provision of public services—is consistent with the type of community and the state in which it is located. This is difficult to accomplish for state legislators in states that may have micropolitan cities of more than one type, therefore with more than one type of economic or financial need. More important, many of the mayors of micropolitan communities who were interviewed indicated that state policy-making was not overly concerned with the needs of smaller communities or those that produced less of the types of tax revenue from which the states themselves provide services.

It should be noted, however, that prior research by this author has yielded a contrary sense from the mayors of larger cities who maintain that too little of their states' tax revenues are used to fuel the "economic engines" of the state (thereby generating even greater revenues) in favor of parts of the states that are in greater need. This is a valid argument with points on both sides, but not a discussion for this research.

It is therefore important to consider the bases from which municipalities in various states finance their provision of public services. For example, suburban micropolitans typically, although not always, base their economies on the support services and infrastructure required by the primary city. Thus, back-office operations, retail establishments, personal services, hotels, and more find homes in the suburban micropolitan city. Many of these have, over time, begun to establish economies of their own, even rivaling those of the downtowns, but this is rather more unusual than the norm.

If the states permit cities to benefit from either a percentage of the sales tax or allow their cities to retain those taxes generated at the point of sale, the city can then budget for public services and plan economic development strategies around the growth of retail. Similarly, if the state allows property taxes to be used by suburban micropolitan cities, then they can generate revenues by regulating the tax rate. However, in some of these states, either legislation or referenda have resulted in caps on property tax rates that seriously hinder the ability of municipalities to pay for public services. In Pennsylvania, for instance, such a cap has forced dozens of communities into Act 47, that state's version of municipal prebankruptcy.

For suburban micropolitan cities that exist within states that permit a local income tax, the city and its ability to generate the tax revenues that pay for public services may be largely dependent upon the economic stability of the primary city. Again, different states have different policies that may affect different types of micropolitan communities that all exist in the same state.

For the hub micropolitan cities, the same kinds of considerations persist but within a different context. Hub micropolitan cities may be 50 miles or more from a larger city. People who live in the greater region in some cases add as many as 100,000 additional residents who depend on the city to buy goods, obtain medical care, access entertainment, and more. This means that hub micropolitan cities can establish their economies, as well as the revenue bases from which they provide public services, on the basis of sales tax revenues and enjoy a relatively stable economy and general fund … if, and only if, they exist in states that permit localities to benefit from the sales tax revenues they are able to generate at the point of sale.

In some of the interviews, it was noted that the sales tax revenues accrue either largely or entirely to the benefit of the states' coffers. In other states, there are no sales taxes. In still other states, the point of sale is irrelevant: the state collects all of the sales taxes and redistributes some of them to localities on an established formula. For a hub micropolitan city, this is an economic development opportunity lost. They could seek to generate greater sales and attract additional retailers but why do so if they will not be able to realize the benefits of their efforts?

The same string of logic applies to isolated micropolitan cities, but again with a different impact. Regardless of how their states authorize communities to constitute their local budgets, these cities are so isolated that they *must* provide for their residents, and those of a very wide region, absolutely all of their needs from employment to housing to education to higher education to health care to entertainment and much, much more. Cities in this situation are dependent on sales taxes, if permitted, and income taxes. For any of these cities that must base their local budgets on the basis of property taxes, the system may be regarded by many as inherently and indefinitely flawed. Property is a fixed asset; borders cannot always expand, certainly not infinitely. This can limit the growth of the real estate tax base while the demands for, and costs of, public services continue to rise.

These are interesting twists to the question of how the municipal budgets are constituted in different states. In some states, the budgets have a high proportion of revenues coming from sales taxes. In some cases, this might imply that a good economic development strategy would be to pursue retailers who generate a high volume of sales and therefore pay a lot of taxes. And, this would indeed be a wise strategy if that micropolitan city is located in a state that permits localities to retain the sales taxes generated "at the point of contact." In other words, the city that houses the retailer that made the sales collects the sales tax revenues. However, that is not always the case. Again, in some states, all sales taxes go to the state and are redistributed by an established formula. In some of the micropolitan cities in this study, that kind of state policy dampened any local enthusiasm about attracting more retailers. In brief, why work to raise funds that will just go somewhere else? This results in many communities trying to find logical economic development strategies in contexts that are often viewed as illogical.

The value of this typology is that, given the state tax policies, micropolitan communities of different descriptions may have a greater or lesser ability to control their own economic destinies. It may mean that these cities have to pursue economic development strategies that are not necessarily the best for the future of their residents but rather those which enable the cities' budgets to satisfy the collective needs for public services.

There was also a perspective voiced by several of the mayors who were interviewed that, in good times, small cities and towns need to prepare the infrastructure, office parks, and other community assets that will help attract new employers when the hard times inevitably arrive. Waiting until there is a problem does not work in terms of bringing new companies to the area. Similar attitudes extended for some to the growth and improvement of local colleges and universities. There was a sense expressed that these institutions create a positive name and image for the city and contribute greatly not only to the tax base but also to city boards and commissions, study groups, and community organizations. Making it possible for the college to expand and succeed has numerous spinoff benefits for the municipality as well. Finally, of course, these colleges can be great sources of new businesses, a new workforce, and retraining opportunities for existing workers.

Several mayors also noted in interviews that when employment decreases, enrollments tend to increase. Many of the micropolitan cities that are homes to colleges are intent upon keeping those resultant revenues local rather than seeing them go off to colleges and universities elsewhere.

There is a broad range of advantages that the leaders of micropolitan cities believe they have over their larger counterparts in terms of economic development. Virtually every mayor interviewed expressed the notion that smaller cities enable their residents to be involved at a more intimate and effective level. They attend meetings to discuss strategies and the future of their cities in large numbers. Their collaboration is that of neighbors, not neighborhoods. The people they are strategizing with are their neighbors and friends and, often, families. They go to church together or their kids are on the same sports teams or in the same scout troops. The mayors maintain that their small towns have what they inevitably refer to as "traditional small town values:" safe neighborhoods, decent schools, friendly folks, and a sense of community that simply isn't possible in larger cities. Of course, this is likely to be less the case in metropolitan micropolitan cities.

There was also a consistent expression by the mayors interviewed of the need for smaller communities, especially the hub and isolated micropolitan cities, to be collaborative. This may be an expression of a sense of strength in numbers, but it was a frequently expressed sentiment. To these mayors, collaboration was an essential element of success both within the cities and without. Inside the city, a clear preference for total inclusion of the community was constantly expressed. To them that means all parts of the city's geography, subpopulation groups, business, education, military, institutions, and the business community. External collaboration includes neighboring cities, counties, residents, airports, military installations, and more. The sense that this was more vital in their smaller micropolitan communities than in larger cities was expressed repeatedly.

Of course, it can be argued that one must sacrifice other benefits of the large cities in order to benefit from those of the micropolitan communities. This may include entertainment; a greater breadth of educational opportunities, especially in higher education; and of course employment opportunities. This is a no-win debate; the ability to choose one's lifestyle is one of the advantages of living in the United States. But, the fact does remain that America's micropolitan cities offer what many people are seeking.

One clear distinction between micropolitan and larger US cities became evident from the first interview and remained a factor throughout nearly all of the interviews conducted. The mayors of micropolitan cities largely are not career politicians. They have often become the mayor after serving on the city council or the planning commission or some other relevant ascendancy. Some come to their office as the result of a specific issue on which they worked and that brought them to public service and the public eye.

But, virtually all of the micropolitan mayors who were interviewed noted that their intention was to return to private life, get back to their businesses, and spend more time with their families. Very few of them were full-time mayors; most were running businesses at the same time and many were personally suffering financially as a result. In fact, many declined to be interviewed, which is something that larger-city career politicians in prior research were less inclined to do.

Another frequent expression was that many almost seem surprised that they were the mayor. Many described their cities in almost loving terms, and followed by saying that they became mayor for that reason: "Someone needed to step up and do something!" And, most were salesmen, perhaps because it came from their fondness for their city and not because they felt they had to sell. Furthermore, with a few exceptions, they were natives of the cities—or from within the region—that they now lead. Their parents lived there, their children live there, and many have grandchildren who live there. The position of mayor is not a stepping-stone to these men and women; the future of their city is critically important to them.

Also related to the nonpolitical nature of the backgrounds of these mayors, nearly all of them noted their dependence on, and respect for, the professional city managers and staffers with whom they work. They typically saw their roles as setting vision and policy but expressed the need for strong local managers who could implement the policies and achieve the vision. More than half of those interviewed spoke in glowing terms of one or more such individuals and cited their value to their cities, and several expressed that the absolute most important role of the elected officials in their communities is to recruit and select the best city managers that are available.

Because so many of the mayors interviewed came from the business community and not from careers in politics, these men and women understood business concepts and consistently spoke of the need to plan, seek returns on investments made in the community, and to build reserves against rainy days and economic downturns. Given the relatively smaller budgets and the resulting inability to move funds around between line items as freely or to attract businesses as readily as in larger cities, the business backgrounds of these mayors seems beneficial and noteworthy for these micropolitan cities.

There is, however, a related downside to the part-time and nonpolitical nature of these mayors' backgrounds. Although they are able to rely on professionals in their cities for the management of programs and operations, there is a role to be played by the senior elected officials vis-à-vis their respective state legislatures. They collectively represent the needs of their communities and constituencies, but if they are either inexperienced or not in office long enough to learn the best methods of using their collective strength, they may not be maximally capable of obtaining the necessary benefits and legislation for their constituents. This may go a long way to explaining the arguments made by micropolitan mayors that their state legislatures favor the needs of primary cities and stronger economies over those of the smaller municipalities. Of course, one must also consider that the primary cities may have greater populations (in the aggregate) than do the smaller communities within the states and thus have greater representation and strength in legislative decision making as well as general needs.

There is a presumption in many of the micropolitan communities represented in this research that the federal government also favors the needs of the larger cities and that such preferences translate into relatively less financial support in the form of grants for smaller localities. The sense of the comments, at least in part, related to the relative numbers of voters, however, there was also the occasional, almost begrudging acknowledgment that larger cities can generate greater returns. Still, the argument was also made that the greater ability of larger cities to generate economic growth and tax revenues, coupled with the greater propensity by federal and state agencies to support cities with greater population bases, creates a sort of "perfect storm" from which the needs of the smaller communities are either ignored or undervalued.

Micropolitan communities also stress economic diversity as an essential element of their future. It is too easy to lose one employer or be hurt by a downturn in one dominant industry. If that is all the city has to count on, smaller cities will be in trouble. In addition, micropolitan cities that were dependent upon certain business sectors, such as extractions or manufacturing or textiles or lumber, are particularly susceptible to negative changes in the macroeconomy. Tourism and personal services can also be particularly susceptible to recessionary influences as they are directly affected by expendable income levels. This diversity should be seen to include federal installations and public institutions such as hospitals, universities, and military bases.

Although greater economic facility was frequently cited as an objective, micropolitan city economies are not, almost by definition, generally large enough to support substantial diversity. For them, the loss of a primary employer means more than the loss of jobs and taxes. It can also mean the loss of the best of the workforce in the city as well as private support for organizations and causes throughout the community. This brain drain is an extremely serious issue for micropolitan cities because it removes their most important economic development asset for recovery.

The worst-case scenario occurs in those micropolitan cities where the primary employer is the only employer of a significant size. These cities are the most susceptible to negative recessionary impacts. Not only will the business in question be lost, but now all of the secondary jobs and support businesses are in trouble. And when they decline or depart the tertiary service economy that depended on their spending also suffers. Ultimately, this means that the entire community is in trouble and that danger is compounded the more isolated the micropolitan community becomes. That is, such impacts may not spell the end for Paramus, New Jersey, a suburb of New York City, or even for Kinston, North Carolina, a hub micropolitan city. It may be a much different matter, however, for an isolated hub such as Pullman, Washington or Uvalde, Texas. When people who lose their jobs move away, the unemployment rates do not necessarily reflect the entire problem. The denominator simply changes with the numerator.

Many micropolitan cities try to bring their youth back when they marry and have families. Often, they want their children to experience the same kind of childhood they had enjoyed while growing up. *Under*employment in these communities can further mask the full impacts of the situation as people can only find part-time employment, work full-time but for less pay than previously, have to accept two or more jobs to make ends meet, or simply stop seeking employment altogether and are thus no longer counted as being in the workforce.

The obverse situation is also being experienced in some micropolitan communities. The brain drain in some cities has created a labor shortage. When an existing employer is ready to expand operations, they will often need to import workers. In response to some of these situations, some cities expressed an interest in becoming a center for immigrants to locate as a means of providing workers for both existing and prospective employers.

Micropolitan cities were often founded around one or more traditional industries, such as manufacturing, agriculture, lumber, extractions, or textiles. Typically, the replacement industries have paid lower wages. The lower wage rates translate broadly into reduced tax revenues for the city. This occurs at a time when the demand for public services is increasing. It also means that the resulting loss of private support for community organizations and programs is felt from everything from scout troops to churches, from Little League to the arts, and from health causes to social services. The "catch-22" is that the community then becomes less attractive to potential new residents and employers.

As relates to the perceptions of mayors about the future economic viability of America's micropolitan cities in general, most were positive about the futures of their cities although there were several who voiced concerns that they might not be able to compete with the larger metropolitan economies in the future. Generally speaking, however, the conclusion was that these cities will flourish. Nearly three-fourths of the cities included in this research saw their populations grow between 2000 and 2005; that percentage holds for the period 2005 to 2010 as well. Some of the growth in that latter period may have been due to the recession during which rural residents may have moved into the micropolitan city, but the growth numbers have been sufficient otherwise to suggest that there is something about life in a city of this size that people still want. Table 7.1 displays the changes in population in the micropolitan cities studied.

Table 7.1 Population Change in America's Micropolitan Cities

City, State		1990	2000	2005	2010
1-	Aberdeen, South Dakota	24,927	24,658	24,098	26,091
2-	Adrian, Michigan	22,097	21,574	21,784	21,133
3-	Albany, Oregon	29,462	40,852	44,797	50,158
4-	Ardmore, Oklahoma	23,079	23,711	24,280	24,283
5-	Athens, Ohio	21,265	21,342	20,918	23,832
6-	Bangor, Maine	33,181	31,472	31,074	33,039
7-	Baraboo, Wisconsin	9,203	10,711	10,927	12,048
8-	Bartlesville, Oklahoma	34,256	34,748	36,249	35,750
9-	Beckley, West Virginia	18,296	17,254	16,936	17,614
10-	Blackfoot, Idaho	9,646	10,419	10,828	11,899
11-	Blytheville, Arkansas	22,906	18,272	16,638	15,620
12-	Bowling Green, Ohio	28,176	29,636	29,793	30,028
13-	Bozeman, Montana	22,660	27,509	33,535	37,280
14-	Brigham City, Utah	15,644	17,411	18,355	17,899
15-	Brookings, South Dakota	16,270	18,504	18,715	22,056
16-	Burlington, Vermont	39,127	38,889	38,531	42,417
17-	Carbondale, Illinois	27,033	20,681	24,806	25,902
18-	Chambersburg, Pennsylvania	16,647	17,862	17,961	20,268
19-	Chelsea, Massachusetts	28,710	35,080	32,518	35,177
20-	Chillicothe, Ohio	21,923	21,796	22,081	21,901
21-	Clarksburg, West Virginia	18,059	16,743	16,439	16,578
22-	Clinton, Iowa	29,201	27,720	27,086	26,885
23-	Clovis, New Mexico	30,954	32,667	33,357	37,775
24-	Coeur d'Alene, Idaho	27,065	34,514	39,100	44,711
25-	Concord, New Hampshire	36,006	40,687	42,336	42,695
26-	Cookeville, Tennessee	21,744	23,923	27,743	30,435

Continued

Table 7.1 (*Continued*)   Population Change in America's Micropolitan Cities

City, State		1990	2000	2005	2010
27-	Covina, California	43,207	46,837	47,850	47,796
28-	Culver City, California	38,793	38,816	39,813	38,883
29-	Danville, Virginia	53,056	48,411	46,143	43,055
30-	Denison, Texas	21,505	22,773	23,648	22,682
31-	Dodge City, Kansas	21,129	25,176	26,104	27,340
32-	Doral, Florida	3,126	22,102	21,895	45,704
33-	Douglas, Georgia	22,099	10,639	10,978	11,589
34-	Durango, Colorado	12,430	13,922	15,501	16,887
35-	Elk Grove, Illinois	33,429	34,727	34,025	33,127
36-	Elko, Nevada	14,736	16,708	16,685	18,297
37-	Elmira, New York	38,083	30,940	29,298	29,200
38-	Enid, Oklahoma	45,309	47,045	46,416	49,379
39-	Eureka, California	27,025	26,128	25,579	27,191
40-	Farmers Branch, Texas	24,250	27,508	26,487	28,616
41-	Findlay, Ohio	35,703	38,967	39,118	41,202
42-	Frankfurt, Kentucky	25,968	27,710	27,210	25,527
43-	Fremont, Nebraska	23,680	25,174	25,314	26,397
44-	Galesburg, Illinois	33,530	33,706	32,017	32,195
45-	Gallup, New Mexico	19,154	20,209	19,378	21,678
46-	Gillette, Wyoming	17,635	19,646	22,685	29,087
47-	Greenwood, South Carolina	20,807	22,071	22,378	23,222
48-	Grand Junction, Colorado	29,034	41,986	45,299	58,566
49-	Hannibal, Missouri	18,004	17,757	17,649	17,916
50-	Hays, Kansas	26,131	20,013	19,632	20,510
51-	Helena, Montana	40,144	25,780	27,383	28,190
52-	Hobbs, New Mexico	29,115	28,657	29,006	34,122
53-	Holyoke, Massachusetts	43,704	38,838	39,958	39,880

Table 7.1 (*Continued*)   Population Change in America's Micropolitan Cities

City, State		1990	2000	2005	2010
54-	Hutchinson, Kansas	39,308	40,787	40,961	42,080
55-	Jamestown, New York	37,314	31,730	30,381	31,146
56-	Jasper, Indiana	10,013	12,100	13,767	15,038
57-	Jesup, Georgia	8,958	9,279	9,851	10,214
58-	Kearney, Nebraska	24,396	27,431	28,958	30,787
59-	Kerrville, Texas	17,384	20,425	22,010	22,347
60-	Kinston, North Carolina	25,295	23,688	22,851	21,677
61-	Kokomo, Indiana	44,962	46,113	44,962	45,468
62-	LaGrange, Georgia	INA*	25,988	27,362	29,588
63-	Laramie, Wyoming	26,687	27,204	26,050	30,816
64-	Lewiston, Maine	39,757	35,690	36,050	36,592
65-	Littleton, Colorado	33,685	40,340	40,396	41,737
66-	Lompoc, California	37,649	41,103	39,985	42,434
67-	Lufkin, Texas	30,206	32,709	33,522	35,067
68-	Marquette, Michigan	21,977	19,661	20,581	21,355
69-	Marshall, Texas	23,997	23,935	24,006	23,523
70-	Marshalltown, Iowa	25,178	26,009	25,997	27,552
71-	Martinsville, Virginia	16,162	15,416	14,925	13,821
72-	Maryland Heights, Missouri	25,407	25,756	26,554	27,472
73-	Mason City, Iowa	29,040	29,172	27,909	28,079
74-	Menomonie, Wisconsin	13,547	14,937	15,180	16,264
75-	Meridian, Mississippi	43,539	39,968	38,605	41,148
76-	Minot, North Dakota	43,639	36,567	34,984	40,888
77-	Moline, Illinois	43,202	43,768	42,892	43,483
78-	Mount Pleasant, Michigan	23,285	25,946	26,253	26,016
79-	Murray, Kentucky	15,058	14,950	15,538	17,741

* INA: Information not available   *Continued*

Table 7.1 (*Continued*)   Population Change in America's Micropolitan Cities

City, State		1990	2000	2005	2010
80-	Muskegon, Michigan	53,459	40,105	39,919	38,401
81-	Muskogee, Oklahoma	37,708	38,310	39,776	39,223
82-	Naples, Florida	32,081	20,976	21,709	19,537
83-	Natchitoches, Louisiana	16,609	17,865	17,701	18,323
84-	New Bern, North Carolina	17,363	23,128	24,106	29,524
85-	Newberry, South Carolina	10,542	10,580	10,659	10,277
86-	New Castle, Pennsylvania	29,849	26,309	25,030	23,273
87-	Nogales, Arizona	19,489	20,878	20,833	20,837
88-	Ossining, New York	22,582	24,010	22,582	25,060
89-	Ottumwa, Iowa	24,488	24,998	24,798	25,023
90-	Owatonna, Minnesota	19,386	22,434	24,133	25,599
91-	Paducah, Kentucky	27,256	26,307	25,575	25,024
92-	Paramus, New Jersey	25,067	25,737	26,545	26,342
93-	Picayune, Mississippi	10,633	10,535	10,830	10,878
94-	Placentia, California	41,259	46,488	49,795	50,533
95-	Plainfield, New Jersey	45,567	47,829	47,642	49,808
96-	Plattsburgh, New York	28,012	18,816	19,181	19,989
97-	Ponca City, Oklahoma	26,359	25,919	25,070	25,387
98-	Portsmouth, Ohio	22,676	20,909	20,101	20,226
99-	Pottsville, Pennsylvania	16,603	15,549	14,764	14,324
100-	Poughkeepsie, New York	28,844	29,087	30,355	32,736
101-	Pullman, Washington	23,478	24,675	25,262	29,799
102-	Quincy, Illinois	39,681	40,366	39,841	40,633
103-	Roanoke Rapids, N. Carolina	15,727	16,957	16,458	15,754
104-	Rolla, Missouri	14,090	16,367	17,717	19,559
105-	Ruston, Louisiana	20,027	20,564	20,667	21,859
106-	Salina, Kansas	42,303	45,697	45,956	47,707

Table 7.1 (*Continued*)   Population Change in America's Micropolitan Cities

City, State		1990	2000	2005	2010
107-	San Luis Obispo, California	41,958	44,174	43,509	45,119
108-	Sedalia, Missouri	19,800	20,339	20,430	21,387
109-	Selma, Alabama	23,775	20,512	19,401	20,756
110-	Shelby, North Carolina	14,669	19,477	21,263	20,323
111-	Shelbyville, Tennessee	14,049	16,105	18,648	20,335
112-	Sierra Vista, Arizona	42,220	37,775	41,908	43,888
113-	Starkville, Mississippi	18,458	21,869	22,131	23,888
114-	Steven's Point, Wisconsin	23,006	24,551	24,298	26,717
115-	Stillwater, Oklahoma	36,676	39,065	40,906	45,688
116-	Texarkana, Texas	31,656	34,782	35,746	36,411
117-	Tifton, Georgia	14,215	15,060	16,327	16,350
118-	Tupelo, Mississippi	30,685	34,211	35,673	34,546
119-	Tuskegee, Alabama	12,257	11,846	11,590	9,865
120-	Twin Falls, Idaho	27,591	34,469	38,630	44,125
121-	Uvalde, Texas	14,729	14,929	16,441	15,751
122-	Valparaiso, Indiana	24,414	27,428	29,109	31,730
123-	Vicksburg, Mississippi	20,908	26,407	25,752	23,856
124-	Walla Walla, Washington	29,437	29,680	30,989	31,731
125-	Warren, Ohio	66,538	46,832	45,796	41,557
126-	Watertown, Wisconsin	19,142	21,598	22,816	23,861
127-	Waynesboro, Virginia	18,549	19,520	21,269	21,006
128-	Wilson, North Carolina	36,930	44,405	46,947	49,167
129-	Winona, Minnesota	25,399	27,069	26,587	27,592
130-	Winter Haven, Florida	24,725	26,487	29,501	33,874
131-	Wooster, Ohio	22,191	24,811	25,668	26,119
132-	Yankton, South Dakota	12,703	13,528	13,716	14,454
133-	Zanesville, Ohio	26,778	25,586	25,253	25,487

Source: United States Bureau of the Census.

Chapter 8

Conclusions

The histories of micropolitan cities are, of course, as divergent as the cities themselves. They can be classified according to any number of factors, including those used herein: metro area micropolitans, hub micropolitans, and isolated micropolitans. One of the commonalities that can be found in many of these locations is the basis for their original establishment.

In many cases, the smaller cities of the United States were formed as an alternative location to larger areas or as the "largest" areas within less-populated regions. In many cases, these cities were formed to provide common services, a social setting, and even some security to rural populations that were first largely dependent upon self-sustaining agricultural production, and later upon agricultural production for export from the community.

Over time, the rigors and uncertainties of farm life encouraged people to seek higher-wage positions in manufacturing enterprises that were located in or near the cities. This new lifestyle came with greater social interaction, educational opportunities for children, and more. Ultimately, this trend was accelerated by the advent of large-scale farming businesses that helped drive out the smaller, less efficient family farming operations.

Once in the cities, this trend led to crowding and sprawl, or what amounted to sprawl for smaller cities and towns. Finally, manufacturing operations declined as overseas competition offering much lower labor costs became more numerous and increasingly aggressive in taking over such industries as timber, steel, and textiles. Now city dwellers, and with farming no longer a viable option, residents either had to move away or find new means of survival. And the cities had to find new ways to survive as well.

What would become of America's micropolitan cities now that they had to face the perfect storm of economic hardships: reduced populations, increased demands for public services, lower-wage jobs yielding smaller municipal budgets, the loss of the best and brightest, and the absence of a highly skilled workforce with which to attract new employers. As manufacturers left these cities, the largest users of water, sewer, and electricity were gone, leaving still more gaps in the state, local, and regional budgets.

Part of the future must include the growth of similar industries, including manufacturing operations, but of a higher order. Manufacturing, for example, must evolve into advanced manufacturing, robotics, and computerization. To make this work, of course, the local workforce needs to learn new skills and gain awareness in the business community for possessing those skillsets.

Could the situation get any bleaker? Many of the mayors interviewed argued that it did because the recent recession was so deep that federal and state programs were aimed at the larger numbers of constituents (and voters) in the larger cities and metro areas, thus making it increasingly difficult for the nation's smaller cities and regions to compete for federal and state assistance.

Micropolitan cities have been left with providing either support services to the residents and companies in larger towns, or bedroom communities for larger urban areas. Often, those bedroom communities grew in states in which municipal budgets were overly dependent upon real estate taxes for their general fund expenditures. In those situations, the bedroom communities in question were required to provide residential public services, including public education, with only residents to provide the real estate tax base. And the declining value of homes at such times yields even greater budgetary pressures.

Today's micropolitan leaders are quite correctly looking to new industries that will strengthen their local economies by providing higher-wage jobs and greater long-term stability. Technology today enables micropolitan cities to offer more than just residences in addition to all the values that are generally associated with a small town, plus the ability to work for major employers for higher wages from a distance. Their economic development strategies—as well as these conversations with mayors of micropolitan cities—indicate that selling small-town quality of life is part of the plan.

Beyond that, micropolitan cities still need to close the asset gaps that make it difficult to attract businesses to town. The metropolitan micropolitan cities need to have the infrastructure that enables their residents to get into jobs in the primary city; hub micropolitan cities need to create ways to attract the types of expenditures that provide their tax base (again, depending upon the states in which they are located), whether that be sales, income, or assorted fees for services; and the isolated metropolitan cities of the United States need to be able to offer their residents and businesses everything: a fully self-contained community.

This, of course, raises the key question of whether America's micropolitan cities can survive. For many, there is a circular challenge to overcome: they need the resources to rebuild in order to be able to generate the kinds of resources they will need in order to rebuild. Right now, they are facing greater problems with fewer resources, both human and capital.

State and federal programs and grants are presented with a difficult decision. Should their similarly minimal resources be focused on the smaller cities and towns of the nation which are likely in the greatest jeopardy, or should they be used to fuel the most promising engines of future growth, the major metropolitan areas and primary cities that have not only the greatest potential for a return on the investment, but also affect far greater numbers of citizens (and voters)? Many will argue that the greatest return on those investments will be needed if the country is going to remain competitive with the up-and-coming BRIC nations (Brazil, Russia, India, and China) and others.

For America's micropolitan cities, survival may come down to one or more of the opportunities for which they may be uniquely prepared. That is, some natural economic development assets can enable smaller cities to sustain the local economies if (and only if) they are properly used. These assets may include a regional airport, a national park or natural settings, colleges and universities, military installations, or other institutions. Many of the micropolitan leaders interviewed expressed a clear recognition of this and discussed either the need for or the action being taken to make their local assets of universities, airports, and more operate more effectively now and plan growth for the future. This is a modified version of the "build it and they will come" perspective in which the growth plans become attractive not only for the community but for the future definitions of those assets themselves. As noted earlier, it helps to make the overall economic development environment conducive to the growth of commerce, which is a difficult though excellent strategy for micropolitan communities.

However, it must be made clear that even with such economic development opportunities, micropolitan cities may or may not succeed largely on the basis of the sources by which the municipal budget is built. That is, enhanced sales do not help the local budget if sales taxes go to the state, and greater incomes are nice but only indirectly support the costs of public services if the local budget is dependent upon sales taxes and income taxes go to the capitol.

Where the mismatches between budget sources and economic base occur, and the situations are exacerbated by steadily declining federal and state dollars, mayors (and perhaps their constituents as well) can become disillusioned. They focus on the positive elements of life in micropolitan cities and on doing what they can to make their cities better places through collaboration and volunteerism. They focus on improving appearances and revitalizing their downtowns. They plan and they work long hours and they do their very best. Even in the worst of situations, they brag about their cities as though they were the very best places in this great nation in which to live, to work, to play, and to raise a family. And for every single one of these mayors, in every single one of these micropolitan cities . . . it undoubtedly is.

Postscript: What's Next?

The beauty of academic research is that it never ends. Every answer leads to many more questions. I rather suspect that the most important sentences in academic discussions and debates start with, "Yes, but ..." This research series (the three books) is no different. It began with generalities and then proceeded to apply them to cities of great populations and those with 10,000 to 50,000 residents.

By speaking to the mayors of micropolitan cities, bright lights were shined on their particular needs and strengths from the perspective of the elected officials who, as sincere and passionate as they may be, are primarily volunteers and short-termers. This begs the question of what the perspective of the professional city manager is to these same issues. Given their longer-term experiences and their often multicity backgrounds, one wonders if their view on the same questions about economic growth, regrowth, and sustainment would be the same.

Hmm. . . .

Bibliography

Books

Cochran, Thomas C. and Brewer, Thomas B. 1966. *Views of American Economic Growth: The Agricultural Era*. New York: McGraw-Hill.

Fleming, David. 2007. *The NFL's Greatest Team and the Stolen 1925 Championship*. New York: ESPN Books.

Gardner, Bruce L. 2002. *American Agriculture in the Twentieth Century: How It Flourished and What It Cost*. Cambridge, MA: Harvard College Press.

Gordon, Gerald L. 2011. *Reinventing Local and Regional Economies*. Boca Raton, FL: CRC Press.

Heidler, David S. and Heidler, Jeanne T. 2011. *Henry Clay: The Essential American*. New York: Random House.

Heilbroner, Robert and Singer, Aaron. 1994. *The Economic Transformation of America Since 1865*. Orlando, FL: Harcourt Brace.

Hindle, Brooke and Lubar, Steven. 1986. *Engines of Change: The American Industrial Revolution, 1790–1860*. Washington, DC: Smithsonian Institution.

Hughes, Jonathan and Cain, Louis. 2007. *American Economic History*, 8th ed. New York: Addison-Wesley.

Jacobs, Jane. 1992. *The Death and Life of Great American Cities*. New York: Random House.

Jacobs, Jane. 1969. *The Economy of Cities*. New York: Random House.

Knox, Paul L. and Mayer, Heike. 2009. *Small Town Sustainability: Economic, Social, and Environmental Innovation*. Basel, Switzerland: Birkhauser.

Rybczynski, Witol. 2010. *Makeshift Metropolis: Ideas About Cities*. New York: Scribner.

Schultz, Jack. 2004. *Boom Town USA: The 7½ Keys to Big Success in Small Towns*. Washington, DC: NAIOP.

Sloan, John W. 1999. *The Reagan Effect: Economics of Presidential Leadership*. Lawrence: University Press of Kansas.

Teaford, Jon. 1997. *Post-Suburbia: Government and Politics in the Edge Cities*. Baltimore: Johns Hopkins University Press.

Internet Citations

Albany's Economy Continues to Climb. September 13, 2011. *The Business Review*. http://www.bizjournals.com

Allbusiness. 2011. http://www.allbusiness.com

Area Vibes. 2011. http://www.areavibes.com

Area Vibes. 2011. Galesburg, Illinois Employment and Jobs. http://www.areavibes.com/galesburg

Badkhen, Anna. 2008. A Warehouse for the Poor: Holyoke Absorbs State's Homeless. http://www.smocingham.org (February 9)

Bauge, Sebastiaen. March 2, 2011. News. http://www.cronkitenewsline.com

Chiri, Toni Walker. August 1996. A New Era for Hobbs, New Mexico. http://www.albuquerque-businessjournal.com

City of Clovis website. 2012. http://www.developclovis.com

City of Lompoc website. 2011. Economic and Community Development. http://www.cityoflompoc.com

City of Lufkin website. 2011. http://cityoflufkin.com

City of Natchitoches website. http://www.natchitochesonthemove.com

City of New Bern. February 2012. Economic Profile. http://www.findnewbern.com

City of Ottumwa. About Ottumwa, Iowa. 2011. http://www.cityofottumwa.org

Coal Decline: Economy Is Shifting. May 24, 2012. http://www.wvgazette.com

Crum, Amanda. May 9, 2012. Scientific Ghost Town: Hobbs, New Mexico. http://www.webpronews.com

Dedman, Bill. 2012. City by City, Here's Your Guide to the Painfully Slow Economic Recovery. http://www.openchannel.msnbc.com

DeWitt, David. August 31, 2011. Area's Congressmen: Economic Growth Will Save Area. http://www.athensnews.com

EconPost. 2011. http://econpost.com

Economic Expansion Expected for Minot. April 30, 2008. http://www.kxnet.com

Economy in Sedalia, Pettis County Has Avoided Some of the Pitfalls Elsewhere. December 14, 2010. http://www.allbusiness.com

Egerstrom, Lee. September 26, 2007. Minnesota Ghost Towns Haunt 500 Endangered Small Cities. http://www.tcdailyplanet.net

Ellis, Sean. October 20, 2010. Blackfoot Firm to Add Up to 70 Jobs. http://www.commerce.idaho.gov

Fier, Jill. April 26, 2011. SDSU Cuts Will Impact Brookings Economy. http://www.brookings-register.com

Forbes. 2011. http://www.forbes.com

Gauchon, Dennis. September 28, 2007. No End in Sight for Idaho's Growth. http://www.usatoday.com

Gauchon, Dennis. April 25, 2011. Ohio is Spending $1.4 Billion to Attract Jobs. Will it Work? http://www.ustoday.com

Godefrin, Shelly. April 24, 2009. Polk Crime Rate Up 45 Percent. http://www.newschief.com

Granholm, Jennifer and Mulhern, Dan. 2011. *A Governor's Story: The Fight for Jobs and America's Economic Future*. New York: Public Affairs.

History, Data, and Stats. 2012. http://www.nevadaregional.com

History of Shelby. 2012. http://www.nps.gov/nr/travel/shelby/history

Hollander, Catherine. June 1, 2012. How Wine Growing in Walla Walla Supports Economy. http://www.news.yahoo.com

Human, Daniel. June 22, 2011. Reports Offer Conflicting Views on Kokomo's Recovery. http://www.indianaeconomicdigest.net

Iowa Cities Need Lawmakers' Help in 2012. 2011. http://www.desmoinesregister.com

Kelley, Kevin. April 26, 2011. Economic Growth Continues in Burlington Despite Recession. http://www.vermontbiz.com

Kennedy, Maura. September 4, 2010. Grand Junction Listed as Only City in State Still in Recession. http://www.krextv.ehcclients.com

Knutson, Jonathan. June 6, 2011. Minot Economy Facing Ag Hit. http://www.afweek.com

Lifestyle of Southern West Virginia. 2012. http://rightlifestyle.com

Little, Ryan L. June 24, 2012. Winter Haven's Economy Improving, Report Says. http://www.theledger.com

Local Area Unemployment Rates Remain High. April 24, 2011. http://www.ucdailynews.com

Lutey, Tom. December 18, 2011. Economy Taking Off: High Tech Businesses, Location Boost Bozeman. http://www.billingsgazette.com

Lynem, Julie. November 9, 2011. SLO County Advised to Put Recession Behind. http://www.sanluisobispo.com

Michigan Unemployment Up Again. June 25, 2009. http://www.woodtv.com

Monaco, Vincent. May 6, 2011. Project Update—City of Kinston: Development-Led Economic Development. http://www.sogweb.sog.unc.edu

Moody's Analytics. 2012. http://www.economy.com

Murray, Calloway County. 2012. http://thinkmurray.org

Nalley, Steven. March 1, 2011. Starkville Leaders Optimistic About Area Economy. http://www.starkvilledailynews.com

Natalie-Lees, Jeff. July 14, 2011. Boomtown: Study Says Beef Plant Will Have Ten Billion Dollar Impact. http://www.articles.aberdeennews.com

National League of Cities. 2012. Daytime Versus Nighttime Population. http://www.nlc.org

Neal, Zachary. September 8, 2010. Cities: Size Doesn't Matter Much Any More. http://www.newgeography.com

Newman, Mark. March 26, 2011. Area Officials Make Bio-Processing Plea to Lawmakers. http://www.ottumwacourier.com

Nicolau, Corinna. Summer 2008. Breathing Life into Pullman's Economy. http://www.wsm.wsu.edu

Nogales USA. 2012. http://www.nogalesusa.com

Northeast Missouri Hotspot–Hannibal http://www.missourieconomy.org/pdfs/led_hannibal.pdf

Ogden, Eloise. June 17, 2010. Oil Field Driving Economy. http://www.minotdailynews.com

Pella Windows Creates Seventy-Five Jobs in Murray, Kentucky. September 7, 2011. http://www.businessclimate.com/kentucky-economicdevelopment

Peralta, Eyder. September 15, 2011. Stagnant: Checking in on the Economy in Chillicothe, Ohio. http://www.wbur.org/npr

Pressley, Carolyn Mullenax. March 1993. Clovis/Portales: Beefing up Economy. *The New Mexico Business Journal*, (March): vol. 17, no.n3. http://trove.nla.gov.au/work/107261477?q=%2Portales%2C+New+Mexico%22&c=article&versionId=120698931

Rapacon, Stacy. 2010. Best Cities 2010: Burlington, Vermont. http://www.kiplinger.com

Ricker, Amanda. February 24, 2011. Bozeman Economy Ranks Seventh in Micropolitan Study. http://www.bozemandailychronicle.com

San Luis Obispo Chamber of Commerce. 2012. http://www.slochamber.org

Shaver, Pat. Ottumwa Unemployment Leads Iowa Cities. October 23, 2009. http://www.allbusiness.com

Sierra Vista. 2012. http://www.sierravistaaz.gov

Sparkman, Worth. April 27, 2012. http://www.sedaliamoed.com

Swallows, Carolyn. September 27, 2011. One in Five in Region Enrolled in Food Stamp Program. http://www.ecdailynews.com

Taschler, Joe. June 8, 2011. Wisconsin Manufacturers and Commerce Survey Turns Optimistic Following Change in Madison. http://www.jsonline.com

Tavernise, Sabrina. April 19, 2011. Ohio County Losing Its Young to Painkillers Grip. http://www.nytimes.com

Thinkmurray. 2012. http://www.thinkmurray.com

Thompson, Angie. February 8, 2011. City Council Hears About Economic Developments. http://www.tiftongazette.com

United States Department of Agriculture, Rural Development. 1999. http://www.rurdev.usda.gov

US Beacon. 2012. http://www.usbeacon.com

West Virginia Economy among Fastest Growing Last Year. 2012. http://www.wvnstv.com/story/18708207/wv-economy-among-fastest-growing-last-year?clienttype=printable

Wilin, Lou. April 29, 2011. Economic Development Plans Outlined. http://thecourier.com/issues

Woodruff, Nick. April 2, 2011. Stillwater Economy Doing Just Fine. http://www.ocolly.com

Young, Dayne. August 7, 2012. New Business Could Bring 1,000 Jobs to Tifton. http://www.walb.com

Zagorski, E.D. December 29, 2011. Sears Closing Another Blow to Baraboo Economy. http://www.host.madison.com

Articles: Journals and Magazines

Porter, Michael E. November–December 1998. Clusters and the New Economics of Competition. *Harvard Business Review*, 77–90.

Porter, Michael E. May–June 1995. The Competitive Advantage of the Inner City. *Harvard Business Review*, 55–71.

Porter, Michael E. April 2003. The Economic Performance of Regions. *Regional Studies*. 37: 549–578. Strategy for the I-29 Corridor.

Unpublished Papers

Abel, Jaison R. and Dietz, Richard. December 2008. Buffalo Branch of the Federal Reserve Bank of New York. New Measures of Economic Growth and Productivity in Upstate New York.

Brookings Economic Development Corporation. 2011 Community Profile.

Brookings Institute. 2010. State of Metropolitan America: On the Front Lines of Demographic Transformation. Washington, DC: Brookings Institute.

Carroll, Michael C. October 2004. Measuring Bowling Green State University's Impact on Ohio's Economy. City of Dubuque. 2009. A Vision of Sustainable Development. Dubuque, Iowa.

Christopherson, Susan. July 20, 2004. Creative Economic Strategies for Small and Medium-Size Cities: Options for New York State. Community Marketing Economics Workshop.

City of Bangor. 2007. Economic Status Update.

City of Baraboo. August 2006. Riverfront Redevelopment Plan.

City of Bozeman. 2009. City of Bozeman Economic Development Plan.

City of Concord, Economic Development Advisory Council. June 30, 2008. New Hampshire's Creative Crossroads: The Concord Creative Economy Plan.

City of Dubuque. 2009. A Vision of Sustainable Development. Dubuque, Iowa.

City of Kerrville, City of Ingram, and Kerr County. September 2008. Economic Development Incentive Policy.

City of Meridian. 2002. Comprehensive Plan.

City of Nogales. 2010. City of Nogales General Plan. The Planning Center.

City of Ossining, New York. August 2008. Ossining Market Analysis for the Waterfront and Downtown.

City of Paducah. Choices 2025, Economic Strategies.

City of Ruston, Louisiana. March 21, 2011. Ruston 21, Comprehensive Plan.

City of Selma, Alabama. March 2009. Comprehensive Community Master Plan.

City of Shelby, North Carolina. March 3, 2005. Strategic Growth Plan.

City of Shelbyville, Tennessee. June 7, 2010. Comprehensive Plan.

City of Watertown, Wisconsin. November 17, 2009. City of Watertown Comprehensive Plan.

City of Waynesboro, Virginia. June 30, 2010. An Economic Assessment Report for Downtown Waynesboro, Virginia.

Cochise College, Center for Economic Research. 2003–2004. Sierra Vista Economic Growth Focus.

Coeur d'Alene Tribe. 2009. Comprehensive Economic Development Strategy.

Cookeville, Tennessee. 2003. Cookeville 2030 Plan.

Cohen, Stephen S. and Eugenia-Garcia, Clara. May 1, 1993. Learning from California: The Macroeconomic Consequences of Structural Changes.

Criddle, Mike. October 2010. City of LaGrange Comprehensive Master Plan.

Dietz, Richard. Buffalo Branch of the Federal Reserve Bank of New York. Winter 2005. Population Out-Migration from Upstate New York.

Dunne, Timothy, and Fee, Kyle. 2011. Metropolitan and Micropolitan Population Growth. Cleveland: Federal Reserve Bank.

Economic Vitality Corporation (EVC) of San Luis Obispo County. November 2010. Clusters of Opportunity: Economic Strategy.

EMSI. 2007. Analysis of the Walla Walla Wine Cluster: Past, Present, and Future.

Gilliam, Frankie, Arkansas State University. May 2009. Quality of Place and Economic Development: A Case Study of the Iowa Great Places Program.

Greenberg Development Services. February 2008. Downtown Danville Market Study Update.

Harris, Thomas R., University of Nevada, Reno. January 2004. Analysis of Socio-Economic Data and Trends for Elko County.

John Locke Foundation. 2008. Agenda 2008.

LHB, Inc. July 2011. Downtown Menomonie, Wisconsin.

Northeast Missouri Hotspot–Hannibal. 2010. Missouri Department of Economic Development.

Oklahoma State University, Spears School of Business. January 20, 2008. The Oklahoma Economy: Stillwater Micropolitan Area.

Partnership Alliance. December 2008. Economic Development Strategic Action Plan, Greenwood, South Carolina.

Sharma, Subhash, Diaby, Aboubacar, and Harfst, Kyle. August 29, 2011. The Economic Impact of Southern Illinois University, Carbondale in the Region and State of Illinois.

Sharp, Helen Burns and Hansen, Heather. Eco Northwest. August 31, 2007. Update of Economic Opportunity Analysis for the City of Albany. Eugene, Oregon.

Siegel, Beth and Waxman, Andy. June 2001. Third-Tier Cities: Adjusting to the New Economy. Washington, DC: United States Department of Commerce, Economic Development Administration.

Surface, Michael K. and Allen, Katie, City of Gillette. February 2010. Developing Gillette.

Talley, Tim. September 6, 2011. Associated Press. Energy Driving Oklahoma Economy, But Diversity Will Sustain It.

Target Industries. 2010. Bartlesville Development Corporation.

United States Department of Housing and Urban Development. May 1, 2005. Analysis of the Grand Junction, Colorado Housing Market.

United States Department of Housing and Urban Development. April 1, 2010. Sherman-Denison, Texas Comprehensive Housing Market Analysis.

Wassmer, Robert and Boarnet, Marlon G. 2002. The Benefits of Growth. Washington, DC: The Urban Land Institute.

Wisconsin Bureau of Aeronautics. 2008. Airports and Economic Development.

Zanesville Summary. 2011.

Additional Reading

A Governor's Guide to Cluster-Based Economic Development. 2002. Washington, DC: National Governor's Association.

A Guide to Preparing the Economic Development Element of a Comprehensive Plan. August, 2003. Madison, Wisconsin: The Wisconsin Economic Development Institute.

Anderson, Deb. June 23, 2010. Economic Development Gets Boost with Expansion Project. http://www.chippewa.com

Artz, Georgeanne. 2003. Rural Area Brain Drain: Is It a Reality? *Choices*. 4th Quarter, pp. 11–15.

Atkinson, Robert D. February 2004. Reversing Rural America's Economic Decline. Progressive.

Asheim, Bjorn, Cooke, Phillip, and Martin, Ron (Eds.) 2006. *Clusters and Regional Development: Critical Reflections and Explorations*. London: Routledge.

Badenhausen, Kurt. September 19, 2010. Sioux Falls Again Top Small City for Business. http://www.msnbc.msn.com

Baraboo Economic Development Commission. 2011. Baraboo Retail Market Analysis.

Barkley, David L. September 2001. Employment Generation Strategies for Small Towns: An Overview of Alternatives.

Barta, Suzette and Woods, Mike. 2003. Targeted Economic Development Case Study. Enid: Oklahoma State University.

Bass, Frank. November 16, 2009. Small U.S. Cities Have Better Quality of Life but Economic Picture is Steadily Worsening. http://www.news.gaeatimes.com

Beef Plant Impact Study is Good News. July 17, 2011. http://www.beefmagazine.com

Berger, Knute. October 21, 2007. New Economy: Will Success Spoil Washington's Walla Walla? http://www.newwest.net

Bernard, Richard M. and Rice, Bradley R. 1983. *Sunbelt Cities: Politics and Growth Since World War II.* Austin: University of Texas Press.

BGSU Provides Seed Money for Two Economic Development Projects. May 20, 2011. http://www.sent-trib.com

Bingham, Richard D. and Mier, Robert. 1997. *Dilemmas of Urban Economic Development: Issues in Theory and Practice.* Thousand Oaks, CA: Sage.

Bingham, Richard D. and Mier, Robert. 1993. *Theories of Local Economic Development: Perspectives From Across the Disciplines.* Newbury Park, CA: Sage.

Blair, J.P. Spring 1998. Quality of Life and Economic Development Policy. *Economic Development Review* 16(1): 50–54; 62 (3).

Bowman, Rex. December 17, 2009. McDonnell Team Takes Aim at Martinsville's Economy. http://www.roanoke.com

Boyce, Dan. January 3, 2011. City Says Economic Development Goals a Good Start, More Needs to be Done. http://www.kbzk.com

Bradbury, Katherine L., Kodrzycki, Yolanda K., and Tannenwald, Robert. March–April, 1997. The Effects of State and Local Public Policies on Economic Development: An Overview. *New England Economic Journal* 1–13.

Brand, Aaron. August 30, 2006. Texarkana Generates Steady Economic Growth. http://www.urbanplanet.org

Brookings Economic Development Corporation. January 2009. Building a Recession-Proof Economy.

Brown, Martin. Living Large in the Small City. http://www.singlemindedwomen.com

Buckles, Susan. Small Towns in South Dakota Are Worried About the Economy. St. Paul, Minnesota: The Northwest Area Foundation. http://programs.nwaf.org

Byczkowski, John B. December 18, 1998. Warren Is Economic Pacesetter. http://www.enquirer.com

Cannon, Ellen. October 1, 2011. Durbin Sees Amtrak Funding Critical to Western Illinois Economy. http://www.examiner.com

Carreira, Robert. April 21, 2010. Sierra Vista Economic Outlook. http://www.wilcoxrange-news.com

Cawthon, Graham. January 9, 2011. Economic Recovery: 2010 Some Job Gains but Will Continued Growth Come Fast Enough? http://www.shelbystar.com

Chambers, Matt. December 2011. Small Firms Are Big Part of Economy. http://www.lagrangenews.com

Chapman, Dan. May 6, 2010. South Georgia Chicken Jobs Coming Home to Roost. http://www.ajc.com

Chura, Hillary. January 9, 2009. Lacking Airlines, Small Cities' Economies Suffer. http://www.nytimes.com

Ciscel, David H. Autumn 1999. Creating Economic Growth in Rural Mississippi Delta Counties. http://www.stlouisfed.org

City Neighborhoods Going Bankrupt: Act 47. November 2, 2003. http://www.old.post-gazette.com

City of Albany Strategic Plan: FY—2011–2015. February 7, 2011.

Clarke, Susan, and Gaile, Gary. 1998. *The Work of Cities.* Minneapolis: The University of Minnesota Press.

Clausing, Jeri. May 8, 2012. Hobbs, New Mexico Picked as Site of Scientific Ghost Town. http://www.yahoo.com

Coon, Lisa. December 30, 2011. Poverty Report: Demand on the Rise for Local Charities. http://www.Galesburg.com

Coppola, Manuel C. September 19, 2008. Violence Surge Is Hurting Economy and Tourism in Nogales, Sonora. http://www.insidetucsonbusiness.com

Corey, Russ and Delinski, Bernie. December 6, 2010. Small Town Woes. http://timesdaily.com

Cortright, Joseph. 2002. The Economic Importance of Being Different: Regional Variations in Tastes, Increasing Returns, and Dynamics of Development. *Development Quarterly*. 16(1): 2– 16.

Curran, Dennis E. February 1, 2011. Southeast Wyoming Is Growing Again. http://www.wyomingbusinessreport.com

Dairy Research May be Cash Cow—Literally—of Idaho's Economy. September 8, 2009. http://www.magicvalley.com

Deffenbaugh, Greg. July 19, 2011. County Criticizes City's Plan for Kohl's Development. http://www.heartlandconnection.com/news/story.aspx?id=642093

Depriest, Joe. January 2011. Wind Power Fuels New Jobs in Shelby. http://www.news-observer.com

Dinesh, Ramde. September 16, 2008. Sour Economy Hits Paper Mills, Small Town Workers. http://www.usatoday.com

Dissart, J.C. 2003. Regional Economic Diversity and Regional Economic Stability: Research Results and Agenda. *International Regional Science Review*. 26(4): 423–446.

Downs, Anthony. 1994. *New Visions for Metropolitan America*. Washington, DC: Brookings.

El Nasser, Haya. June 27, 2004. Small Town USA Goes "Micropolitan." *USA Today*.

Elsbree, Amy and Miller, John. Small Cities Council Focuses on Economy, Green Technology. http://www.nlc.org

Estill, Lyle. 2008. *Small Is Possible: Life in a Local Economy*. Gabriola Island, Canada: New Society.

Expanded Gaming Will Aid Local Economy. August 25, 2011. http://www.chelsearecord.com

Fadali, Elizabeth and Harris, Thomas R. University of Nevada, Reno. May 2006. Estimated Economic Impacts of the Cattle Ranching and Farming Sector on the Elko County Economy.

Fisher, R.C. 1997. The Local Effects of State and Local Public Services on Economic Development. *New England Review*. March–April: 53–82.

Florida, Richard. 2004. *The Rise of the Creative Class: And How It Is Transforming Work, Leisure, Community, and Everyday Life*. New York: Basic Books.

Friedman, Benjamin M. 2005. *The Moral Consequences of Economic Growth*. New York: Vintage Books.

Garreau, Joel. 1998. *Edge City: Life on the New Frontier*. New York: Doubleday.

Gittell, Ross J. 1992. *Renewing Cities*. Princeton, NJ: Princeton University Press.

Gordon, Gerald L. 2009. *The Formula for Economic Growth on Main Street America*. Boca Raton, FL: CRC Press.

Gordon, L. and Scheffer, Leo J. Fall, 1990. Air Service: A Vital Ingredient in a Developing Economy. *Commentary*, 14(3). Washington, DC: National Council for Urban Economic Development.

Gottman, Jean. 1961. *Megalopolis: The Urbanized Northeastern Seaboard of the United States*. New York: Twentieth Century Fund.

Governor's Office for Economic Analysis. March 2001. Kentucky Economic Forecast.

Grand Opening of Hamlet Protein Factory. 2012. http://findlayhancocked.com

Grayson, Katherine. March 16, 2008. Multiple Factors Fueling Economic Growth in Western Wisconsin. http://www.bizjournals.com

Greene, Stephen. April 1, 2002. Doing Business in Texarkana Sometimes Means Going Over the Line. http://www.allbusiness.com

Halseth, Greg. July 7, 2010. Rural Renaissance: British Columbia's Small-Town Economy. http://www.bcbusinessonline.ca/bcb

Hannah, James. December 26, 2002. Cities Use Arts to Boost Economies: Strategy to Drive Economic Development. http://www.enquirer.com

Heg, Deena. October 2003. Spreading the Wealth: Building a Technology Company in Small and Medium-Sized Regions. http://www.brookings.edu.reports

Heilman, Wayne. September 13, 2011. Springs Economy Growing—So, Where Are the Jobs? http://www.gazette.com

Henton, Douglas. 1994. *Grass Roots Leaders for a New Economy: How Civic Entrepreneurs Are Building Prosperous Economies.* San Francisco: Jossey-Bass.

Henricks, Mark. June, 2005. Rural Economies: Can Entrepreneurs Help Boost Small Town Economies? *Entrepreneur Magazine.* http://www.entrepreneur.com/article/78232

Henry, Mark, and Drabenscott, Mark. Second Quarter 1996. A New Micro View of the U.S. Rural Economy. *Federal Reserve Review.* pp. 53–70. http://www.kansascityfed.org/Publicat/Econrev/pdf/2q96henr.pdf

Higgins, Suzanne. December 17, 2010. Economy Hurting Charity Fundraising. http://www.wvpubcast.org

Howard, Lee. December 13, 2011. Economists Predict Glowing 2012 for Region. http://www.theday.com

Hudnut, William H., III. 1998. *Cities on the Rebound: A Vision for Urban America.* Washington, DC: The Urban Institute.

Huszai, Steve. November 30, 2011. Newell Moving Distribution Out of Wooster. http://www.thedaily-record.com

Idaho's Economic Growth Lags Nation's, Report Says. September 13, 2011. http://www.idahostatesman.com

Inergy Automotive to Expand in Adrian. November 13, 2007. http://michiganadvantage.org

Innovation Center, Biotech Institute Awarded $500,000 to Boost Economic Development. August 27, 2011. http://www.athensohiotoday.com

International Economic Development Council. March 29, 2010. Creating Quality Jobs: Transforming the Economic Development Landscape. Washington, DC: 161–182.

International Economic Development Council. January 2006. Economic Development Strategic Plan. Prepared for the City of Tulsa.

James, Winston. 2009. Officials: Nioxin Closing Huge Loss to Local Community and Economy. http://www.times-georgian.com

Jarrett, Emily. March 2, 2012. Pettis County Proud of Its 2012 Record of Retail Growth. http://www.sedaliamo.com

Johnson, Brett D. 1993. Down the Drain: As River Towns Tally the Cost, Most of Illinois Economy Is High and Dry. http://www.lib.niu.edu

Johnson, Charles S. December 18, 2011. Stalled by Government: Fed, State Pay Freeze Thwarts Helena Growth. http://www.billingsgazette.com

Johnson, Patak. July 6, 2004. Small Cities Cope with Crime Surge. http://www.csmonitor.com

Johnson, Sharna. October 18, 2008. Local Banks, Economy Stable. http://www.pntonline.com

Katz, Anne. March 20, 2007. The Arts and the Creative Economy: An Investment for Small Town Wisconsin. Hudson, Wisconsin: The Leadership Hudson Program.

Kay, David L. September, 2007. Role of Services in Regional Economic Growth. *Growth and Change.* 38(3): 419–442.

Kelley, Kevin. July 17, 2009. Vermont's Growth Engine Is Sputtering as Recession Drags On . . . and On. http://www.vermontbiz.com

Kindleberger, Charles H. and Herrick, Bruce. 1977. *Economic Development*, 3rd ed. Dallas: McGraw-Hill.

Kingsley, G. Thomas and Pettit, Kathryn L.S. December 18, 2002. Population Growth and Decline in City Neighborhoods. *Change in Urban America.* Washington, DC: The Urban Land Institute.

Knight Foundation. September 29, 2009. Economy Not Key in Residents' Love for Aberdeen. http://www.knightfoundation.org

Kort, J.R. 1981. Regional Economic Instability and Industrial Diversification in the United States. *Land Economics.* 57(4): 596–608.

Kotkin, Joel. 2000. *The New Geography: How the Digital Revolution Is Reshaping the American Landscape.* New York: Random House.

Kotkin, Joel. 2010. *The Next Hundred Million: America in 2050.* New York: Penguin Press.

Kuestener, Kristina. September 14, 2011. Grand Junction Lags Behind in Economic Growth. http://www.krextv.com

Kures, Matt and Wise, Greg. November 5–6, 2008. The Role of Small Cities in the New Regional Economy. Stevens Point, Wisconsin: The 17th Conference on the Small City and Regional Community.

Lambe, Will. December 2008. Small Towns, Big Ideas: Case Studies in Small Town Community Economic Development. Chapel Hill: University of North Carolina.

Leroux, Andre. Summer, 2009. New England's Small Cities: A Mostly Untapped Resource. *Communities and Banking,* 19–21.

Lewis, Paul G. 1996. *Shaping Suburbia: How Political Institutions Organize Urban Development.* Pittsburgh: University of Pittsburgh Press.

Lofton, Lynn. August 1, 2005. Nine Proposed Casino Projects Could Mean Growth for Economy. http://www.findarticles.com/p/articles

Lufkin Industries Creating 120 Oil Sector Jobs in Texas. January 20, 2011. http://www.areadevelopment.com

Lynch, Robert G. 2004. *Rethinking Growth Strategies: How State and Local Taxes and Services Affect Economic Development.* Washington, DC: Economic Policy Institute.

Lynch, Robert L. 2007. Arts and Economic Prosperity. Washington, DC: Americans for the Arts.

Madrick, Jeff. 2002. *Why Economies Grow: The Forces that Shape Prosperity and How We Can Get Them Working Again.* New York: Basic Books.

Mansfield, Howard. 1990. *Yesterday's Cities of the Future.* New Brunswick, NJ: Center for Urban Policy Research, Rutgers University.

Markley, Deborah M. Winter 2006. A framework for developing rural entrepreneurship. *Economic Development America.* US Department of Commerce. pp. 4–6.

Markusen, Ann R., Lee, Yong-Sook, and DiGiovanna, Sean (Eds.) 1999. *Second Tier Cities: Rapid Growth Beyond the Metropolis.* Minneapolis: University of Minnesota Press.

Mast, Tom. September 11, 2011. Job Growth Quickens in Laramie County. http://www.trib.com

Matthews, Anne. 1992. *Where the Buffalo Roam.* New York: Grove Weidenfeld.

McGeehan, Patrick. November 12, 2009. Pfizer to Leave City that Won Land Use Case. http://www.nytimes.com

McGuire, Jim. City of Gillette. April 2011. Developing Gillette 2010.

McKay, Becky. January 18, 2009. Trends for Rural Small Businesses in 2009. http://www.smallbiztrends.com

McNulty, Robert H. 1985. *The Economics of Amenity*. Washington, DC: Partners for Livable Places.

Meet Elko. 2012. http://nenevadaregional.com

Michigan Economy: Will Taxes Stunt Growth? July 25, 2011. http://www.dailypress.net

Mills, Edwin S. and McDonald, John F. 1992. *Sources of Metropolitan Growth*. New Brunswick, NJ: Center for Urban Policy Research.

Minot Chamber of Commerce. 2011. Economic Profile. http://www.minotchamber.org

Mitchell, Jeffrey. University of New Mexico. April 2007. Hobbs Main Street Community Economic Assessment.

Mouhcine, Guettahl. Oklahoma State University. February 19, 2012. Bartlesville Economic Outlook 2012.

Mullin, Jeff. 2009. Vance Is Economic Anchor Despite Struggling Economy. http://www.enidnews.com

Murphy, Sean. October 4, 2011. Treasurer: Oklahoma Economy Continues Steady Growth. http://www.tulsaworld.com

Myers, David. Fall 2007. Partnership builds a knowledge economy in Ponca, Oklahoma. *Economic Development Journal*, 16(39–42). Washington, DC: International Economic Development Council.

Nacker, Roger. January 2002. Facilitating Entrepreneurial Growth Companies in Wisconsin. Madison: Wisconsin Economic Development Institute.

Nacker, Roger. October 2002. Measuring Economic Development Return-on-Investment Models. Madison: Wisconsin Economic Development Institute, Inc.

National Association of Development Organizations. 2011. Mobilize Maine: Asset-Based Regional Economic Development.

National League of Cities. 2012. Number of Cities and City Population. http://www.nlc.org

Nelson, Margaret K. and Smith, Joan. 1999. *Working Hard and Making Do: Surviving in Small Town America*. Berkeley: University of California Press.

North Carolina Poverty Rates Staggering. November 25, 2009. http://www.witn.com

O'Sullivan, Arthur. 2007. *Urban Economics*. New York: McGraw-Hill/Irwin.

Ohio University, Voinovich School of Leadership and Public Affairs. July 2011. The 2010 Economic Impact of Ohio University's Innovation Center.

Olson, Mark W. July 26, 2002. Economic Change in Rural America. Remarks to the Fergus Falls Rotary Club, Fergus Falls, Minnesota.

Oregon Economic Forecast. June 2012.

Ovellana, Cynthia K., Quirk, Melissa, Spencer, Melanie N., and Villa, Yvette. Tufts University. April 2006. An Assessment of Community Impacts of Economic Development Projects in Chelsea, Massachusetts.

Pack, Jane Rothenberg. *Growth and Convergence in Metropolitan America*. Washington, DC: Brookings Institute, 2002.

Pagano, Michael A. and Bowman, Ann O'M. 1995. *Cityscapes and Capital: The Politics of Urban Development*. Baltimore: Johns Hopkins University Press.

Parker, Rosemary. February 28, 2009. Despite Poor Economy, Small Family Farms Are Taking Root. http://www.mlive.com

Pennsylvania General Assembly. 2006. Municipal Fiscal Distress and Recovery.

Pitts, Cindy. September 2012. County Unveils Tactical Economic Development Plan. http://www.newberryobserver.com

Plosila, Walter. Winter 2005. Building Innovation-Driven Regional Economies in Small and Mid-Sized Metro Centers. *Economic Development America.* Washington, DC: International Economic Development Council. pp. 7–10.

Polk County Economic Barometer. 2011. Central Florida Development Council.

Poor Counties Are Least Healthy. April 2012. http://www.lgrangenews.com

Powalskie, Katie. 2006. Visiting Federal Lawmakers Study Dropout Issue in Shelbyville. http://www.aypf.org

Pulver, Robin, et al. November, 2005. Small Towns Fact Book. Raleigh, North Carolina: The Rural Center.

RDG Planning and Design. February 2012. The Kearney Plan.

Regional Technology Strategies, Inc. June 2010. Pressing the Advantage: A Regional Growth.

Ridgeway, Jennifer. December 2009. Minnesota's Composites Cluster. http://www.positively-minnesota.com

Rosenfeld, Stuart A. May 12, 1995. Business Clusters That Work: Prospects for Regional Development. Carrboro, North Carolina: Regional Tech Strategies.

Russell, Victoria. Winter 2002. Downtown Main Street, Douglas, Georgia. *Economic Development Journal.* Washington, DC: International Economic Development Council. pp. 35–41.

Sappington, Brant. February 2011. Leaders Have to Take Advantage of Opportunities for Economic Success. http://www.dailycorinthian.com

Sarzyonski, Andre, Brown, Marilyn A., and Southworth, Frank. 2008. *Shrinking the Global Footprint of Metropolitan America.* Washington, DC: Brookings.

Saunders, Forrest. October 18, 2010. Yankton, South Dakota Business Announces Expansion, Adds Jobs. http://www.ktiv.com

Schaeffer, Peter V. and Loveridge, Scott. 2000. *Small Town and Rural Economic Development: A Case Studies Approach.* Westport, CT: Praeger.

Schneider, Mark. 1989. *The Competitive City: The Political Economy of Suburbia.* Pittsburgh: University of Pittsburgh.

Schramm, Jim. May 11, 2010. What Recession? Tax Report Shows Minot's Economy on a Roll. http://www.minotdailynews.com

Shaffer, Ron. May 1995. Dying Communities. *Community Economics Newsletter.* Madison: University of Wisconsin. (223).

Shaffer, Ron. 2004. *Community Economics: Linking Theory and Practice.* Ames: University of Iowa Press.

Slanina, John B. January 2006. Knowledge-Based Economic Development Strategies for the Youngstown-Warren, Ohio–Pa. Metropolitan Area.

Soubly, Kevin. August 22, 2011. Muskegon Seen as Key Link in Wind Energy Development. http://www.mibiz.com

Sperling's Best Places. 2012. http://www.bestplaces.net/economy/city

Sprague, Mike. August 8, 2011. Bad Economic Times Create Problems for Homeless Shelters. http://www.sgvtribune.com

State of Connecticut. May 3, 2005. The Contribution of the Groton Naval Sub Base and the Electric Boat Company to the Economies of Connecticut and Southeastern Connecticut.

Status of Education in Rural America. 2006. Washington, DC: National Center for Education Statistics. http://www.uses.ed.gov

Still, Tom. December 7, 2009. In Western Wisconsin, Regional Economic Growth Has Momentum of Its Own. http://www.wtnnews.com

Stillwater Economy Doing Just Fine. April 3, 2011. http://www.ocolly.com

Strickland, Tonya. June 8, 2012. Brighter Year Forecast for Central Coast Economy. http://www.sanluisobispo.com

Summers, Laura. February 18, 2011. Steady Recovery Predicted for Bartlesville Area. http://www.tulsaword.com

Swafford, Rindy. November 11, 2007. Tech Economy on the Rise in Ruston. http://www.research.latech.edu

Timmons, Eric. December 9, 2010. Census Offers Grim View of Galesburg. http://www.pjstar.com

TMRC has $415 Million Impact on Local Economy. June 1, 2012. http://www.tiftongazette.com

Troske, Kenneth R., University of Kentucky, Gatton School of Business and Economics. January 2008. Economic Growth in Kentucky: Why Does Kentucky Lag Behind the Rest of the South?

Tweh, Bowdeya. June 13, 2011. Sputtering Economy Leads to Growth Doubts. http://www.nwitimes.com

United States Department of Commerce, Bureau of the Census. 2010a. Small Cities Lose Luster in Downturn. http://msnbc.com

United States Department of Commerce, Bureau of the Census. 2010b. Metropolitan and Micropolitan Statistical Areas. http://www.census.gov

United States Department of Homeland Security. August 2007. Long-Term Community Recovery Plan, Greensburg, Kansas.

Wacker Announces $23.7 Million Expansion. December 16, 2009. http://www.techumsa.com

Waddington, Lynda. March 5, 2009. Alliant Nixes Plan for Marshalltown Coal Plant. http://www.iowaindependent.com

Waits, Mary Jo, Rex, Tom, and Melnick, Rob. April 1997. Cluster Analysis: A New Tool for Understanding the Role of Public Policy. Phoenix: Arizona State University, Morrison Institute for Public Policy.

Wallem, Paul. January 18, 2010. Survey Gives Gillette High Marks for Economic Strength. http://www.basinradio.com

Waugh, Danielle. September 27, 2011. Economic Development Along Bangor Waterfront. http://www.wlbz2.com

Weinstein, Bernard L. 1985. *Regional Growth and Decline in the United States*. New York: Praeger.

Wells, Barbara. 2002. Smart Growth at the Frontier. *Strategies and Resources for Rural Communities*, Northeast-Midwest Institute.

West Virginia University, Bureau of Business and Economic Research. 2009. Beckley MicroSA Outlook.

Wheaton, Bob. December 2009. Adrian Tries to Fill Industrial Park Despite Sour Economy. http://www.lenconnect.com/news

Wilks, Victoria. May 18, 2011. Many Jobs on the Prairie, but No Place to Live. http://www.npr.org

Willett, Heather. April 2, 1995. Cities Face Similar Situations: Most Try to Rebound After Hard Times. http://www.predergastlibrary.org

Wolman, Harold and Spitzley, David. 1996. The Politics of Local Economic Development. *Economic Development Quarterly*. 10: 115–150.

Wyoming Center for Business and Economic Analysis, Inc. September 2011. Economic Indicators for the Laramie Economy.

Zavadi, Chris. January 2, 2010. Business Growth Makes Others Envious. http://www.fremonttribune.com

Index

Page numbers followed by f indicate figure
Page numbers followed by t indicate table